VARSITY LETTERS

Documenting Modern Colleges

and Universities

Helen Willa Samuels

The Society of American Archivists
and
The Scarecrow Press, Inc.
Metuchen, N.J. & London
1992

British Library Cataloguing-in-Publication data available

Library of Congress Cataloging-in-Publication Data

Samuels, Helen Willa
    Varsity letters : documenting modern
    colleges and universities / by Helen
  Willa Samuels.
      p. cm.
    Includes index.
    ISBN 0-8108-2596-1
    1. Universities and colleges — United States — Archives.
2. Universities and colleges — Archives.   3. Documentation — United
States.   4. Documentation.
CD3065.V37 1992
025.2'1877 — dc20   92-24126

Jacket design: Betsy Chimento
Composition: Resolution Graphics

For my father

Irving Samuels
B.A., City College, 1930
M.A., Columbia University, 1931

Acknowledgments

The longest chapter in this book describes the need to sustain colleges and universities. People must also be sustained, and I feel most fortunate that colleagues and friends have been generous with their counsel and patience and have thereby sustained me throughout this long project. During the early phase of the project, Bridget Carr and Beth Sandager served as valuable research assistants. Many colleagues at MIT and other institutions read portions of this work and were generous with their expert advice. My thanks to Greg Anderson, Paul Barrett, David Bearman, James Bess, Allan Bufferd, Terry Cook, Richard Cox, Jack Currie, Margaret dePopolo, John Dojka, Mark Duffy, Terry Eastwood, Tim Ericson, Ken Fones-Wolf, Robert Friedel, Margaret Hedstrom, Carol Johnson, Sally Kohlstedt, Joan Krizack, Jay Lucker, Bill Maher, Avra Michelson, Jutta Reed-Scott, Robert Root-Bernstein, Nancy Schrock, Lee Stout, Donna Webber, Lisa Weber, Tom Wilding, and Beth Yakel. Special thanks to Jim O'Toole and Megan Sniffin-Marinoff, who served as advisors throughout the project. I am very grateful for their advice and encouragement.

Support for this project was provided by the Andrew W. Mellon Foundation. My thanks to James M. Morris and the Foundation for their confidence in the project and their willingness to wait for the final product. Thanks also to Jay K. Lucker and the staff of the MIT Libraries for providing a home for this work. Special thanks to the staff of the Institute Archives, whose advice and patience throughout the project were greatly appreciated.

Rose Engelland opened the rich photographic archives of the *Chronicle of Higher Education* to me, and I thank her for her assistance. Lois Beattie's careful attention to the preparation of the manuscript was invaluable. Betsy Chimento's skillful and creative design made it possible for this project to come to a successful conclusion.

Finally, my thanks to Greg, Ted, and Phoebe Anderson, who gave me the last and best reason to finish this book.

Contents

1

Convey Knowledge 53

Foster Socialization 75

Conduct Research 107

Sustain the Institution 135

Provide Public Service 229

Promote Culture 243

Institutional Documentation Plan 253

Rationale for the Functional Approach

Varsity Letters is a functional study of colleges and universities intended to aid those responsible for the documentation of these institutions. The method used in this book, labeled an institutional functional analysis, is a new tool that supplements archival practice and turns it around.

The volume, duplication, dispersal, and transient nature of modern documentation require a reexamination of archival appraisal theory and practice. The premise of *Varsity Letters* is that new tools are needed for the analysis and planning that must precede collecting today. The book argues that archivists must start their selection activities not with a consideration of specific sets of records, but with an understanding of the context in which records are created. A functional approach provides the means to achieve a comprehensive understanding of an institution and its documentation: a knowledge of what is to be documented and the problems of gathering the desired documentation. Such knowledge enables the archivist to establish specific documentary goals and collecting plans. Institutional functional analysis, therefore, is the appropriate first step for all institutional archivists.[1]

Varsity Letters is intended for two audiences. First, the work is for archivists, records managers, administrators, historians, librarians, and others concerned with documenting modern academic institutions. For this audience, the book offers specific advice about the records of modern colleges and universities and proposes a method to ensure their adequate documentation. The volume contains descriptions of the primary functions of colleges and universities and explores the problems of documenting them.

Second, the work is addressed to those responsible for the documentation of other modern institutions: hospitals, banks, churches, museums, governments. For these readers, the volume offers a method to analyze and plan the preservation of records for any type of institution. This chapter is directed to the second audience to show how *Varsity Letters* contributes to archival practice in general and how an institutional functional analysis can be adapted to deal with the documentary problems of other sectors of modern society.

Background

For the last two decades archivists have criticized the capacity of their profession to document modern society. Acknowledging past deficiencies, archivists recognize that the complexity and volume of modern records require new approaches, especially to selection. When F. Gerald Ham explored why archivists carry out their selection responsibilities so badly, he commented, "A handful of critics, however, have suggested that something is fundamentally wrong: our methods are inadequate to achieve our objective, and our passivity and perceptions produce a biased and distorted archival record."[2]

Archivists utilize a body of accepted theory and practice to guide their selection of records. The selection process, known as appraisal, generally emanates from an analysis and evaluation of specific sets of records. Collection by collection selection processes, however, are inadequate and unrealistic in light of the volume of records archivists face. "The size of the annual accumulation of recorded evidence, and the variety of its sources of creation, prohibit archivists, even collectively, from ever coming into con-tact with all but a tiny percentage of it....If somehow archivists could review it all, how much manpower would be required to appraise it, using present approaches?"[3] Archivists use collection policies to articulate the goals of an archival repository and provide the context that guides the selection of individual collections. Generally, however, collection policies are vaguely worded, open-ended statements of goals that are not specific enough to guide selection or documentary activities.

Selection is also guided by archivists' knowledge of their institutions, which is traditionally obtained by reading historical works, studying organi-zation charts, and examining records. *Varsity Letters* supports this focus on institutions but suggests starting the selection process with a different set of questions: focusing first not on the specific history, people, events, structure, or records of an institution, but on an understanding of what the institution does — what are its functions. A knowledge of the broad range of the functions provides the context that institutional archivists need to for-mulate their collecting policies and select specific collections.

As part of F. Gerald Ham's exhortation to the profession that "conceptuali-zation must precede collection," he asked for "empirical studies on data selection. For example, why don't college and university archivists compare the documentation produced by institutions of higher education with the records universities usually preserve, to discover biases and distortions in the selection process and provide an informed analysis on how archivists should document education and its institutions?"[4] This book responds to the idea of providing an analysis of the institution and its documentation as the background information needed by archivists to make informed selection decisions. Such an approach is in harmony with Hugh Taylor and Terry Cook, who suggest that "the focus of appraisal should shift from the actual record to the conceptual context of its creation, from the physical to the intellectual, from matter to mind."[5] *Varsity Letters* transforms these calls for contextual information into an analytic process that can become a part of archival practice.

Method Used

Varsity Letters builds upon traditional archival practice and is intended to supplement it. The work uses a functional approach to achieve an understanding of a specific type of institution — colleges and universities — in order to ensure an adequate documentation. Archival practice stresses the need to understand institutions and has used an examination of functions as a method to achieve this goal. This work departs from traditional archival approaches, however, in certain fundamental ways: in the level at which the functional analysis takes place; in the objectives of the analysis; in the scope of documentary problems examined; and in the role of the archivist in the process. This introductory chapter examines the different assumptions and approaches taken in this work.

Varsity Letters is the second study of modern documentation funded by the Andrew W. Mellon Foundation undertaken by the Institute Archives and Special Collections of the Massachusetts Institute of Technology (MIT) Libraries. The purpose of both studies was not only to prepare useful appraisal guidelines for specific areas but also to develop better appraisal methods in general. The first project used science and technology as a case study to formulate approaches to the documentation of particular subject areas. *Appraising the Records of Modern Science and Technology: A Guide*,[6] the book produced by that project, presents descriptions of the component activities in the scientific and technological processes. Records are evaluated for the evidence they provide about each activity. The authors hypothesize that their method can be adapted to analyze the records of other subject areas.[7]

Most archivists, however, focus their activities not on a specific subject area, but on the institution they work for. *Varsity Letters*, therefore, studies the documentation of institutions. Colleges and universities were chosen as the case study for this project because they provide a good example of complex modern institutions and because there is a large community of college and university archivists who can make use of the findings.

Level of Analysis

Professionals as diverse as anthropologists, sociologists, and business managers use functional analysis as a descriptive technique to facilitate the examination of patterns across structures and cultures. The archival literature encourages the use of functional analysis, but until recently such proposals had not been developed into accepted procedures. "It is probably more important to relate the records to a particular function than it is to relate them to an organizational component because there may be no relationship between the organization and the function."[8] David Bearman and Richard Lytle's emphasis on the power of provenance is essentially an argument for an emphasis on functions. "Functions are independent of organizational structures, more closely related to the significance of documentation than organizational structures, and both finite in number and linguistically simple."[9] Bearman and Lytle argue persuasively for the use of functions, especially for descriptive purposes. *Varsity Letters* demonstrates how a study of functions can support appraisal and documentary activities as well.

Increasingly, archivists are using functional approaches in diverse ways. In *Understanding Archives and Manuscripts* James M. O'Toole examined the functions of records to fulfill basic human motivations to record and document activities.[10] Clark Elliott has examined the function of individual documents.[11] Bearman and Lytle have discussed the functions of both organizations and offices.[12] The MARC AMC bibliographic record contains a field for information on the function of the office that created the records. Although the simultaneous application of functional analysis at all of these levels may create some confusion, each application is valid and useful. Functional analysis frees the observer from focusing on the particulars, such as the name of the office that created the record, and promotes greater understanding of the purposes for which the records were created. Functional analysis also reveals common patterns that permit comparison across traditional institutional boundaries. It is imperative, however, that the level of application be clear.

Varsity Letters applies a functional approach at an institutional level by asking, what are the functions of colleges and universities? The work argues that applying functional analysis at the institutional level is essential to understand the nature of modern institutions and the broad range of activities that they encompass.

Archival practice has always placed great emphasis on a knowledge of institutions. Archivists study the history and organization of their institutions to help them analyze records, develop institutional collecting policies, and describe their collections. Formal published histories; organization charts; and volumes of rules, regulations, and policies are all used for these investigations. The purpose of these institutional studies is generally to understand a set of records or the activities of a specific office. Archivists have used functional analysis as part of this effort, but the application has been synonymous with a structural analysis. The question archivists have asked is what is the function of a given office?

The traditional focus on administrative structure may be increasingly obsolete in light of the changing nature of modern institutions and their documentation. American appraisal theory and practice were developed at the National Archives and Records Administration and reflect the need to manage the records of hierarchical institutions — specifically the federal government. Though these theories may have been useful to the federal government in the 1930s, they are inadequate for managing the records of complex institutions in the 1990s and beyond.

The size, scope, and pace of modern institutions require a new kind of organizational structure. The traditional pyramid with power concentrated in the hands of a few has yielded to organizations "differentiated not vertically, according to rank and role, but flexibly and functionally."[13] Appraisal studies of modern science and technology, business, and academe reveal that traditional hierarchical analysis is not applicable where power and decision making cut through organizations rather than being concentrated at the top. Modern organizational structures are more fluid, responding as needed to changing responsibilities and economic conditions. Automated integrated databases reinforce the need to analyze functions, not administrative structures. The question of which office creates, uses, and owns records must be transformed when many offices enter, alter, and share information in a common database. Modern institutions require an alteration in appraisal practice that focuses the analysis on what organizations do rather than who does it.

While the internal structures of modern institutions have altered, so too have the relationships among institutions. Traditional appraisal practice supports the analysis and collection of records of individual institutions. Today, however, complex relationships exist among institutions. Government, industry, and academe — the private and public sectors — are linked through funding and regulations. Records mirror the society that creates them. Integrated functions affect where and how the records of activities are created and where they are retained.[14] Documentary studies provide greater understanding of these related but divided sources and support coordinated appraisal decisions.

5

The documentation of modern institutions requires appraisal techniques that reflect their true nature. Rapidly changing organizations demand a mode of analysis that shifts attention from volatile structural issues to more consistent patterns of functions. Appraisal techniques must include the analysis of the functions of an institution no matter where they occur — within the organization or outside.

By applying functional analysis at the institutional level, the study aims to avoid the problems of shifting structures while also broadening the analysis to examine how functions are carried out within and outside of official administrative structures. Such an analysis leads to an understanding of the multiple actors whose activities need to be documented.

To study the full spectrum of activities that constitute academic institutions, this work examines seven functions: *confer credentials, convey knowledge, foster socialization, conduct research, sustain the institution, provide public service*, and *promote culture*. The goal was to identify a minimum set of functions that reflected activities at all colleges and universities to one extent or another. These categories and terms were derived from a careful examination of the literature on higher education and particularly the vocabularies the academic community uses to describe and evaluate itself. Consideration was also given to the categories and concepts familiar to the archivists responsible for these records. Therefore, the functional terms are in harmony with the way both the higher education and archival communities analyze and describe their universe.

Objectives of the Analysis

What does it take to document an institution? An archivist's response to that question dwells primarily on the analysis and control of institutional records and the responsibility to assemble and preserve official records. Archival practice focuses attention on the activities and individuals who generate official records. This emphasis is natural enough, but it runs the risk of narrowing consideration of the scope of activities to be documented and the evidence needed to document the institution. Traditional archival practice can obscure the multiple actors who play roles at all levels of an institution as well as the activities that produce little documentation. Though the care of administrative records may remain the archivist's primary responsibility, the official administrative records should not be considered a full and adequate record of the institution. By looking along rather than across administrative lines, archivists are impeded from achieving a holistic understanding of their institutions.

While some institutional archives (because of legal or institutional constraints) confine their activities to the care of official records, other repositories do collect non-official records in their archival or special collections. Canadians, and archivists in other countries that apply the concept of "total archives," combine a responsibility for official archival records and non-official manuscripts in their mandates and collecting policies. In the United States, however, there has been a perceived dichotomy between the motivations of institutional archivists and those of special collections curators. College and university archivists/special collections curators collect faculty papers, records of student clubs, and student "ephemera" because at some level they realize that this material contributes to a knowledge of their institution. The collection of these non-official materials, however, is often perceived as extraneous to the official documentary responsibility.

An objective of the analysis in *Varsity Letters* is to demonstrate that both official and non-official materials are required to achieve an adequate documentation of an institution. This work shows how the two types of records complement each other and why they must be examined in an integrated approach. With the emphasis in this book placed first on what is to be documented, the location of the record (which office or individual actually holds the material) becomes a secondary issue. If the function *convey knowledge* (the process of teaching and learning) is to be documented, for example, the archivist must acknowledge that official administrative records offer little understanding of what actually happens in the classroom. The documentation that does illuminate teaching and learning resides with the faculty and students.

Functional analysis aims to broaden a sense of the activities and actors that must be documented to achieve a full understanding of the institution. If the breadth of activities that constitute an institution is to be documented, we must acknowledge that the official administrative record is not enough.

Appraising in Light of Future Research Needs

This work argues that a broader functional understanding of institutions provides a more useful guide to what should be documented than some of the traditional values archivists have used, such as the consideration of research needs.

Archivists have been directed to plan for the future uses of records when making appraisal judgments. As early as 1963, W. Kaye Lamb called upon archivists to "practice the difficult art of prophecy...[and] attempt to antici-pate needs."[15] Maynard Brichford has said that "the appraiser should approach records...evaluating demand as reflected by past, present, and prospective research use....The archivist must appraise records that will come into their greatest use in the next two or three generations."[16] Although we come to our work with varied training, few archivists are skilled soothsayers. Bruce Chatwin wrote in his novel *Utz*, "History is always our guide for the future, and always full of capricious surprises. The future itself is a dead land because it does not yet exist."[17]

Brichford and others also recommend that archivists use their skills as historians and their knowledge of historical research when they appraise. This is useful advice. William Joyce's analysis of the research use of archives notes that "whatever the disciplinary affiliation of the academic user of archives, most come to the archives using an historical way of thinking...and approach their topics with a retrospective or sequential understanding."[18] Archivists can do a great deal to improve their knowledge of the methods applied by historical researchers: how they frame questions and use sources. Little can be done, however, to anticipate future research trends that alter the questions asked or the use of the documentation. Did archivists anticipate quantitative history, social history, women's history? No. These all represent new ways of thinking both for historical researchers and for archivists.

Rather than relying on subjective guesses about potential research, appraisal decisions must be guided by clearer documentary objectives based on a thorough understanding of the phenomenon or institution to be documented. Since archivists cannot predict future research, the best they can do is to document institutions as adequately as possible. A representa-tive record of the full breadth of an institution is the best insurance that future researchers will be able to answer the questions they choose to ask. Functional analysis makes it possible to select such a record.

No analysis or selection process, of course, is totally objective. The analytic methods proposed in this book are, of necessity, grounded in current values and perceptions, for, like historians, archivists cannot "divest [them-selves] of [their] own knowledge and assumptions....for everything we see is filtered through present-day mental lenses."[19]

Scope of Documentary
Problems Examined

The presentation in *Varsity Letters* places equal emphasis on descriptions of the functions and on analyses of the problems associated with documenting them. The approach taken in these analyses differs from usual archival practice in two important ways: first, the evidence examined as potential sources includes not only archival and manuscript but also published, visual, and artifactual materials; second, the documentary problems examined include not only managing abundant records but also responding to the scarcity or absence of documentation for some functions.

Information about modern society exists in many forms: unpublished, published, visual, aural, and artifactual sources all provide parts of the total documentary record. Archivists are not responsible for the preservation of all forms, but they must be aware of other types of evidence as they make selections. For example, scientific journals and technical reports are preserved in a library, but archivists should understand the general role and content of this literature as they select a manuscript and archival record to complement the published documentation.[20]

The modern documentary record reflects the changing nature of communication. Arthur Schlesinger commented, "In the last three-quarters of a century, the rise of the typewriter has vastly increased the flow of paper, while the rise of the telephone has vastly reduced its importance."[21] Since Schlesinger made these comments in 1967, the copy machine has increased the paper flow, while electronic mail and database systems have further altered our means of communication. Archivists acknowledge that these developments create significant alterations in the documentary record.

The record is affected not only by technology but also by the very nature of human activity. While many human endeavors produce records as a natural by-product, other activities leave no tangible evidence. Colleges and universities create many formal records as they examine and alter their curricula, but the actual teaching, learning, and socialization processes often leave few records. Yet these are vitally important activities. Such documentation techniques as oral history and photography are used occasionally by archivists, historians, and others who recognize that the written record is incomplete. Although archivists acknowledge the deficiencies of modern records, they have not systematically included the analysis of these deficiencies among their tasks or initiated activities to fill in these gaps.

Archival and records management techniques focus attention on the management of records. The archivist's problem is perceived as controlling the abundance of modern records and selecting the small percentage of documentation that should go to the archives. The documentary analyses in this work suggest that there are other documentary problems for the archivist to address as well.

Quality vs. Quantity

Primarily, however, this work supports the process of selecting evidence from existing sources. The purpose of the documentary analysis in *Varsity Letters* is to understand the available forms of evidence so that their relative worth can be evaluated. These evaluations should not only help archivists make selection decisions but also provide qualitative measures to support the reappraisal of collections already in archival repositories.

In recent years archivists have begun to use collection analysis to test the effectiveness of their collecting policies and practices. Survey techniques are used to evaluate the holdings of a repository and develop more detailed collecting objectives. Collection assessment projects at the State Historical Society of Wisconsin, the Minnesota Historical Society, the Bentley Library at the University of Michigan, and the Immigration History Research Center at the University of Minnesota all provide useful models of these efforts.[22] In each case, appropriate lists of subjects or topical areas were used to guide the evaluation of the collections. Descriptive controls and the collections themselves were examined to assess the subject strengths of the holdings. The difficulty with the existing collection analysis process is that it supports primarily a quantitative not a qualitative analysis of the holdings. Lacking sufficient knowledge about the nature and value of evidence, archivists can assess only the amount of material assembled on a specific topic, not the potential value of the evidence to support research.

The assessment project at the State Historical Society of Wisconsin, for example, left some doubt about the impression that their holdings are a rich source of information about religion. The survey found a considerable quantity of records documenting religious activities, but closer examination revealed that the records came from only three denominations and that 90% of them were baptismal and marriage records. These records contribute very important pieces of information, but they fail to document the religious experience in Wisconsin fully.

Archivists' documentary efforts often proceed directly from defining a topic to be documented to a survey to determine what records are available. Rather than asking what exists, the question should be what is the value of the available information to provide evidence about the phenomenon. Information exists in many forms and the sum total makes up an integrated record. An evaluation of each form of evidence determines its particular value in relation to the other forms of information.

In the last decade the archival profession has benefited from numerous projects that have examined the nature of documentary evidence. These studies demonstrate that the potential value of records is best understood by examining their creation and original use and their relationship to other evidence. While the National Archives study of the FBI records, the Massachusetts study of judicial records, and the more recent RAMP study of case files by Terry Cook[23] follow a long tradition of examining particular types of records, the archival community has also begun to produce studies that focus on the documentation of specific topical areas and types of institutions.

Understanding Progress as Process, Appraising the Records of Modern Science and Technology, The High-Technology Company: A Historical Research and Archival Guide, and the reports of the Center for History of Physics, of the American Institute of Physics, study the nature of scientific and technological documentation by examining the institutions and activities that generate records.[24] The study of the records of Congress being conducted by the Congressional Papers Roundtable of the Society of American Archivists (SAA) and the study of the health care industry directed by Joan Krizack will improve archivists' ability to document these sectors of society by providing information about these institutions and their documentary problems.[25]

All of these studies have essentially taken functional approaches that aim to examine the nature of a specific institution or phenomenon and the nature of the evidence of that institution or phenomenon. By examining the evidence — whether published, manuscript, visual, or artifactual — in relation to the activities that are to be documented, the quality of the evidence is assessed. The studies of science and technology, for instance, evaluate the role and worth of the published scientific and technical report literature and describe the particular types of archival and manuscript evidence that are needed to document the scientific process more fully. The functional descriptions in *Varsity Letters* clarify the activities to be documented, while the documentary analyses assess the ability of the available evidence to provide adequate information. For example, the finances section of the chapter *Sustain the Institution* evaluates published financial reports as sources of information and then identifies the key records that are needed to supplement those reports.

Understanding the nature of the function or activity to be documented is necessary for the evaluation of whether the evidence provides useful information. The integrated analysis of the available evidence makes possible the evaluation of the relative worth of each source. A greater understanding of the relative value of the evidence supports the qualitative reevaluation of collections already in archival repositories, the establishment of planned collecting efforts, and more informed selection of individual collections.

Role of the Archivist

Without analytical methods that provide an understanding of institutions, archivists focus on the records themselves. The records, not the institution, become the guiding force, and the archival record becomes synonymous with the documentation of the institution. The archivist's task becomes the management of existing records rather than the assembly of an adequate documentation for an institution. The archivist relies on records management and survey techniques to manage the voluminous records generated by modern society. The dictum to study institutions and appraise records in light of the total documentation translates all too frequently into a records survey which, as F. Gerald Ham pointed out, "is a logistical device we often mistake for an acquisition strategy."[26] Surveys simply uncover what records exist, and the end product is generally a plan to manage those records. A survey does not indicate what material is actually needed to document the institution.

Is the archivist's responsibility to manage existing records or to play a role in assuring the adequate documentation of an institution? The approach taken in this work suggests the larger, more active role for archivists. To meet the challenges posed by modern documentation, archivists and their colleagues must become active participants in the creation, analysis, and selection of the documentary record. This places archivists, librarians, and other curators in the role of documenters of their institutions, rather than simply keepers of their records.

To be a documenter requires a comprehensive understanding of the institution to be documented and the nature of its documentary problems. By examining all areas, a functional study encourages the documentation of the full multiplicity of activities that make up modern institutions. A functional understanding helps the archivist select wisely from the abundant records while planning appropriate strategies to document those functions that create few records.

Archivists have conflicting reactions, however, to activities that engage them in the creation of records. Since the early 1970s, when Howard Zinn challenged the profession to relinquish their passive "keeper" mentality and become "activist archivists," there have been debates about such interventionist roles. Archivists acknowledge the importance of records management techniques to control aspects of the creation and retention of records. The profession has also had to face the necessity of intervening at the creation of electronic records to assure that they will exist and continue to be useful. Archivists are more ambivalent, however, about their appropriate role in creating documentation when it otherwise would not exist. They recognize that certain phenomena will not be documented without active intervention: an archival record of a dance company requires the creation of a moving image record of the dances, and a more durable record of a culture that uses oral tradition will only be captured if visual and aural records are deliberately created.

Archivists have come to acknowledge and participate in such documentary activities, but a professional consensus has not emerged about their legitimacy or necessity as a regular part of the responsibility of any institutional archivist. As archival practice focuses primarily on activities that produce records, the documentation of activities that do not is not an integrated and accepted part of the archivist's job. Yet, if archivists perceive their responsibility as documenting an institution, then the intervention to create or ensure the creation of records must be an integrated part of their documentary mission.

Archivists, however, need not be the people who actually create records. Their most important roles are as analysts, planners, and agents who create an awareness of documentary problems. Archivists can then work knowledgeably with appropriate individuals to carry out oral history, photographic, video, or other documentary projects as needed. To be able to articulate a coherent documentary plan, archivists must do archival research, which must not be confused with historical research. The goal of archival research is to understand the nature of an institution and its documentary problems. Historical research, on the other hand, is a process of answering specific questions through the interpretation of sources.

Relationship to Archival Practice

Archivists use a variety of techniques to help them carry out their documentary responsibilities. These techniques form a continuum from traditional appraisal methods that guide the selection of individual collections to more recently proposed practices designed to coordinate the activities of many institutions. Institutional functional analysis and documentation strategies are both appraisal methods, but since this latter concept has become better known it is important to clarify the similarities and differences between them.

Much has been written and spoken about documentation strategies since the idea was first described in 1986.[27] Although confusion and concern remain about documentation strategies, this author believes that what is most important and valid is the fundamental ideas that underlie the concept: analysis and planning must precede documentary efforts; and institutions must work together because modern documentation is linked across institutional lines.

Documentation strategies are multi-institutional activities, as they are intended to coordinate and plan the natural dispersion of the integrated documentation of modern society. Documentation strategies require an analysis of the phenomenon to be documented and an understanding of the value and availability of evidence. The analysis of the documentary problems must precede the logistical challenge of determining where the documentation resides and should be retained. The current project of the Congressional Papers Roundtable of SAA on the documentation of Congress is a very appropriate application of these ideas. The record of Congress is created by senators, congressmen, congressional aids, committees, the press, and many others. These records are eventually dispersed and held by Congress, the National Archives, and numerous other private and public archives that collect and preserve the personal and professional papers of senators and congressmen. Members of the Roundtable have undertaken an extensive research project to ensure the adequate documentation of Congress. Archivists of government repositories, university special collections, and historical societies are working together to study what Congress does (its functions), how it performs its work, and what records are required to document its activities. The study's findings will help ensure the coordinated placement and appraisal of these voluminous records.[28]

The intellectual approach that underlies documentation strategies is the same as that for institutional functional analysis: analysis and planning must precede collecting. The techniques, however, are to be applied at different levels. Documentation strategies are intended to coordinate the collecting activities of many institutions. Institutional functional analysis is intended to be used by individual institutions to improve their own documentation. Documentation strategies and institutional functional analysis are, therefore, separate techniques but are mutually supportive.

Documentation strategies rely on strong institutional archives: the strategies are planning and coordinating mechanisms, not collecting activities. Although documentation strategies can focus on geographic areas, topics, or phenomena, the material identified for preservation is not brought together to form artificial collections, but rather preserved in the archives of the institution that created the documentation.

In the course of a documentation strategy for software carried out by the Center for the History of Information Processing of the Charles Babbage Institute, MULTICS was identified as an early development that should be thoroughly documented. As the MULTICS software was developed at MIT, the Babbage asked the Institute Archives at MIT to participate in their project. A search of the published, manuscript, and archival holdings determined that the Institute Archives already held some administrative records and published technical reports on this development. The Babbage Institute's interest highlighted the importance of MULTICS to MIT's history and therefore suggested that the documentation should be improved. The staff of the Babbage informed the Institute Archives of the laboratories and individuals who developed MULTICS and suggested the specific types of documentation that should be sought from them. The documentation strategy identified the need and the documentation sought, and the institution responded by strengthening its own holdings. Indexes at the Babbage Institute inform researchers of the location of documentation on software held by many institutions.

Documentation strategies require a thorough knowledge of institutions and their documentation, which is best supplied through a series of functional appraisal studies. Functional studies provide the foundation for both institutional collecting plans and cooperative collecting activities such as documentation strategies. For instance, a documentation strategy for the State of New York can use *Varsity Letters* to analyze and plan the cooperative collecting objectives for higher education in the state. At the same time, SUNY-Albany and Cornell University can use the book to assess their own holdings and devise collecting plans that reflect both their own needs and the documentation objectives and plans of the state.

To conclude this examination of how *Varsity Letters* relates to archival practice, it is appropriate to return to the fundamental concepts that guide archival activities, including provenance. How does this work relate to these and other basic concepts? How and where do archivists utilize traditional archival principles, and when do they use this work?

The central chapters of this book present descriptions of the functions that make up academic institutions. These chapters describe the potential full range of activities at colleges and universities. Clearly, these functions manifest themselves differently at each campus. The elements that constitute the function *foster socialization* will be different at commuting and residential campuses. The scope of *conduct research* differs at a research university such as MIT, a liberal arts college such as Swarthmore, and a community college. The complexity of managing an institution that enrolls 50,000 students makes the function *sustain the institution* different from that of a college that enrolls 5,000.

College and university archivists who want to use this book must translate these general descriptions so that they are applicable to their institutions. The Institutional Documentation Plan at the end of the volume will guide archivists through that translation process and assist them in preparing detailed documentation plans that meet the needs of their institutions. The translation process utilizes traditional archival tools such as administrative histories and collection analysis, and a knowledge of the concept of provenance.

The translation process begins by studying each function and evaluating its importance to the institution through historical investigations. The result of these studies is a clear understanding of what is to be documented and what documentation is needed. The challenge is then to locate that documentation. For the archivist, that problem requires an additional translation process to determine who created the documentation and therefore where it must be sought. The preparation of administrative histories guides the archivist through the second process. Fundamental to this work, then, is an understanding of the principles of provenance that rely on a knowledge of the office that created the records as a means to locate, arrange, and describe them. The functional analysis provides an understanding of why specific documentation is sought. Archival principles determine how those records are located, arranged, and described.

How To Adapt This Work for Other Institutional Types

Functional guides are a new tool to provide background knowledge of the phenomenon to be documented and guide the activities of archivists and their colleagues. Functional studies are critical to archival practice because their findings support all levels of activities from the selection of individual collections to cooperative documentation strategies involving many institutions.

It is the premise of *Varsity Letters* that its method can be replicated to provide functional descriptions of many other institutional types. If this test case is successful and proves useful, archivists can adapt this functional appraisal process to hospitals, museums, banks, courts, churches, and businesses. Seven functions are described in this study as comprising the activities of colleges and universities. A similar list could be developed for any other type of institution.

While certain functions, such as *sustain the institution* and *foster socialization*, will apply to many institutions, some functions must be altered to reflect the specific nature of an institution. For instance, while a list of functions for a religious institution might include *sustain the institution* and *foster socialization*, sanctify, evangelize, maintain tradition, and minister are functions unique to religious institutions.[29] It might also be possible to produce a generalized list of functions that each institutional type could adapt to its setting. Using the functional method, a series of institutional guides could be produced to support the documentary activities of the archival and historical communities. These guides would not only help each institution to document itself but also aid cooperative collecting activities, such as documentation strategies, by providing information about the nature of institutions and their documentation.

The author hopes that *Varsity Letters* will be accepted as a useful addition to archival practice and that colleagues will develop functional guides for other institutions that are vital to modern society.

Notes

1 It should be understood that although scientists and others use the term functional analysis to refer to specific analytic processes, in this work the term is used more freely to describe the use of functions to structure the study.

2 F. Gerald Ham, "The Archival Edge," *American Archivist* 38, no. 1 (January 1975): 5.

3 David Bearman, *Archival Methods*, Archives and Museum Informatics Technical Report, vol. 3, no. 1 (Spring 1989), 9.

4 Ham, "The Archival Edge," 12.

5 Terry Cook, "Mind over Matter: Towards a New Theory of Archival Appraisal," in festschrift for Hugh Taylor to be published by the Association of Canadian Archivists in 1992.

6 Joan K. Haas, Helen Willa Samuels, and Barbara Trippel Simmons, *Appraising the Records of Modern Science and Technology: A Guide* (Cambridge, Mass.: MIT, 1985; distributed by the Society of American Archivists).

7 Joan K. Haas, Helen Willa Samuels, and Barbara Trippel Simmons, "The MIT Appraisal Project and Its Broader Applications," *American Archivist* 49, no. 3 (Summer 1986): 310-314.

8 Thornton Mitchell, "Appraisal" (Paper prepared for the Society of American Archivists' advanced workshop on appraisal, UCLA, May 1979), 8.

9 David Bearman and Richard Lytle, "The Power of the Principle of Provenance," *Archivaria* 21 (Winter 1985–86): 22.

10 James M. O'Toole, *Understanding Archives and Manuscripts* (Chicago: Society of American Archivists, 1990), 10–13.

11 Clark A. Elliott, "Communication and Events in History: Toward a Theory for Documenting the Past," *American Archivist* 48, no. 4 (Fall 1985): 357–368.

12 Bearman and Lytle, "The Power of the Principle of Provenance."

13 Warren Bennis quoted in Alvin Toffler, *Future Shock* (New York: Bantam Books, 1971), 144.

14 Helen W. Samuels, "Who Controls the Past," *American Archivist* 49, no. 2 (Spring 1986): 109–124.

15 W. Kaye Lamb, "The Archivist and the Historian," *American Historical Review* 68 (January 1963): 385.

16 Maynard Brichford, *Archives and Manuscripts: Appraisal and Accessioning* (Chicago: Society of American Archivists, 1977), 13.

17 Bruce Chatwin, *Utz* (New York: Viking, 1989), 119.

18 William L. Joyce, "Archivists and Research Use," *American Archivist* 47, no. 2 (Spring 1984): 131.

19 David Lowenthal, *The Past Is a Foreign Country* (Cambridge: Cambridge University Press, 1985), 216.

20 Haas, Samuels, and Simmons, *Appraising the Records of Modern Science and Technology*, 69–76.

21 Arthur Schlesinger quoted in Ham, "The Archival Edge," 15.

22 Judith E. Endelman, "Looking Backward to Plan for the Future: Collection Analysis for Manuscript Repositories," *American Archivist* 50, no. 3 (Summer 1987): 340–353.

23 National Archives and Records Service, *Appraisal of the Records of the Federal Bureau of Investigation* (Washington, D.C.: NARS, 1981); Michael S. Hindus, *The File for the Massachusetts Superior Court, 1859–1959: An Analysis and Plan for Action* (Boston: G.K. Hall, 1980); Terry Cook, *The Archival Appraisal of Records Containing Personal Information — A RAMP Study with Guidelines* (Paris: UNESCO, 1991).

24 Clark A. Elliott, ed., *Understanding Progress as Process: Documentation of the History of Post-War Science and Technology in the United States: Final Report of the Joint Committee on Archives of Science and Technology* (Chicago: Distributed by the Society of American Archivists, 1983); Haas, Samuels, and Simmons, *Appraising the Records of Modern Science and Technology*; Bruce H. Bruemmer and Sheldon Hochheiser, *The High-Technology Company: A Historical Research and Archival Guide* (Minneapolis: Charles Babbage Institute, University of Minnesota, 1989); Joan Warnow, Allan Needell, Spencer Weart, and Jane Wolff, *A Study of Preservation of Documents at Department of Energy Laboratories* (New York: American Institute of Physics, 1982); *American Institute of Physics Study of Multi-institutional Collaborations in High-energy Physics* (New York: American Institute of Physics, 1991).

25 Karen Paul, et al., *Congressional Documentation Project Report*, to be published by the U.S. Senate, Spring 1992; Joan Krizack, *The NHPRC Health Care Records Project Report* (Forthcoming).

26 Ham, "The Archival Edge.

27 Samuels, "Who Controls the Past"; Larry J. Hackman and Joan Warnow-Blewett, "The Documentation Strategy Process: A Model and a Case Study," *American Archivist* 50 (Winter 1987): 12–47; Richard J. Cox, *American Archival Analysis: The Recent Development of the Archival Profession in the United States* (Metuchen, N.J.: Scarecrow Press, 1990).

28 Paul, et al., *Congressional Documentation Project Report*.

29 This list of functions was suggested by Beth Yakel.

The Functions of Colleges and Universities: Structure and Uses of *Varsity Letters*

Clark Kerr, the former president of the University of California at Berkeley, is reported to have said that the perfect university provides sex for the students, sports for the alumni, and parking for the faculty. Sex, sports, and parking seem a far cry from the traditional depiction of colleges and universities as institutions of teaching, research, and public service. Clark Kerr's list suggests the transformation of modern academic institutions from Thomas Jefferson's "academical village" into modern collegiate cities.

The purpose of *Varsity Letters* is to describe these complex modern institutions of higher education in order to promote their adequate documentation. The premise of the book is that a full understanding of the institution and its documentation is needed to realize this goal. For this reason, a functional approach has been chosen: the core of the book contains descriptions of the seven functions that constitute modern academic institutions. These seven functions are a part of every college and university, although their scope and emphasis differ at individual institutions. The descriptions are therefore intended to provide broad knowledge about the functions and their documentary problems. The last chapter, *Institutional Documentation Plan*, provides a method to transform the general findings of the book into an appropriate documentation plan for a particular institution.

This chapter begins with an explanation of how the seven functions were selected and then provides a definition of each one. Following a discussion of the structure and uses of the book, the chapter concludes with an exploration of the assumptions and themes that underlie the study.

The Functions

Colleges and universities are traditionally assigned three missions: teach, conduct research, and provide public service. This three-part mission may have adequately described nineteenth- and early twentieth-century academic institutions, but it fails to reflect the full multiplicity of activities that constitute modern colleges and universities.

In a little over a hundred years, higher education in the United States has been transformed from scattered small denominational colleges to a modern complex of more than three thousand public and private institutions varying in size and scope. As colleges and universities have grown and diversified, their original missions and purposes have expanded. Many colleges and universities have evolved into large multi-purpose institutions, with sprawling physical plants and endowments and expenses in the millions of dollars.

Several factors account for this extraordinary growth. Academic institutions have expanded along with the development of new and increasingly specialized knowledge. Faculty with subject expertise are required to staff new departments that splintered off from the traditional departments. The expansion and specialization of knowledge increased the need for professional, technical, managerial, and service workers with particular training.

In response, colleges and universities have broadened and diversified their curricula. The number of students attending institutions of higher education has increased dramatically in the twentieth century, growing from 4% of college age youth in 1900 to 27.9% in 1986. More recently, part-time and adult learners have become a significant part of the student population.

The rate of growth, however, has not been uniform. While some institutions evolved into multi-purpose universities with graduate and professional schools, others have consciously retained their small size and specialized focus. Therefore, the diversity among academic institutions is at least in part a result of differing rates of growth. Modern institutions of higher education range from small selective private liberal arts colleges enrolling 2,000 students to large public research universities enrolling 50,000 students, and from community colleges with open admissions policies to specialized, selective schools such as theological seminaries and engineering institutes.

For the purpose of this study, then, the three traditional mission terms had to be transformed into a group of functions that more accurately describe modern colleges and universities. The literature on higher education was consulted to determine if there was an agreed upon vocabulary that could be adopted for this purpose. The most useful list was found in the *Program Classification Structure* (PCS) issued by the National Center for Higher Education Management Systems.[1]

The PCS provides a common language to support program oriented planning and management of higher education. "The *Program Classification Structure* is a set of categories and related definitions which allows its users to examine the operations of a postsecondary education institution as they relate to the accomplishments of that institution's objectives. Specifically, the PCS is a logical framework for arraying information in a hierarchical disaggregation of *programs*, in which a 'program' is defined as an aggregation of activities serving a common set of objectives."[2] The nine categories established by PCS are instruction, research, public service, academic support, student service, institutional administration, physical operations, student financial support, and independent operations. Though useful, the categories predominantly reflect a management perspective.

The objectives of *Varsity Letters* required altering the PCS categories because the functions had to reflect the activities of not only management but also other actors including students, faculty, staff, and members of the community outside the institution; support an examination of documentary issues; and harmonize with categories familiar to archivists and their colleagues. For this project, then, the PCS categories were modified and the three missions expanded into the following seven functions:

1 Confer Credentials

describes the process of recruiting, selecting, and admitting students; providing financial aid and academic advice; and finally, graduating the students.

2 Convey Knowledge

covers the formulation and delivery of the curriculum as well as the learning process.

3 Foster Socialization

includes the informal learning that takes place outside the classroom in a planned and unplanned manner through residential life, extracurricular activities, and personal counseling.

4 Conduct Research

describes the endeavors of the faculty and graduate students in the search for new knowledge.

5 Sustain the Institution

covers those areas, including governance, financial and personnel management, and physical plant, that are required to assure the continuity of the institution.

6 Provide Public Service

examines those activities, including technical assistance and continuing education, that are primarily directed to outside communities.

7 Promote Culture

explores the role of the institution as collector and disseminator of culture through the operation of museums, libraries, and archives.

These categories were established to facilitate the analysis of the functions, but clearly many activities may appear to belong in more than one function. As the purpose of the book is not to classify activities into particular functions, but rather to provide an understanding of those functions, this ambiguity should not distract readers but rather aid their understanding. For example, in this work athletics is discussed in the function *foster socialization*. When informed of this fact, a group of archivists disagreed: athletics belongs in *provide public service*, suggested an archivist from a large midwestern state university, while another colleague felt that it belonged in *promote culture*; an archivist from a "Big Ten" institution suggested that they were both wrong as clearly athletics belongs in *sustain the institution*. The point is that they are all correct. These archivists have identified nuances of athletics that are important at their institutions and that suggest what should be documented. At MIT, and other NCAA Division III institutions, understanding the role of athletics in the socialization process is sufficient.

Structure and Rationale of the Book

The main portion of *Varsity Letters* is devoted to an examination of the seven functions. The subdivisions of each chapter are dictated by the particular activities or issues that are unique to that function. The presentation for each activity or issue, however, follows a parallel structure throughout the book: a description of the activity precedes a discussion of its documentation. The documentation sections explore the problems, including the management of an abundant record as well as the absence of evidence for a given activity, and suggest the potential value of particular evidence and appropriate documentary goals. Introductory sections, when needed, explore concerns that are relevant to several activities. Each chapter of the book concludes with a brief bibliography.

Although some issues may be addressed in more than one section of the book, cross references have been avoided. The reader should use the index to locate all of the places where a given topic is discussed.

Guidelines, not Directives

The documentary analysis and recommendations in this book are guidelines, not directives. Selection and documentary decisions can only be made in the context of a specific institution, and, therefore, these recommendations must be evaluated by curators before they can be applied. The book describes academic institutions as broadly and fully as possible, but the functions may not be of equal importance to all institutions. It may not be necessary or desirable for an archival program to document all of the functions equally. The legal environment, nature of the institution, and goals of the archival and library programs, among other things, will affect the way these findings should be applied. The Institutional Documentation Plan guides archivists and their colleagues through the transformation of the general findings presented in each chapter into a detailed documentary plan suitable to a specific college or university. The Institutional Documentation Plan sets out a procedure that uses functional analysis as well as more traditional archival techniques such as administrative histories, collection assessment, and surveys to develop goals and a plan of action.

Official Responsibility of the Archivist

The archivist has a responsibility to assemble and preserve records of legal, administrative, and fiscal value to protect his or her institution as a legal entity and promote its efficient management. At the same time the archivist assembles evidence that is of historical value not only to the institution but to other researchers as well. The analyses and recommendations about documentation contained in *Varsity Letters* aid archivists with their official responsibilities by discussing the possible legal, administrative, and fiscal values of records. Throughout the volume, however, are reminders that laws and regulations differ from state to state, and that requirements may vary for public and private institutions. The recommendations, therefore, must be verified in their particular legal setting before they are applied.

"Faculty Papers"

Archival repositories frequently make a distinction between the official records of the institution and the personal and professional papers of the faculty, administration, staff, and alumni. Legally, this is an appropriate distinction. Official records are transferred to an archives, as legally they belong to the institution. Faculty papers are deemed to be the property of the individual and must be given to the institution through a legal deed of gift. This book, however, evaluates evidence available to document specific activities without regard to the legal questions of how it must be obtained, and therefore without labeling the evidence as "administrative" or "faculty" papers. For the purposes of this analysis, all of the evidence, no matter in whose hands it resides, is considered part of a common pool of potential documentation.

Multiple Actors

Colleges and universities include many actors: administrators, students, faculty, staff, and individuals outside the institution. The abundance of administrative records often focuses undue attention on just one segment of the population. The approach in this book is to examine the role all of these groups play in each function and to explore the documentary problems of capturing their particular contributions.

More To Be Done

The quantity of published literature on higher education provides a sobering reminder that there is much to understand about modern colleges and universities. Certainly, this volume does not cover everything. The author hopes, however, that what is included and the approach taken prove useful, and that additional research and writing on the documentation of colleges and universities will supplement these findings.

Uses of the Book

Varsity Letters is written for individuals concerned with the documentation of colleges and universities. The primary audience is archivists, records managers, administrators, librarians, museum curators, data archivists, and others who share the responsibility of documenting an academic institution. *Varsity Letters* is not a general manual on the administration of college and university archives; it deals specifically with the selection of documentation and is a collection development tool. In addition, the descriptions of the functions and the evaluations of potential sources of documentation may help archivists and other curators provide better descriptive controls and reference service. In conjunction with William Maher's *The Management of College and University Archives,*[3] *Varsity Letters* can be used to plan a new archival program for a college or university or evaluate a program already in existence.

As *Varsity Letters* provides an overview of the activities that constitute colleges and universities, it could prove useful not only to curators but to anyone who needs to understand more about academic institutions and their documentation. Managers working in colleges and universities can examine their relationship to the rest of the institution and the adequacy of their services through a consideration of these functions. The administrators of an academic library tested this idea by using the list of functions to evaluate if their activities responded sufficiently to all parts of their institution. Additional experimentation will suggest other applications.

Recurring Themes about the Institutions and the Documentation

Throughout the descriptions of the functions and discussions of the documentation, certain themes recur and therefore underlie *Varsity Letters*. It is useful to explore a few of these in general terms before they are dealt with more specifically in the chapters that follow.

General Issues about the Institutions

Relationship to Society

An understanding of modern colleges and universities requires a knowledge of the complex interactions between these institutions and the larger society. Whether public or private, colleges and universities are shaped by many outside pressures including economic conditions, social values, and government laws and regulations. In turn, academic institutions influence society in many ways including the values they inculcate in their students, the knowledge they create through the research process, and their role as social critics. A fundamental tension exists because academic institutions are perceived as both preservers of culture and agents of change and innovation. As preservers of culture, they play a conservative part by assuring cultural continuity and stability, while they act as agents of change in their research capacity.

Autonomy and Independence vs. Dependence and Responsiveness

American colleges and universities are independent and autonomous in that they are free from direct government control and have the ability to govern themselves. Their independence is, however, tempered by their dependence on outside factors and the need to be responsive to society.

All academic institutions — private as well as public — depend on society for resources such as students, faculty, and financial support. To compete for these resources, colleges and universities must consider the changing values and needs of society. Their response is demonstrated through the academic programs and services they offer, the students they admit, and the research they pursue.

Societal pressures are strong. Government agencies, professional societies, and accrediting bodies exert increasing influence over colleges and universities. In many cases now, responsiveness to outside needs and values is actually mandated by federal, state, and local laws and regulations.

Competition

The pressures to acquire financial resources and attract students and faculty create competition among colleges and universities. Competition does not generally occur among all schools, but rather within a peer group of institutions: public institutions within the same region compete for state appropriations and in-state students; institutions with similar programs, such as library or medical schools, compete with each other regardless of their location; and the large research universities, such as Stanford, Harvard, and MIT, compete for faculty, students, and resources within their specialized group.

Academic institutions compete for the prestige that enables them to procure resources. The quality and quantity of those resources determines the status of an institution: quality of students and faculty, size of the endowment and budget, number of books and journals in the library, quality of laboratory equipment, volume of research support, success of athletic programs, and kinds of jobs and salaries that students obtain upon graduation.

These concerns about the institution's relationship to society and the competition for resources form a backdrop to the discussion of all of the functions.

General Issues about the Documentation

Each chapter of *Varsity Letters* contains relevant discussions of documentary issues. The introductory sections to *Sustain the Institution* and *Foster Socialization* have particularly lengthy general discussions about their documentary problems. The following is a summary of many of the problems that will be explored at length throughout the book.

Abundance vs. Absence

Records are the natural by-products of many activities, but not all. Voluminous records are the product of most bureaucratic activities such as financial management and personnel administration. Few records exist, however, that capture other critical activities such as the interaction between student and teacher in the classroom, the life of the student outside the classroom, and the role of the staff.

Both the abundance and the absence of documentation pose serious problems. Records management and archival skills are required to manage the voluminous record and identify the small portion that has long-term value. On the other hand, attention must be paid to the possible need to create a documentation of activities that would otherwise remain uncaptured.

Duplication and Dispersal

The records that are created often exist in duplicate copies held by many offices at the same institution. At the same time, the numerous ties to the outside world create a dispersal of related records among the academic institution and the government, athletic, academic, professional, and foundation offices that regulate and fund colleges and universities. Coordinating this duplicative and dispersed record is a complex task.

Multiformat
The documentation of colleges and universities exists in many formats and is the shared responsibility of many curators. Each type of evidence — published, manuscript, archival, visual, and artifactual — contributes some information which taken as a whole constitutes an integrated body of documentation. Selection decisions can only be made when the value of each form of evidence is appreciated as a part of the integrated record. The documentary analysis in *Varsity Letters* explores, for instance, the relationship between a published annual report or scientific report and the supporting unpublished records, and suggests when the published record might serve as sufficient evidence.

Automation
A particular documentary concern is the growing use of automation to monitor, analyze, produce, and communicate information. An extensive discussion of the problem of capturing and preserving these transient records appears on pages 141–146 in *Sustain the Institution*. Though solutions to these problems do not yet exist, it seems clear that archivists must work with systems designers and administrators as automated systems are set up to ensure that information of long-term value will continue to be available.

Legal Environment
The most pervasive external influence on colleges and universities is the complex legal environment in which these institutions now operate. Government regulations have a direct and dramatic impact on the documentation of colleges and universities as the creation of specific records, their retention for specified periods, and the access to them can be mandated by regulations. The particular legal environment of an institution, and therefore the effect of the government upon it, is defined by its public, private, church, or secular status. Archivists and others responsible for the documentary record must work closely with legal counsel, compliance officers, and auditors, who monitor the institution's legal affairs and records-keeping practices.

Each of these documentary problems is explored more fully in the appropriate chapters which follow.

Notes

1 Douglas J. Collier, *Program Classification Structure*, 2d ed. (Boulder, Colo.: National Center for Higher Education Management Systems, 1978).

2 Ibid., 2.

3 William Maher, *The Management of College and University Archives* (Metuchen, N.J.: Scarecrow Press; Chicago: Society of American Archivists, 1992).

1

Confer Credentials

Introduction:
The Students

The diplomas that graduates receive certify the completion of their academic work and confer credentials on them. This ritual is the final step in the long process of obtaining these credentials. *Confer Credentials* examines all of the administrative activities that lead up to this final moment including the recruitment, selection, and admission of students; the funding of their education; the advising and counseling of students about their studies and careers; and the process of graduation.

The description of each function in this book attempts to account for the roles played by administrators, faculty, students, and staff. Students, however, are the central focus of *Confer Credentials* and also of *Convey Knowledge* and *Foster Socialization*. A brief account of the current demography of these students and the legal environment that determines their relationship to the institutions forms the introduction to these functions.

Demography

The image is persistent: the eighteen-year-old student, living in a college dormitory, studying in the library, pursuing four consecutive years of higher education. Hollywood perpetuates this image of the undergraduate, but college administrators recognize that it is no longer accurate.

These are the facts:

Fewer than half of the nation's undergraduate students are under the age of 22. Full-time students tend to be younger than those attending part-time: two-thirds of the full-time students are 21 or younger, compared to one-fifth of the part-time students.

Among graduate students, 58% of the full-time students are under the age of 30, compared to 34.8% of the part-time students.

Only two million, or about 17% of American college and university students, live on campus. The rest are commuters.

While 57% of all students attend college full-time, 43% attend part-time. In the past decade, part-time undergraduate enrollment has risen by 22% while full-time enrollment has risen by only 13%.

Of students 25 years of age and older, 74% attend classes part-time because they are employed, have additional family responsibilities, or both; 58% of these adult students are women.

Attendance at two-year institutions has risen to 4.7 million students, and most of those enrolled attend on a part-time basis.

This changing profile requires considerable readjustment in many areas. Administrative, business, and library services must be available for more hours each day to meet the needs of commuting and part-time students. Financial aid policies that provide funds only to full-time students must be altered. To respond to the more mature and part-time students, faculty must rethink the content of their courses and the times when they are offered. College admissions officers must determine what credit should be awarded for "life's experiences." Orientation programs and services must be redesigned to inform and help the "non-traditional" students.

Archivists, too, must make readjustments. Stereotyped visions of the student body must give way to an accurate knowledge of the age and enrollment patterns of the undergraduate and graduate populations. Archivists must document how and why the population changed and how that change affected the institution. Although final transcripts for most students look quite similar, the experience of resident teenaged students is markedly different from that of women with children or working 40-years-olds pursuing undergraduate degrees part-time. Documenting the academic and social life of any student is a difficult task, and documenting the experience of adult, part-time, and commuting students presents additional challenges. These documentary problems are discussed more fully in this chapter and the two that follow.

Legal Environment

Since the 1960s, the legal environment governing the relationship between students and their colleges or universities has changed dramatically. Several factors are responsible: the lowering of the age of majority, the recognition of the constitutional rights of students, the acknowledgment of students as consumers, and the increase of government regulation of education.

In 1913 *Gott* v. *Berea College* stated that "college authorities stand *in loco parentis* concerning the physical and moral welfare and mental training of the pupils, and we are unable to see why, to that end, they may not make any rule or regulation for the government or betterment of their pupils that a parent could for the same purpose." Since 1971, when the Twenty-sixth Amendment of the federal Constitution lowered the voting age to eighteen, the states have responded by establishing eighteen as the age of majority, thus making *in loco parentis* obsolete. Today, most students are legally adults, and their relationships to their colleges and universities are governed by contractual and Constitutional law.

In 1969 the United States Supreme Court decision in *Tinker* v. *Des Moines Independent School District* stated, "It can hardly be argued that either students or teachers shed their constitutional rights to freedom of speech at the schoolhouse gate." Since then, the Constitution — especially the First, Fourth, and Fourteenth Amendments — has played a significant role at colleges and universities. The United States Constitution directly controls public but not private institutions, although private institutions have come to accept similar policies as the courts increasingly view students as individuals who have rights in contractual relationships. Federal regulations, including the Civil Rights Acts and the Family Educational Rights and Privacy Act of 1974, known as FERPA or the Buckley Amendment, apply equally to students at public and private institutions of higher education. In addition, considerable control of higher education is exercised by the states. The rights of individual students at private and public institutions are protected by provisions in the state constitutions.

In addition to federal and state constitutions and regulations, students gain protection through their contractual relationship with their institutions. Under state law, students of the age of majority are protected as consumers and have challenged their institutions over tuition charges, disciplinary actions, admissions decisions, academic dismissal, change in academic programs, and degree revocation. Students have tended to win cases involving rules and regulations regarding conduct, but the institutions have generally prevailed in cases relating to academic matters. Academic institutions now scrutinize their published materials, policies, contracts, and activities to minimize their contractual liability. Contractual relationships are two-sided: just as the student can sue the university for breach of contract, so too can the university sue the student for, for instance, non-payment of fees and infraction of the social or academic rules.

General Documentary
Issues about Students

Against this legal backdrop, colleges and universities create and maintain a wide variety of information about their students including administrative, financial, academic, and medical records, as well as information on social and personal activities. These records are voluminous, highly dispersed, and often heavily duplicated. Increasingly they also exist in machine-readable form. Official student records are created and maintained by many offices: admissions, registrar, dean of students, bursar, employment, medical, and others. Additional academic records are created and maintained by departmental offices, instructors, and advisors. While these academic files often contain copies of records generated by administrative offices, there may also be unique information documenting the student's choice of courses, selection of thesis topic, job or graduate school selection, and relationships with faculty members.

Information about personal and social activities is maintained in dormitory and club offices, in the files of those who serve as personal advisors, and by the students themselves. This diverse set of records provides documentation about the many facets of the students' college experience.

Discussions of the specific documentary problems and forms of evidence are included in the three chapters that follow. The overriding goal, however, is that an adequate record about students be preserved. The significant problems in achieving this goal must be considered first, as they shape all decisions governing student information. These problems can be categorized as managerial, technical, historical, and legal.

The dispersed and duplicative nature of student records creates managerial problems for the institution. Assembling one coherent file or coordinating the retention of specific material in diverse files is a complex task. Establishing retention policies requires the coordination of administrative, financial, and academic offices. Records of long-term value are interfiled with routine transactional forms in many files around the campus, and the task of separating and gathering the archival records while eliminating the records of short-term value is not insignificant. For the institution and the archivist as well, the size of the student body exacerbates this problem: coordinating information about 40,000 full- and part-time students is a significantly more difficult task than dealing with the records of 2,500 full-time undergraduate students.

Technical problems present themselves whether records exist in paper or automated form. The paper record presents space and physical preservation problems for the administrative offices as well as the archives. Both the registrar and the archivist must be concerned about the preservation of the paper records deemed to be of long-term value. Machine-readable files lessen the concerns about space but generate different problems. The transient nature of machine-readable records requires archivists to work with administrators and systems designers to ensure that retained data remain usable in the future. There must be assurance that databases contain the information required for short- and long-term needs, that the information is maintained and not altered without approval, and that steps are taken to retain and update the system documentation (the technical documentation of the data structure and content values represented in the data).

Historical considerations are relevant not only to outside researchers but to the institution as well. Institutional self-studies rely on access to adequate information. While aggregate information about the students can suffice for certain investigations, more detailed data about individuals are needed for others. Information about the background and academic careers of the students is needed to understand a wide variety of issues including how and why students come to a college, how they select their academic programs, and how their training does or does not prepare them for their jobs.

Finally, there are legal considerations. The creation and maintenance of information about students is heavily regulated by the federal and state governments and the courts. The most significant control over student records is imposed by the Family Educational Rights and Privacy Act of 1974 (FERPA), the purpose of which is to protect the rights of students by controlling the creation, maintenance, and access to educational records. The Act defines student records very broadly as all "those records which (1) are directly related to a student, and (2) are maintained by an educational institution or by a party acting for the agency or institution" (20 U.S.C. 123g(a)(4)(A); 34 C.F.R. sec. 99.3). Five exemptions are made for personal and private records of institutional personnel, specific campus law enforcement, student employment and health care records, and information about individuals once they are no longer students (alumni records) (Kaplin, p. 359). Also excluded from regulation is directory information, which generally includes the student's name, address, telephone number, date and place of birth, major field of study, participation in officially recognized activities and sports, weight and height of members of athletic teams, dates of attendance, degrees and awards received, the most recent previous educational agency or institution attended, and other similar information. FERPA regulations apply only to records of students who are admitted to and attend academic institutions; therefore, admission applications are not covered.

FERPA gives students the right to inspect and challenge the contents of their records and prevents the institution from disclosing identifiable information without the approval of the student. Institutions must issue written procedures to comply with FERPA, advise students of their rights, and maintain records both of requests for access to material and of the names of the students who have waived their rights to access.

Many problems exist for administrators and archivists alike since student records must be administered in accordance with FERPA regulations whether they are housed in administrative offices, a records center, or the archives. Archivists and administrators must deal with federal regulations, such as FERPA, that can conflict with state laws, and they must interpret legislation that often contains no provisions for long-term historical use. An initial reaction to FERPA and similar legislation was to destroy student records. Intervention by archivists and amendments to the original bill clarified that student records can be retained, and retention policies are left to the discretion of the institution. Colleges and universities are required to formulate written policies, but as FERPA is descriptive rather than prescriptive legislation, there is latitude about many issues. In establishing its institutional policy, each campus must balance the FERPA regulations against local laws and attitudes.

Archivists have a role to play in the formulation and implementation of the FERPA policy. The legal and archival literature provides some useful guidance (see Bibliography), and further advice is available to archivists and administrators alike from the Family Policy and Regulations Office of the United States Department of Education.

For archivists, a primary concern is the question surrounding the use of student records for research, as FERPA prohibits the reuse of records without the student's prior approval. Section 99.31 makes exceptions to the prior approval provision by permitting the reuse by the institution itself and other educational agencies for aggregate studies. Some universities have extended this provision to include aggregate research conducted by scholars in the archives, justifying this access as contributing to the self-study of the institution. Researchers then are required to give a copy of their final research product to the archives, where it is made available to the institution. Research on individuals or on small groups where individuals could easily be identified requires prior permission from the individual students. In most states, privacy is a right that is generally considered to cease at death; therefore, archivists need not restrict the use of records of deceased students. Each institution, however, must clarify these issues in light of FERPA, state laws, and its own institutional policies.

The American Association of Collegiate Registrars and Admissions Officers (AACRAO) provides valuable guidance for administrators and archivists on the management of student records. Their publication *Retention of Records: A Guide for Retention and Disposal of Student Records* is a useful accumulation of legal considerations and retention recommendations and is therefore a good place to begin. In addition to FERPA, AACRAO's publication covers other federal regulations including those issued by the Veterans Administration and the Internal Revenue Service. Although an archivist served on the committee that prepared the 1987 retention guide, archival concerns are still not fully reflected. The retention recommendations delineate only the minimum required to comply with the law. Archivists therefore must build on these recommendations to ensure that an adequate record is preserved.

Here, as in many other chapters of this book, consideration must be given to three different levels of documentation: policies and procedures, aggregate data, and information about individuals. While the main focus here is on records of individual students, the documentary sections that follow discuss the need to preserve the records of the policies and procedures that control the students (their admission, graduation, conduct, academic performance, etc.) and aggregate information about students (size and demography of the student body, enrollment and housing patterns, degrees awarded, etc.) that is needed for administrative and historical research.

The most detailed and voluminous record and the most difficult to manage is, however, the information about each student. Institutions that enroll 40,000 may be able to keep little more than the final transcript. The decision about what types of information should be retained about each student (e.g., transcript, admissions material, correspondence, evaluations, thesis proposals), by whom, and in what form must be a cooperative decision made by the appropriate officials of the institution, with advice from the archivist and legal counsel. The information and legal needs of the institution and of the students must be evaluated. These deliberations must include consideration of the future uses of the records and should clarify under what circumstances and with whose permission student records can be used for aggregate and individual research both during the student's lifetime and after his or her death.

There is no single solution to this problem. Each institution must weigh the institution's and students' needs against the burdens of gathering and preserving these records and the legal risks of retaining or destroying them. The long-term administrative, legal, and historical value of the records must justify the costs and risks of retaining them.

Recruiting, Selecting, and Admitting Students

Admission to Undergraduate Education

Admissions Policies

Each academic institution establishes an admissions policy in light of its mission, history, resources, and goals. Admissions policies at American colleges and universities range from the highly selective to open enrollment. These policies are influenced heavily by changing societal attitudes about the need for a college education and who should have access to it. Changing economic and social values influence both public and private institutions. Government policies reinforce societal trends and influence who is admitted to college by obliging institutions to comply with regulations that further social programs, such as civil rights and affirmative action. Admissions policies, therefore, represent a balance of internal and external concerns.

Simultaneously, another selection process takes place as students choose the institutions they want to attend. The socioeconomic backgrounds of the students and their impressions of the colleges they are familiar with are strong factors influencing such choices. The two sides of the process converge as college and university admissions officers actively recruit prospective students.

Private institutions have greater autonomy over their admissions policies than do public institutions. For example, state and city legislators can mandate open enrollment policies and control the number of in-state and out-of-state students accepted by public institutions. Public as well as private institutions have other pressures: alumni exert pressure for the acceptance of their children; faculty and staff lobby for special consideration of academically and athletically talented students; additional pressures may exist for racial, geographical, religious, and social diversity.

All of these factors are weighed when institutions establish their admissions policies, and the most senior officers of an institution are involved in this process. The sensitive nature of these deliberations, however, means that little written documentation may exist of how the policy evolved. Torn between compliance with government regulations, external pressures, and their own internal goals, colleges are understandably wary of committing selection policies to writing. What is documented is the implementation of the policy — the process of recruiting and admitting students.

The Recruiting Process

Realizing the goals embodied in the admissions policies is the task of the admissions officers. They have several responsibilities: identify and attract applicants; establish screening and selection criteria; receive and evaluate applications; select and admit students.

The selection of students may be the most visible and lasting product of the admissions office; however, it is only the last step in a long process that begins with marketing activities. Multimedia presentations, brochures, and advertising campaigns are used by academic institutions to attract students and encourage them to apply. Special targeted efforts are made to fulfill recruiting goals for specific categories of students: minorities, women, native Americans, etc. In addition, as demographic projections have drawn attention to the possibly diminishing pool of college students, general marketing is undertaken to ensure continuing sufficient applicants.

Working with faculty and administrators, the admissions office establishes the qualifications to be sought and the process of evaluating the applicants. The admissions application elicits academic, social, and financial information about each applicant. Entrance examinations such as the Scholastic Aptitude Tests, although criticized widely, continue to be used by many institutions as a screening technique. Faculty, alumni, students, and admissions staff may be called upon to interview prospective students and to screen applications as they arrive. Finally, the admissions committee makes its selection and informs the applicants of its decisions.

The number of applications and the time constraints relating to the selection process make this a complex task. While the pool of prospective students may be diminishing, the competition to get into college continues to increase. In 1988, 37% of the incoming freshmen had applied to three or more colleges, but only 68% were admitted to their first choice. For the college and university admissions office, this means processing increasing numbers of applications: in 1990 the University of Michigan processed 17,926 applications to admit 10,602, of whom 4,763 actually enrolled as freshmen.

Admission to Graduate Education

Admission to graduate programs is equally if not more competitive than undergraduate admissions, but the selection process differs. While admission to autonomous schools, such as law, medicine, and business, is generally administered by the individual school, admission to graduate programs at a university (history, chemistry, anthropology) is usually controlled by the faculty of each department. The university controls which departments can offer doctoral programs and the number of students in each program through the allocation of resources (funds and space). The faculty, however, have a strong hand in admitting students, as they must weigh the availability of research and teaching assistant funding and match the research interests of prospective students with the faculty as they judge the caliber of the candidates.

Recruiting, Selecting, and Admitting Students: Documentation

There are four facets of these activities to be documented: the establishment of policy, the implementation of that policy, and both an aggregate and individual documentation of the students.

Records of governing boards, senior officers, and admissions committees suggest the actors involved in setting admissions policy and may indicate changes that resulted from outside pressures. Some admissions goals are recorded clearly and pursued actively. Many institutions prepare specific literature to publicize their efforts to attract minorities and other specific communities; for example, MIT's effort to increase the number of women undergraduates is revealed in its published literature. Evidence of the setting of quotas will be more difficult, if not impossible, to document; policies relating to reserving places for minorities, children of alumni, and athletically or academically gifted students may not be reflected in written records but revealed only through oral interviews.

The admissions policies of state colleges and universities may be formulated by a board of higher education and documented in its records. For public and private institutions, the records of senior administrators may contain correspondence about formulating and implementing the policies, though this may be inferential rather than direct evidence. Interviews with key administrators can provide more detailed information.

The records of marketing campaigns designed to locate and recruit students shed light on admissions policies by revealing the targeted groups, the geographical areas covered, and the particular kinds of students that the institution wishes to attract. Audiovisual and written materials are a useful record not only of the efforts to attract applicants but also of the institution's image of itself.

The records of admissions officers, who develop and implement the process of tracking and evaluating applications, may indicate changing attitudes toward the use of screening exams, modifications in the information required in applications, and alterations in the purpose and style of applicant interviews. Blank application forms are themselves useful documents as they chronicle changes in the information solicited from applicants over time.

The actual deliberations and selection of successful applicants — the most critical and probably the most difficult part of the selection process — are not documented. The impressionistic nature of these decisions and the required confidentiality suggest that this will remain so. Studies of the selection process have been conducted, and admissions directors may be willing to discuss some aspects of these activities.

Aggregate analyses of the students admitted may be available in a published annual report of the registrar, admissions director, or senior officer for student affairs. Such reports should provide evidence of the number of applications received, the number admitted, and those who chose to attend. Computer databases now facilitate analysis of the social, racial, and economic background of applicants. Reports can often be obtained from the admissions office in published form, printouts, or automated databases which facilitate future remanipulation of the data.

The result of the admissions process is available in the list of students admitted to the institution and eventually the list of students who accept the offer to attend. Some institutions issue a separate directory of incoming freshmen, often with their pictures; others rely on a published directory containing information about all undergraduate and graduate students.

The most voluminous record of the admissions process is the application form with its supporting documents. The information is gathered in one or more forms: a folder for each applicant that contains the completed application, high school transcript, letters of recommendation, evaluations by interviewers and staff, essays, photographs, and supporting documentation (including tape recordings and video tapes); card files summarizing the data and tracking the application; and increasingly an automated database containing background and summary information that also tracks the application process.

Folders for accepted and rejected applicants should be treated differently. Legally, institutions are not required to retain the records of rejected applicants. The American Association of Collegiate Registrars and Admissions Officers (AACRAO) recommends a minimal retention period of one year after application; IRS and VA regulations require that admissions documents for rejected applicants and for those who are admitted but do not enter be retained for three years. The voluminous nature of these files and problems of confidentiality encourage their destruction. It is difficult to justify the retention of even a sample for administrative or historic purposes.

Folders for admitted students receive differing treatments. Some institutions, such as Harvard University, make the application folder part of the permanent student record that is stored eventually in the archives. At other institutions the officer in charge of students (e.g., dean of students) or the student's major department retains part or all of the file, but eventually it is destroyed. The overwhelming volume of this material may force larger institutions to destroy these records, but in most cases the essential data are transferred to permanent academic records. Archivists should assist admissions and academic officers to determine if all or a selected portion of the file should be retained. Then, to prevent the dispersal and possible loss of the record, the selected admissions materials should become part of the primary folder that follows the student throughout his or her academic career.

The admissions folders, card files, and automated databases of information about applicants can be used to study individuals as well as aggregate classes and can support administrative and historical analyses of the admissions process. Analyses can be conducted of the financial, racial, and religious backgrounds of the students; reports can be generated about the educational and extracurricular preparation of the students; and studies can even be done on why students choose not to attend. While both paper and automated data can be used to answer these and other questions, machine-readable files facilitate the manipulation of information. Care must be taken, however, to ensure that the automated records needed for short-term and long-term studies are properly stored and the system documented. (See pages 141–146 for further details on automation.)

Financial Aid

Admissions policies establish goals to achieve a diversified student body. To a great extent, the ability to attract and retain students is dependent on the availability of financial aid. Such aid, in the form of grants and scholarships, loans, and work-study support, is used to defray tuition and living costs and other expenses such as books and supplies. There is a long tradition of individual colleges and universities and states making scholarships available to students attending their institutions. In recent years, however, federal student aid has become dominant. At first this aid was available primarily as grants, but, in recent years, increasingly the funds are available only as loans. At graduation students now face the prospect of years of paying off substantial debts. This change in policy has created significant problems, especially for many lower income students. As tuition and other costs continue to rise rapidly, institutions and students are trying to solve the problem of how to finance higher education.

As part of special and general fund-raising efforts, colleges and universities try to raise money for scholarships. Sufficiently endowed scholarship funds give academic institutions the ability to attract the students they seek. While most of these funds are raised from alumni, some funds also come from corporations and private foundations willing to support scholarships for specific segments of the population. Academic institutions and state governments are also experimenting with investment plans that encourage parents to set money aside years in advance to fund their children's college education.

Students are forced increasingly to make academic decisions on financial grounds. Unable to afford four years of tuition, students select two-year degree programs. Students choose to attend public institutions, where the tuition is often significantly lower, rather than private institutions. Local institutions are favored over distant colleges and universities to keep housing and travel costs as low as possible. And part-time rather than full-time enrollment is often chosen to enable students to support themselves as they pursue their education.

When a student is admitted and financial support is required, the school negotiates a package comprising grants, loans, and work-study income. The academic institution then has to hope that the sums offered are sufficient to attract the applicant.

Financial Aid: Documentation

Once again it is appropriate to consider the documentation of four facets of these activities: the evolution and implementation of the policy that governs financial aid, as well as an aggregate and individual picture of its award.

Records of senior officers and individuals responsible for student aid capture the evolution of aid policies. Development records and campaign literature demonstrate whether the institution gave priority to the acquisition of scholarship support for particular groups of students or the student body in general, and how they attempted to raise these funds.

Various publications, including handbooks for prospective students and the annual report of the treasurer, provide lists of funds and scholarships available to students. Published lists of annual recipients might also be available. Records of the financial aid office and of appropriate committees document the process by which these funds are allocated, the restrictions on their use, and to whom they are awarded.

The annual report and records of the officer in charge of student financial aid should provide considerable aggregate information. For administrative and historic purposes, it is useful to document the changing patterns of funding for students. What kinds of grants and loans are used to support students? What percentage of the student body funds their own education? How many receive school grants and how many rely on government grants and loans? How have the patterns changed over the years? How many students do not accept the offer to attend, or drop out of the institution, for financial reasons? Other aggregate reports can be generated from financial aid databases to supplement published reports and provide consistent information to allow long-term comparisons.

The management of financial aid produces extensive documentation about each grant or loan. Some records must be retained for long periods to comply with federal reporting and auditing regulations. Institutions are required to retain the records of payment until government loans are paid off, which may be many years after graduation. AACRAO recommends that records of financial aid be retained for five years after an annual audit has been accepted by the U.S. Office of Education.

Once legal and administrative needs have been fulfilled, little evidence is needed of the means by which a specific student funded his or her education. Questions of confidentiality make personally identifiable financial information difficult to administer. While aggregate studies of funding patterns are of continuing value to the institution and historical researchers, detailed financial aid records have no archival value and should therefore be handled through records management. As these records are voluminous and need to be kept for long periods, thought can be given to the use of microfilm to lessen the volume, or to the use of automated systems as a substitute for the paper record. The cost of microfilm or the retention of the automated database, however, may not be justified if low-cost records storage is available.

Advising

Academic institutions provide advice from many sources to help students deal with academic, financial, career, and personal problems. In the past, interactions with faculty were thought to provide sufficient guidance to students. While faculty still play a major role, other academic and administrative officers are now also available for counseling purposes. The presence of a professional counseling staff not only attests to the diverse needs of a student body but also recognizes that advising and career guidance have developed into legitimate fields of their own. Academic and career advising are discussed in this section, while personal counseling is discussed in *Foster Socialization*.

The academic advising process often begins during the summer before students start their first year with orientation programs, remedial course work, and discussions. Once the student is enrolled and declares a major, a great deal of academic advice is provided by the department and the student's principal faculty advisor. More comprehensive academic advice is available from the student affairs and other administrative offices responsible for coordinating and planning academic programs.

The present emphasis on career skills has brought career guidance and placement officers into the academic advising process. Students want to be sure that they acquire the training sought by prospective employers. Placement officers advise students during their academic careers, assist students in finding their first jobs after graduation, and may be available to graduates on a continuing basis for future job changes.

Advising: Documentation

The availability of advising services versus their actual use presents two very different documentary problems. Evidence exists in catalogs, handbooks, and directories of the advising services made available to students. Requirements may even be spelled out for meetings with advisors to approve academic plans. The use of the services by the students, however, may be more difficult to document. Academic plans may be signed by advisors, but little evidence exists of the less formal ways in which students avail themselves of advice. It is even harder to ascertain if the students followed the advice offered to them and if they felt in the long run that the advice was useful. Academic institutions that offer considerable freedom in the choice of courses, such as Brown University, rely heavily on the faculty to guide the students. Studies have shown that students' failure to take advantage of the advice available to them is often a weak link in academic programs.

Faculty members and counseling staff may keep notes on meetings with individual students; these are regarded as confidential records not available to the student under the FERPA regulations. The person who creates the notes generally retains them only as long as needed and then destroys them. Faculty and administrative advisors are frequently called upon to prepare letters of recommendation when students apply for jobs or graduate school, and these are more often retained. Though many counseling relationships are perfunctory, in some cases a faculty advisor becomes a mentor to the student. These relationships and the influence they have on attitudes and career choices are most often undocumented, although sometimes the faculty member and the student may have some correspondence if they stay in touch. Without permission of students and staff, information about the process of advising most likely cannot be captured, retained, or made available for reuse. It may be that studies of the advising system based on interviews with faculty, staff, and students provide the best available record of this experience.

There may be more of a record available of the placement and career paths of individual students. Some career placement offices create annual resume books of students looking for employment. They may also maintain files on students seeking employment, but space and privacy constraints may discourage retention of such placement folders. If placement information is maintained in a database, however, consideration should be given to retaining it for aggregate and individual research purposes. For instance, if information about previous jobs is retained when the system is updated, career paths can be tracked, and aggregate studies correlating academic preparation and career paths can be undertaken. This database can also be used for development purposes by making it possible to identify students employed by specific organizations.

Graduating

Commencement exercises are one of the traditional rites of passage in American society. In highly visible ceremonies, academic officials present diplomas to students and confer on them the credentials they have earned. Although the primary agenda is to honor the graduates, commencements serve several other purposes as well. First, the institution wishes to leave its graduates with a positive feeling about the school; they are now, after all, the newest alumni/ae who soon will receive letters of solicitation to support their *alma mater*. The commencement itself acts as a fund-raising activity as reunion classes — 10th, 25th, and 50th — are often asked to return and march in the academic procession. Finally, the exercises are used as an opportunity to bring prestige and visibility to the institution by inviting prominent individuals to speak and to receive honorary degrees.

Responsibility for planning commencement exercises varies, but decisions about the event are generally guided by a committee of administrators, students, and faculty. Before commencement begins, the registrar must certify that the graduates have earned their degrees and the governing authority must approve their award. One of the final requirements for many undergraduate and advanced degrees is the completion of a thesis, the size and scope of which vary enormously, reflecting the interests of the students and faculty and current questions in the disciplines. It is not uncommon for students in particular disciplines to use aspects of their own institutions as thesis topics. These theses, therefore, not only fulfill an official requirement and serve as a record of research at the institution, but also may represent an additional source of information about the institution.

Graduating: Documentation

Graduation is one event that is usually very well documented. The records of commencement committees trace the decisions made, including the choice of guest speakers and reunion activities. The record of the planning and carrying out of commencement is a useful administrative document for future committees. Honorary degrees may be recommended or even chosen by a committee of faculty, administrators, and students but must generally be approved by the governing board.

Official evidence must be preserved of the degrees awarded to individual students. A list of graduates and the degrees they received may be part of the commencement program or exist as a separate document generated by the registrar's office. The commencement program may also contain the titles of master's theses and doctoral dissertations, or again, a separate list of the theses may be issued by the registrar. A collection of blank diplomas (or samples collected from alumni) can be preserved to trace the changing form and style of these documents over time.

Since theses are submitted as partial fulfillment of the degree requirement, they are an official record. Most institutions submit their doctoral
dissertations to University Microfilms, Inc. (UMI) to be microfilmed,
reported, and distributed. The institution should retain a paper and/or
film copy of all theses. While this is often the responsibility of the
archives, the library is an alternative place where theses can be
preserved.

Beyond these official records, a selection of visual, aural, and published
material should be collected to preserve a sense of the graduation ceremonies. This record is often useful for exhibit and public relations
activities. Both the campus news office and the local papers contain
extensive documentation. A more personal record is produced by the
graduates and their families, whose photographs and videos preserve
their participation in the ceremony.

Bibliography

American Association of Collegiate Registrars and Admissions Officers. *Retention of Records: A Guide for Retention and Disposal of Student Records*. Provo, Utah, 1987.

Barr, Margaret, ed. *Student Services and the Law*. San Francisco: Jossey-Bass Publishers, 1988.

Barritt, Marjorie Rabe. "The Appraisal of Personally Identifiable Student Records." *American Archivist* 49, no. 3 (Summer 1986): 263–275.

Elston, Charles B. "University Student Records: Research Use, Privacy Rights and the Buckley Law." *The Midwestern Archivist* 1, no. 1 (1976): 16–32.

Hendrickson, Robert M., and Annette Gibbs. *The College, the Constitution, and the Consumer Student: Implications for Policy and Practice*. Washington, D.C.: Association for the Study of Higher Education, 1986.

Kaplin, William A. *The Law of Higher Education: A Comprehensive Guide to Legal Implications of Administrative Decision Making*. San Francisco: Jossey-Bass Publishers, 1985.

Knowles, Asa S., ed. *Handbook of College and University Administration*. New York: McGraw-Hill, 1970.

Convey Knowledge

The three traditional missions of academic institutions are usually referred to as teaching, research, and public service, the term teaching being used to describe the process of conveying knowledge. Education, however, encompasses both teaching and learning, and this chapter examines both the delivery of the curriculum and the engagement of the student in the learning process. *Convey Knowledge* describes the roles of teachers, students, and administrators in the teaching and learning process; the method by which knowledge is conveyed and its substance; and how the process is evaluated. Teaching and learning are inseparable, but for the purpose of this study, they are analyzed separately. This chapter begins with a consideration of the curriculum, as it defines the educational philosophy of the institution; the sections on teaching and learning that follow address the realization and delivery of the curriculum by individual faculty members and its reception by students. The chapter concludes by examining how the institution evaluates these processes.

Curriculum

The college catalog contains statements of educational objectives, descriptions of annual course offerings, and requirements for graduation. This information is the final product in the long process of forming a curriculum. The curriculum articulates the educational goals of the institution and defines how they will be achieved by providing the structure and content of the course offerings.

Curriculum planning is a negotiated process influenced by factors inside and outside the institution. One set of negotiations takes place as the college judges what society values and considers necessary to study in relationship to the institution's educational objectives. In addition, the curriculum is shaped by internal negotiations among administrators, faculty, and students, each of whom has different needs and visions.

The curriculum is dynamic. Departments and schoolwide committees continually evaluate, modify, add, and delete courses. Major reconsiderations of the curriculum occur with some regularity nearly every twenty years. Often influenced by external societal concerns about the effectiveness of higher education, as they were in the 1980s, colleges and universities are challenged to reevaluate significant portions, or the curriculum as a whole.

Outside Influences

The most general outside influence on college and university curricula is society's changing vision of what an educated citizen should know: what preparation makes an individual useful to society. Attitudes shift continuously between an emphasis on broad general knowledge and the ability to reason and an emphasis on specialized knowledge and vocational preparation. Often these changing notions are influenced by economic factors and current needs in the workforce. Colleges and universities must respond to society's requirements for trained individuals and at the same time to the graduates' desire to obtain the employment they seek.

The changing definition of the workforce and the skills required are linked to the expansion of knowledge. New fields of knowledge precipitate redefinition of disciplines, transform and create new jobs, and demand new training. For example, as computers became an integral part of most work activities, the need for electrical engineers and "computer literate" individuals increased. New curricula are required to prepare students to apply the new knowledge.

The discipline-based professional organizations play a key role in responding to advances in knowledge by defining the educational requirements for their fields. Organizations such as the American Chemical Society and the American Psychological Association have a direct impact on academic curricula as they specify the knowledge and skills needed to become a part of their particular professions. When educational requirements are established and enforced by a consensus of the members of a professional organization, the faculty impose these needs through their role in influencing and formulating the curriculum at their own academic institutions. In some professions, educational requirements are enforced through an accreditation process, in which case the curriculum is mandated rather than negotiated. When professional organizations structure graduate education, they also influence undergraduate curriculum by imposing requirements for admission to graduate programs.

Internal Influences

Outside influences create curricula that are, in their general scope, very similar from institution to institution. It is the internal influences that mold these general patterns to reflect the specific mission, resources, and interests of a particular institution. The curriculum is shaped by the priorities of the individual institution and is the result of negotiations among academic departments, faculty members, students, and the administrators who oversee the process. Differing concerns and motivations create tension among these actors. Academic administrators want the curriculum to embody the institution's educational goals, to ensure that its graduates are well prepared and employable. At the same time, they must address practical considerations such as the resources and the facilities required to provide the desired curriculum. Academic departments are concerned that the curriculum channels sufficient students to their courses to maintain respectable enrollment levels.

Faculty members play multiple roles in developing curriculum, as they first plan it and then teach it. While responding to institutional needs and priorities, they also hope to teach their own areas of specialization. Students influence the curriculum through the choices they make about their majors and the courses they select. They also influence the selection other students make through informal advice and, on some campuses, published course and faculty evaluation guides. On many campuses students now participate more directly in curriculum planning as they attempt to exercise some control in shaping their own education.

Curriculum Planning Process

Against this background, curriculum planning takes place. Senior academic officers, working with the faculty, establish the educational philosophy, objectives, and overall structure of the curriculum; the academic departments design the specific sequence and courses to fulfill these objectives; and individual faculty members develop the content of the courses they are assigned to teach. Though described in a linear fashion, these tasks actually overlap and influence one another.

Each institution has internal procedures to oversee ongoing modifications to the curriculum. Departmental committees review existing courses and recommend new offerings which are approved by faculty committees and senior academic officers. Periodic reexaminations of the entire curriculum are generally carried out by special committees composed of administrators, faculty, and possibly students.

Shaping the curriculum involves transforming educational objectives into the specific content and structure of the offerings. The objectives are usually realized by establishing a balance between the three separate components that make up the undergraduate curriculum: general education, concentrations, and electives. General education courses provide a breadth of understanding about the primary disciplines: humanities, social sciences, and physical and biological sciences. Learning in depth is provided through a sequence of courses in an area of concentration (major). The unrequired part of the curriculum, the electives, is the courses that the students choose to complete the degree requirements and satisfy their other interests. These components, balanced in different ways, constitute the curricula of the majority of American colleges and universities, although not all of them: some colleges form their curricula around interdisciplinary concerns, work experiences, or, more recently, competency-based programs.

Recurring debates throughout this century have focused on the problem of the appropriate balance between depth and breadth of the curriculum, between specialization and general education. The value placed by academic institutions in the middle of the twentieth century on a core curriculum as a method of providing general education has now regained acceptance after a period in which students had more freedom to select.

Curriculum: Documentation

The social context of curriculum reform is captured in the books and articles that document educational controversies. Alan Bloom's *The Closing of the American Mind*, Ernest L. Boyer's *College*, E.D. Hirsch, Jr.'s *Cultural Literacy*, and Derek Bok's *Higher Learning* are four works that provoked and commented on the latest round of curriculum reform in American higher education. Newspapers, magazines, and television programs also contribute to and record the debate. In addition, there is a voluminous literature of research on curriculum: sponsored by such organizations as the Carnegie Foundation for the Advancement of Teaching and the Carnegie Council on Policy Studies in Higher Education, studies have been produced on theories of curricula and the process of curriculum formulation. The sum total of this literature is a documentation of the external factors that influence curriculum reform. College and university archivists need not collect this literature, but it serves as a useful source of background information.

The final articulation of the curriculum is printed in college catalogs. The catalogs and supplementary literature explain the structure of the curriculum and delineate the areas in which students must take courses. Students are informed how to fulfill their general education and concentration requirements and how many electives they may take. How individual students partake of the curriculum is, however, another issue: while the college catalog and published literature including the registrar's reports suggest an aggregate picture of the curriculum, only individual transcripts reveal the particular combinations and choices made by each student.

Curriculum development should be recorded by documenting the process that lies behind both major reform activities and the ongoing review and modifications. This documentation has long-term administrative and historic uses. Curriculum reform is a cyclical phenomenon, and each new committee formed to examine and revise the curriculum should value access to the work of previous committees. While the new committee may reach different conclusions, important insights can be gained from the records of earlier debates that reveal the issues considered and the conclusions formed at that time. Correspondence of the president, provost, and deans may document why major curriculum studies were undertaken and what they hoped to achieve. The records of the committees assigned to carry out such studies provide greater detail of the process and the debate. Depending on the formality or informality of the process, correspondence and minutes of the committee may be in the hands of participating faculty members or with the chair. If the proceedings were recorded, audiotapes or transcripts may also exist. The final report of the committee should contain a summary of the process and the conclusions. If the report had to be approved by the faculty, deans, provost, president, or governing board, their records may contribute information about the negotiations surrounding the acceptance and implementation of the report.

In addition to the records of special curriculum studies, documentation must be gathered of the continuing modifications to the curriculum, as these also have long-term administrative value. Administrators and faculty frequently need to determine when particular courses were approved and what they were intended to cover. These decisions are contained in the records of the faculty committees that oversee changes in the existing curriculum and acceptance of new courses. Minutes of departmental meetings and correspondence files of chairmen and individual faculty members record the process by which sequences of courses for majors are constructed and individual courses are formulated and approved.

For long-term historical research, curriculum records provide valuable information about the development of disciplines. It is particularly important to capture the transfer of new knowledge from the research process into course offerings.

Many schools have pioneered in the design of curricula that turned out to be highly influential on other institutions. For instance, the cooperative education program in which students study at college and work in industry at the same time was conceived by Herman Schneider, then Dean of the School of Engineering at the University of Cincinnati. Such innovative programs should be thoroughly documented for administrative and historical purposes. Unique failures should also be documented.

Teaching

To understand the teaching process requires a knowledge of who teaches, what is taught, and how it is taught.

Who Teaches

In the last few decades there has been a significant shift in the demography of the American professorate. Since 1970, full-time faculty appointments have grown slowly while part-time appointments have surged from one-fifth of the academic profession in 1969 to one-third in 1979. The largest growth in faculty positions has occurred in the two- and four-year colleges rather than the universities: in 1979, 46% of faculty members worked at four-year colleges, 22.4% at two-year community colleges, while barely one-third worked at universities.

While these changes have occurred, a more competitive labor market has elevated the general educational preparation of the faculty, and an increasing percentage have doctorates in their subject areas. In addition, the surge of hiring that took place in the 1960s to meet the needs of growing enrollments created a faculty whose members are now predominantly more than 50 years old. The aging trend is also reflected in the percentage of faculty with tenure: while 46.7% of the faculty had tenure in 1969, by 1979 that percentage had increased to 56.1%. The 1990s will witness a rapid change as older faculty members retire and young Ph.D.'s take their places.

Affirmative action goals of the last years have stressed the need to add women and minorities to the faculty. Some small change has occurred for women, who now constitute more than a quarter of the faculty, while as recently as 1960 they had represented only one-fifth of the ranks. However, although the numbers have increased, most of the jobs for women are still concentrated in two- and four-year institutions, not in universities. Minorities have fared less well: blacks still make up only 3% and Hispanics only 1% of the faculty.

An ongoing issue in the effort to convey knowledge relates to the qualifications of the professorate to teach. Faculty members are trained in their subject areas, not in pedagogy. Graduate education stresses the mastery of specialized knowledge and research skills, not the acquisition of teaching skills. To a great extent, the faculty develop such skills by adapting the methods of their own teachers, consulting with professional colleagues, and acquiring experience on the job. Students, parents, and legislators have all complained about deficiencies in teaching skills. Some academic institutions and professional organizations have addressed this problem by providing training and literature for new faculty members, especially for teaching assistants.

Faculty teaching loads vary widely: individuals at two-year institutions are required to carry considerably more course hours than those at four-year colleges and universities. Teaching loads must be balanced with the other demands placed on the faculty by administrators and students. Higher proportions of time allocated to research and administrative or community service mean smaller teaching loads.

With the exception of two-year community colleges and some four-year institutions, the reward system for higher education emphasizes research above teaching. The lower value placed on teaching is railed against by students and the public. The value placed on research is caused, in part, by the fact that there are accepted means of measuring and evaluating research while similar criteria do not exist for teaching. Scholarly literature can be judged by outside peer groups, and prestige comes to the institution from the quality and quantity of the publications and the scholarly reputations of its faculty, not from their teaching skills. Students do evaluate their teachers, but these judgments are not deemed very useful or reliable in making decisions about promotion and tenure. Academic administrators, however, continue to seek acceptable procedures to judge teaching and incorporate its value into promotion and tenure decisions.

What Is Taught

With the general curriculum as the guide, faculty members teach the specific courses they are assigned and seek opportunities to offer courses in their specialized areas. In courses structured by a syllabus that outlines the work to be covered and the assigned readings, faculty members have little opportunity to make changes. In contrast, faculty members have considerable autonomy when asked to develop a new course or courses in response to departmental or institutional needs. Finally, faculty members seek opportunities to develop courses featuring their own areas of specialization or current research. Proposals for new courses are generally submitted to a department or school committee for approval.

The total course offerings reflect the intellectual boundaries drawn by the institution's curriculum, which constantly expand in response to the interests and research of the faculty.

Intellectual and administrative tasks are required to prepare new courses and revise existing ones. Intellectual preparation is required to define the purpose and scope of the course, develop the syllabus, select the readings, and prepare the lectures or presentations. Behind the intellectual preparation are scholarship and research activities. Scholarship encompasses the broad reading and investigation that is required to keep knowledgeable and current in an academic discipline; research is directed toward advancing current knowledge and developing new findings. Course materials are drawn from both: ongoing scholarship generates revisions and updates of course materials; research findings may lead to the development of new courses. The administrative aspects of course preparation start with the submission of the course description and syllabus to the faculty for approval. Then books must be ordered; materials placed on library reserve; audiovisual equipment ordered; and syllabus outlines, reading lists, and assignments prepared.

How It Is Taught

When course assignments are determined, a decision is also made about the teaching method that will be used to convey the knowledge: lecture, seminar, case study, laboratory, etc. Although the faculty member has autonomy about many aspects of the delivery, the style or method the teacher employs may be determined in large part by the size of the class, the discipline, or the level of the topics to be covered.

While the shortcomings of the lecture method are widely recognized, it is still the most expedient method of teaching large numbers of students. To respond, in part, to the problems of the lecture format, subgroups of the class may meet to discuss the lectures with teaching assistants.

During the twentieth century, interactive instructional methods have been encouraged as more effective in engaging students in the learning process. When size and subject matter permit, seminars, discussions, laboratory work, and problem solving techniques are employed.

Experimentation in teaching methods was encouraged first by the advent of audiovisual materials and now, in a potentially more revolutionary fashion, by automation. Computers are being used in many aspects of the teaching process to reinforce and enhance classroom activities. Writing courses have taken advantage of the capabilities to edit, revise, and comment on papers in on-line classrooms where all of the students can follow and participate in the process. Programs are being made available to students to review the work covered in class and to increase their knowledge through the opportunity to apply it. A computer game entitled "Go for Baroque," developed at Carnegie-Mellon University, is used in conjunction with university history courses:

> *The objective of the game is to make students in European history aware of the forces affecting religious affiliation during the baroque period in Europe. The program asks them to play the roles of Jesuit, Calvinist and Anabaptist missionaries who must make decisions about which European cities they should visit in order to make converts, weighing the risks of failure, arrest and execution against the gains of conversion.*

—Campus of the Future, p. 19

Computer graphics and simulations have the potential to enhance learning by visualizing concepts and creating situations that could otherwise not be known. Science students can study the atmosphere of a planet by simulating the flow of gases around its equator; language students can practice their skills in simulated real life situations; and students of urban planning can "walk around" Paris, Bombay, and Boston with the help of video disc technology.

Computers also expand the potential for self-learning. The availability of computer programs promotes the philosophy that teaching does not take place solely in the classroom; students are encouraged to take their education into their own hands and learn at their own pace.

Finally, the process of producing effective computer programs forces attention on teaching methods. Development of new materials requires the shared expertise of subject and computer specialists to analyze what is to be taught and determine how best to present the material. A problem for all concerned, however, is that this is a very labor-intensive process. It is estimated that 200 hours of preparatory work is required for every hour of programmed instruction.

In 1991 EDUCOM published *The Joe Wyatt Challenge: 101 Success Stories of Information Technologies in Higher Education.* The stories were assembled in response to a challenge made by Chancellor Joe B. Wyatt of Vanderbilt University to identify 100 cases in which information technologies improved undergraduate education. The abstracts printed in this publication "demonstrate a wide variety of technologies supporting many disciplines, student populations, institution sizes, and educational and institutional goals."

Technological applications are still new, and their ultimate effect on the teaching process has yet to be evaluated. (The impact of computers on the learning process will be discussed later in this chapter.) However, computers can clearly enhance the classroom experience and focus more attention on effective teaching methods.

Professional and Graduate Teaching

Graduate education in the arts and sciences relies on seminars, individual tutorials, research, and laboratory experiences to convey specialized knowledge and develop research skills. Professional education still features the lecture method, especially to instruct first-year students in law, business, and medicine. Business and law schools, in particular, utilize the case-study approach to develop a systematic way of thinking about the problems characteristic of their professions. The medical profession has begun to experiment with the case method as well.

Teaching: Documentation

Who Teaches

An accurate record of the faculty and their teaching responsibilities is needed for administrative and historical purposes. For promotion and tenure decisions, administrators must have an accurate record of each faculty member's course offerings. Students and graduates sometimes must confirm the content of specific courses and the name of the person who taught them. For historical research on the evolution of disciplines and the transfer of knowledge, researchers need to be able to trace the courses given by specific faculty members, the development and offering of new courses, and their acceptance or transformation by other teachers.

Catalogs and telephone directories contain lists of the teaching staff, although these are rarely fully accurate. A complete list of the teaching staff, including the part-time faculty and teaching assistants, is generated by the senior academic officer or the registrar and may exist as both a machine-readable and paper record. Some institutions, or parts of institutions, publish brochures containing brief biographies of the faculty and their areas of research and courses taught. These may not include the full teaching staff, but they do provide useful information about some of the faculty.

Detailed information about the teaching staff exists in personnel files held by the senior academic officer, individual schools, departments, and personnel and benefits offices. These files include information about salaries, benefits, tenure, leaves, sabbaticals, grants, and negotiations about teaching assignments and loads. Policies governing access to faculty records are less uniform than those for student records. The proliferation of litigation related to promotion and tenure is forcing institutions to clarify their policies on access to and retention of these files. (Personnel records of the faculty are discussed in greater detail in the chapter *Sustain the Institution*, pages 206–212.).

What Is Taught and How It Is Taught

Archivists should recognize that teaching, one of the central tasks of higher education, is actually very difficult to document. Although who taught what course can be recorded easily, what was actually taught and how it was taught is much more difficult to capture. For this reason, the problems of documenting the material taught and the methods by which it is conveyed are considered here together.

Documentation of what is taught is found in college catalogs, although these are often printed before all appointments and teaching assignments are made and may therefore be incomplete. Entries may state that a given course is to be taught by "department staff." Registrar's records in machine-readable and paper form are needed to supply an accurate list of the courses offered, the instructors for each class, the teaching assistants (if any), and where and when the classes met. The registrar's office may also be able to answer the question of who took what course by generating class lists.

Clearly, not every course must be fully documented. Some records, however, should be maintained to supplement the bare description of the courses printed in the catalog. The subject matter covered, the sequence of topics, and even a sense of the methods used to present this information are documented in reading lists, syllabi, problem sets, and exam questions. Library reserve book rooms generally receive at least the reading lists and in some cases also the syllabi. Academic departments sometimes ask faculty members to submit such material to them so that they can maintain a central reference file on their courses.

Reading lists, syllabi, and the texts used in a given course tell much about the subject matter covered, but they provide little information about how the course was presented to the students in the classroom. What is lacking is an understanding of how the information was conveyed and the message that the teacher brought to the students. What themes and principles were stressed in the presentations? How did the teacher use student participation, and how did this add to (or detract from) the learning experience? How did the teacher use and interpret the readings? Without the answers to these questions, the documentation of teaching remains incomplete.

Some faculty members write out full lectures, while others speak from the barest outlines. Lecture notes are reused and recycled over time, and another reader may or may not be able to decipher the notes. Whether complete or not, lecture notes and course handouts provide important detail and should be solicited along with other materials gathered from faculty members. Students' notes, which are often valued as a record of teaching, may actually be a more accurate record of the learning process. Such notes do suggest the information covered, but usually provide more insight into what the students considered relevant and how they interpreted the material.

On the whole, then, few records exist that capture the information conveyed and the style of delivery. Long-standing attitudes toward academic freedom and the autonomy of the faculty have discouraged the creation of a record of classroom presentations. Recently some faculty have consented to a videotape record of their lectures to be used by students to review class sessions. These videotapes should be acquired by archives. Then, selectively, courses and specific faculty members could be targeted for fuller documentation. Attention should be paid not only to the exemplary but also to the more routine courses. A schedule could be established to ensure that each department is targeted for fuller coverage on a regular basis. Special attention should be given to departments undergoing rapid intellectual change (e.g., departments of biology in the 1970s and 1980s during the development of molecular biology and genetic engineering). With permission of the faculty, videotapes could be made of the standard introductory courses, courses taught by key faculty members in their specialties, and courses offered for the first time in a new disciplinary area. Cost may prohibit doing a great deal, although financial assistance could be sought from the departments, media center, or alumni for such projects. The product of a videotaping effort would be a fuller and more accurate record of teaching.

Learning

On the other side of the lectern sit the students — listening, taking notes, asking questions, and, it is assumed, learning. But what is the nature and degree of the learning taking place, and what is actually being learned?

Researchers in cognitive psychology, higher education, artificial intelligence, and philosophy have devoted considerable time to attempting to understand the learning process: how does learning take place? what facilitates learning? and how can learning be measured and evaluated? If learning is a difficult process to understand, it is even more difficult to document.

The most visible sign of learning is the acquisition of facts. Examinations judge the acquisition of knowledge and the ability of the students to use what they have acquired. However, this is only one type of learning. Support is increasing for the belief that the ability to reason and apply knowledge may be of greater value than the acquisition of facts. A new emphasis on critical thinking and problem solving demonstrates that educators are trying to teach different skills.

Learning involves a variety of processes that help students absorb information, make it part of their knowledge, and enable them to apply their new skills as needed. Students learn by listening to faculty and fellow students, taking notes, studying, asking questions, carrying out experiments or other practicum activities, and writing papers and exams.

Research is also viewed as an active learning experience in which students must ask questions, direct their own learning, and thereby absorb new knowledge. Some institutions use writing requirements in many subjects as a means to help students articulate what they have learned. When successful, these processes force students to apply their new knowledge and initiate their own learning.

Students acquire a variety of cognitive skills that teach them how to learn. The concept of "hidden curriculum" describes the intangible and tacit forces that shape the academic and nonacademic learning experience. Knowledge acquired from the stated and unstated messages of teachers and fellow students guides the learning process by providing information on reasoning skills, as well as more practical concerns such as what the teacher expects the student to know to pass an exam. Students may be given conflicting signals from a teacher who encourages them to be creative but rewards rote memory on tests. Teachers are aware that the informal messages they impart to their students shape and add value to the learning experience.

It is generally assumed that in the teacher-student relationship the teacher teaches and the student learns. It should be recognized, however, that teachers are also learning, both about their subject matter and about their teaching skills, through the interaction with their students.

Learning: Documentation

Documenting learning presents significant problems but also significant opportunities. If the educational process is recorded solely through teaching activities, then the role of the faculty is documented but not that of the student. Although difficult to achieve, some evidence of learning is required to comprehend fully the impact of the educational experience.

Students take notes to record classroom lectures and discussions and their independent study and research. Papers, essays, laboratory reports, and exams for any given class may be retained by students or faculty members. The increased emphasis on writing encourages some students to maintain journals of their intellectual and social progress. Although often impressionistic and far from complete, these sources provide some evidence of the learning process of individual students. A program to collect notebooks, journals, essays, and exams from students could contribute useful information. Based upon the size of the college or university, the notebooks and related materials created by a designated group of students during their education could be collected by the archives. Another approach would be to gather the materials created by all or selected students attending specific classes. In the latter case, the selection should correspond to the documentation gathered from the faculty so that a record of the teaching and learning processes is developed for the same classes.

The increased use of computers in teaching may provide an opportunity for the archivist, as it does for the educator, to capture the learning process. Computer programs provide evidence of the information the faculty member wants to impart and the learning skills to be developed. Capturing the student's actual use of the program could provide some evidence of the process of learning. Although such a record may not be actual proof of learning, it may document the learning process better than other methods. The archivist still has the intellectual problem of making an appropriate selection as well as the physical problem of preserving the machine-readable record and the technical documentation of the automated system. As educators, subject specialists, and computer programmers study the comparative merits and uses of classroom and computer learning, archivists can benefit by capturing their findings and seeking new ways to document learning.

Surveys and research studies of students are also potential sources of information about learning. From time to time, faculty, administrators, and even alumni associations undertake studies to assess what students learned during their college education and what proved useful to them once they were employed. Cognitive psychologists/psychiatrists, educators, and other researchers have conducted long-term longitudinal studies of the learning process. Students become part of these studies while still undergraduates and are then interviewed every five or ten years to trace changing attitudes towards their education and their life.

The findings from the surveys and studies provide aggregate information about the learning process. Some researchers may establish files for the individuals they are tracking; with the permission of the faculty member and the students/alumni, these files could come to the archives and be made available for research. In any case, long-term studies may provide one of the only opportunities to capture the students' perceptions about their learning.

Evaluation

A number of methods are employed to measure the effectiveness of the curriculum and the teaching and learning processes. Although most evaluation techniques are deemed less than perfect, they are still used extensively.

Faculty committees examine the curriculum and add, delete, and modify classes. Students evaluate the curriculum when they select their courses and write evaluations of the ones they take. At some institutions, the students issue their opinions in published guides, commenting on the content of course offerings and the quality of the instructors. Although student evaluations of teachers have become more widespread, their usefulness has been questioned. Student comments often provide a personal response to the style of delivery rather than an accurate assessment of the quality of the teaching and the learning that took place. Standard methods for peer review of teaching have yet to be developed and accepted by the academic community.

While some institutions use only written comments or pass/fail grading systems, graded exams are usually used to test students and thereby evaluate the learning process. What examinations and grades reveal about learning is a widely debated issue, but examinations are generally considered a more accurate measure of the capacity to master a body of facts than of the ability to retain and use knowledge creatively.

Competition has made grades an integral part of the academic system. Institutions use grades to determine admission, retention, and the award of scholarships and honors. For students, grades provide motivation, feedback, reward, and punishment. Although students and faculty seek more accurate measures, grades remain central to the evaluation system.

Thus, neither examinations nor grades provide a satisfactory evaluation of the learning process. Recent demands for accountability made by state legislators, parents, and students suggest that academic institutions may be forced to devise methods that more accurately evaluate the effectiveness of teachers and the learning accomplished by their students.

Evaluation: Documentation

As researchers undertake studies to compare the value of classroom versus computer teaching, develop tools to measure the knowledge acquired during a college education, and establish accepted criteria for evaluating teaching, interest may be stimulated in evaluative policies and practices. Numerous records are generated by evaluation processes, and whether these evaluative mechanisms are flawed or not, they are an integral part of the educational process and should be documented. The records associated with evaluating the curriculum have been covered (see page 56). This section stresses the documentation issues related to evaluating teaching and learning.

Evaluation policies and procedures are established by the administration and faculty. Senior academic officers and department heads play a role in determining how to evaluate the teaching performance of their faculty. If student evaluations, visits to classrooms, and other monitoring devices are used in promotion and tenure decisions, the administration determines the weight they are given. Records evaluating teaching performance, whether generated by students or other faculty members, appear in departmental personnel files of individual faculty members, and consideration should be given to retaining some as examples of these reactions. Summaries and analyses prepared by other faculty members for promotion and tenure decisions are generally more valuable. However, without agreed-upon standard procedures to evaluate teaching, the existing records are at best impressionistic. If institutions preserve a selection of videotapes of faculty members teaching, historical researchers may perform their own evaluations in years to come.

Students and administrators need records documenting the policy and procedures associated with evaluating students. Administrators and faculty need to trace grading and testing policies over time, and students need such evidence when they challenge a grade or the procedure used to evaluate their work. Educational historians use such evidence to examine the theories behind grading and the effectiveness of the evaluation procedures.

Academic administrators and the faculty as a whole play a role in establishing the procedures for evaluating students. In this process the use of written evaluations, pass/fail systems, grades, and exams as well as issues such as grade inflation are considered. Within the general guidelines established by the institution, individual faculty members exercise considerable leeway in their own classrooms. Retaining samples of students' work will facilitate subsequent analysis of the evaluative process. Exams, essays, projects, and laboratory work can provide evidence of the way testing was used as an educational and evaluative tool and of the quality of the students' work.

Each student folder, as well as the official record maintained by the registrar, contains evaluations including remarks by advisors, informal notes, and comments on the learning accomplished by each student. While most exams, essays, problem sets, etc., are returned to the student, grades are noted in the instructor's records, and the final grades are given to the registrar to be entered into the permanent record.

Bibliography

Bloom, Allan David. *The Closing of the American Mind*. New York: Simon and Schuster, 1987.

Bok, Derek Curtis. *Higher Learning*. Cambridge: Harvard University Press, 1986.

Boyer, Ernest L. *College: The Undergraduate Experience in America*. New York: Harper & Row, 1987.

Eble, Kenneth Eugene. *The Aims of College Teaching*. San Francisco: Jossey-Bass Publishers, 1983.

EDUCOM. *The Joe Wyatt Challenge: 101 Success Stories of Information Technologies in Higher Education*. Washington, D.C.: EDUCOM/EVIT, 1991.

Finkelstein, Martin. *The American Academic Profession*. Columbus: Ohio State University Press, 1984.

Hirsch, E.D., Jr. *Cultural Literacy: What Every American Needs to Know*. Boston: Houghton Mifflin, 1987.

Information Resources for the Campus of the Future. *Campus of the Future: Conference on Information Resources* (Co-sponsored by OCLC and the Johnson Foundation). Dublin, Ohio: Online Computer Library Center, 1987.

Snyder, Benson R. *The Hidden Curriculum*. Cambridge: MIT Press, 1973.

Foster Socialization

Outside the classroom, another spectrum of activities occupies the students. Although these extracurricular activities may be viewed by skeptical parents, state legislators, and even archivists as somewhat extraneous to the "real" purpose of higher education, increasingly this other aspect of college life is recognized as an essential element in the learning process and an integral part of the educational experience. The most practical lesson gained from higher education may not be the facts acquired in class, but rather the ability to learn and function in society.

Sociologists and psychologists use the term *socialization* to describe the process of interacting with others and accepting group values. While this is seen most clearly in professional education, in which the student acquires a professional identity, during undergraduate education the student also acquires a set of attitudes and beliefs. Socialization attempts to instill educational values based on reasoning abilities, the commitment to continued learning, and a tolerance for diversity. This process occurs as individual students establish their own identities by observing behavioral patterns and accepting values of their peers as well as their teachers.

In this book the socialization process is considered within a larger context that includes all of those activities that foster the social, cultural, and physical development of the student outside the formal academic program. These activities manifest themselves quite differently based upon who sponsors the activity and why they do so.

Socializing activities occur in three ways:

They are initiated by the institution:
The administration and faculty of the college or university issue rules and provide facilities and services for activities that foster its values and the socializing process.

They are initiated by students, but officially sanctioned, fostered, or supported by the administration:
Students initiate their own publications, meetings, performances, and sporting events, but they are both encouraged and controlled by administrative rules and the availability of funds and facilities.

Students act on their own:
The largest category may be the independent socialization activities carried on by students, including conversations with roommates, pick-up games of touch football, and informal chamber music practice.

The other large variable is the institutional setting in which these activities take place. Socializing activities differ markedly at resident and commuter institutions: although commuting students may participate in cultural and athletic activities, interaction with other students is much diminished. Small liberal arts colleges appear to be most successful at fostering a specific set of values through the socialization process; large universities provide more activities, but the institution may be less able to use its program to convey a coherent set of goals.

Students are the most obvious actors in the socialization process. All individuals at academic institutions, however, including administrators, faculty, and staff, are participants as they interact with and serve as models for students and members of their own peer groups.

General Documentary Issues

Many barriers make the documentation of the socialization function a considerable challenge. Many socializing activities are not normally recorded in any form. Little evidence exists of the bulk of athletic, musical, and social activities, and even less information exists on the effect that these activities have on the development of students. The documentation that does exist is generally created by the administration and the faculty as they establish rules, provide facilities, state goals, and carry out the activities they control. This material is, of course, important, but it documents only one part in the equation. Some evidence should be sought of the student in the socializing process.

Examining the socialization function on three levels — policy, aggregate, and individual — guides the analysis of the documentation. Rules governing the conduct of students are readily available in published handbooks, but it may be more difficult to locate statements of the philosophy that underlies published regulations. Although some institutions articulate coherent goals for socializing activities, others have diverse reasons for the multiple opportunities provided to the students. Recruiting materials, statements in the catalog, and handbooks for students may provide some evidence. Offices and committees that oversee the conduct of students, particularly the dean of students (men/women), should have materials documenting the evolution and implementation of policies and procedures. Periodically, institutions conduct formal studies to examine some of these issues. Such investigations are often precipitated by a current problem such as a housing shortage, increase in the use of drugs, racial unrest, or the occurrence of rapes or suicides. These studies, involving the administration, faculty and students, and even officials of the local community and parents, may include an evaluation of socializing activities.

An aggregate understanding of the socialization process and implementation of the institution's policies can be achieved by gathering information on the range of activities available and how the students participate in them. Directories of sports facilities listing hours and services, programs of cultural events, and descriptions of housing facilities all provide evidence of what is available. Annual reports of the director of housing, athletic director, and deans often provide aggregate figures for the numbers of students housed in specific facilities, attendance at sporting and cultural events, and use of athletic facilities by individuals. These reports provide a general sense of the volume and pattern of socializing activities.

More information about these activities and organizations is available in written and visual documentation. Housing units and student organizations create some formal records. Officers of dormitories may keep minutes of meetings and issue their own rules. Many student organizations create records as a natural part of their activities — student publications, programs of performances, souvenir books of athletic events, programs of worship services — but other less formal organizations and activities produce no records.

While written documentation is scarce, for many aspects of the function *foster socialization* there is an abundant visual record. Visual records are most often created and used for illustrative purposes, but archivists and historical researchers are developing the skills required to use these images as historical documents. Photographs, films, and videos can provide insights into the student's experience that few other forms of documentation offer. Such images reveal friendships, social groups, styles of dress, and the physical environment in which the students study, sleep, and play. Photographic files can be collected from the school newspaper office, information office, individual students, faculty, and staff. The same critical apparatus must be brought to visual images as to any other form of evidence, but when carefully appraised and described, the visual evidence may prove to be the most valuable documentation of this function.

Even so, what individual students have gained from social activities and how these experiences have altered them remain elusive. The activities of the star athlete or concert performer may be chronicled in publications and film, but the normal socializing process of individual students is likely to be lost without a conscious effort to capture it. Letters home and diaries are scarce in a world in which students call home and visit on a regular basis. At some institutions, students are encouraged to maintain journals as a way to improve their writing and analyze their educational experience. The visual record, created both by the students and the administration, supplements these scarce sources.

Published studies and background research materials generated by sociologists, anthropologists, and psychologists studying socialization can provide a closer examination of the experience of individual students. The extensive interviews that are often carried out as part of these projects present problems of confidentiality, but could provide valuable information if permission can be obtained for their reuse (even if the transcripts must be made anonymous).

A fuller record may only be achieved through conscious documentary efforts. Archivists may wish to ask student organizations, housing groups, and alumni clubs to undertake special documentary projects. Organizations can be urged to maintain records of their activities, photograph events, and interview their members. Individual students can be encouraged to keep diaries or participate in oral history projects. Training and guidance will be required, but such records, though self-consciously created, could fill a significant documentary gap.

The following sections explore aspects of the function *foster socialization*, first by examining the official role of the administration in establishing rules, regulations, facilities, and services, and then by describing the role of the administration and students in specific extracurricular activities.

Academic Rules and Regulations

The conduct of students is guided and controlled by rules and regulations issued by the administration. While each institution wants the rules to reflect its own philosophy, constraints are imposed by the legal environment and norms of society. With the age of majority set at 18 rather than 21, the relationship between the institution and the students is now based on contractual and Constitutional rights rather than the concept of *in loco parentis*. The rules and regulations therefore represent a balancing act as the institution tries to protect both its own rights and those of its students, faculty, and staff.

Colleges and universities can try to influence behavior by articulating standards to govern the personal conduct of the students. Regulations are imposed to ensure that the institution can function without disruption and to protect the physical well-being of the students, personnel, and surrounding community. These regulations are influenced by a recognition of the students' rights of privacy, expression, and association, as well as their rights as citizens. Where regulations are established, institutions must specify the sanctions that will be imposed and the process by which actions will be reviewed and judged.

Regulations are typically imposed to achieve the following objectives:

To protect physical property

To protect the personal freedoms and privacy of students and staff

To protect the institution from disruptions

To promote the safety, health, and well-being of students.

Rules are formulated by the administration, but students increasingly have a role in this process. Officers and committees are charged with the dissemination and oversight of these rules, as well as their modification.

Academic Rules and Regulations: Documentation

At the very minimum, published rules and regulations should be preserved in the archives. Rules and regulations are issued and updated on a regular basis; they may appear as a separate handbook or contained in the college catalog. The records of the officers and committees charged with formulating and overseeing these regulations track their evolution, modification, intent, and influence. Records of discipline committees and the campus police department are often considered too confidential to be given to an archives, but if personal privacy can be protected (e.g., restrict records for 75 years), such records could offer a valuable source of information on the conduct of students, their infractions of the rules, and the penalties imposed. Flagrant violations of the rules are often reported in both the campus and local newspapers.

These records track the violations and problems. Harder to document is the effect of the rules on the everyday conduct of the students, their acceptance or rejection of them, and the effect that these rules have on the campus environment.

Facilities and Services

The facilities and services the institution offers to its students and members of its community embody its attitude toward socializing activities by creating an environment that promotes or discourages certain kinds of behavior.

Housing

For residential campuses, the housing supplied by the institution and the regulations governing where the students may live provide the strongest influence on the socialization process. Rules may require that the students live on campus for one or more years and may also restrict their selection of campus living arrangements. Although the economics of building and maintaining dormitories may impose severe limitations, the architectural design and services provided in these facilities say a great deal about the environment the institution wishes to create for its students. Housing four students in a room in contrast to providing single bedrooms with a common living room creates a very different living environment and promotes different relationships among the residents, as do coed versus single sex dormitories, or fraternities and sororities. The provision of common areas (meeting rooms; dining, laundry, and athletic facilities) also influences the interaction of the students. The role of the resident supervisor affects the environment as well: is the residential staff there to impose discipline or to provide psychological and educational counseling? Using members of the faculty as dormitory residents may reflect a deliberate effort to integrate educational activities into the residential life.

The administration has greater control over students occupying institutional rather than off-campus housing or independent living arrangements such as fraternities and sororities. Yet the pattern in recent years indicates that students prefer the atmosphere, services, safety, and convenience of dormitories. Changing attitudes toward housing that discriminates by sex, race, and economic status as well as current mores about sex and the use of alcohol have generated a reexamination of fraternities and sororities. For the "Greek way" to survive, changes may be necessary in their means of recruiting and the conduct of the residents.

Colleges and universities face additional housing problems for their graduate students, married students, faculty, and staff. These individuals and families must seek shelter in apartments and houses in the communities that surround the institution, thereby having a considerable impact on the real estate market in that area. The availability and cost of housing can be greatly affected by the needs of an academic institution, and these demands can create conflict between the institution and its neighbors who can be priced out of the housing market.

Some institutions, especially those in urban areas, are finding that the prohibitive cost of housing is making it increasingly difficult to recruit and retain graduate students, faculty, and staff. Academic institutions in some cities (The Rockefeller University and Columbia University in New York City and Stanford University in Palo Alto) provide subsidized housing for their faculty and staff to lessen this problem. Increasing numbers of institutions are helping faculty members and staff with down payments on houses.

Housing: Documentation

Both institutional policy and aggregate information about housing should be documented. It is important to know what housing options are available to students and staff, what factors influence the decision of where to live, and how many live in what type of housing. It is also important to achieve some understanding of the impact of these housing decisions on the local communities.

A variety of published sources document the housing options available to the students as well as the regulations governing their options and residency. Promotional literature, catalogs, freshman handbooks, and housing guides detail the options and procedures for making a selection. Records of the officer in charge of student affairs trace the evolution of policies concerning housing, and periodic studies of housing needs and the campus environment yield more detailed evidence of the factors that influenced housing decisions. Records of the student housing office document the process of administering the dormitories and assigning space to the students. The records of off-campus housing offices (which help students, faculty, and staff locate housing in the surrounding communities) provide evidence of the number of people who use these services and the relation of the institution to the community.

Student and staff directories confirm where members of the academic community reside, but it is neither possible nor desirable to document the housing decisions made by each person. Chronicling the everyday existence of the student in the dormitory or off-campus residence is difficult. For campus residents, the buildings themselves can provide considerable information about the ambiance, living arrangements, and potential activities and interactions. Fund-raising literature for new dormitories explains why new facilities are needed and what is to be achieved for the residents. Building programs submitted to architects clarify the intent and uses of the dormitory and specify the facilities and services to be included. Interior and exterior photographs depict the completed building and its relationship to the rest of the campus. Finally, photographs of activities in the building, once it is occupied, show how the students actually lived in the facility over time.

Some formal records may be created by dormitory residents as part of their own governance. Additional materials may be compiled by a "historian" of the house, who is charged to write about and gather material in a collection of records or a scrapbook. More often, the documentation is less formal and consists primarily of photographs taken by the residents. As discussed in the general documentary section above, what is not documented but is of critical importance to the development of the students is the informal relationships among the residents. The study groups, friendships, and daily contacts have a lasting effect.

Records of the president and provost and real estate and off-campus housing offices may provide some evidence of the institution's policy and procedures for providing housing to graduate and married students, faculty, and staff. Published literature prepared for incoming students and faculty may describe the housing situation and opportunities both on campus and in the local area. Statistics generated by the off-campus housing office may yield information on the numbers of units listed, the numbers of people placed, and the interactions with the community. Correspondence with prospective students, and especially faculty and staff, could reveal the role housing problems play in decisions to attend particular universities and in negotiating offers of employment.

Documentation about the impact of academic housing needs on neighboring communities can be found both in administrative offices at the academic institution and in the records of local municipalities. Studies or legal actions undertaken by local governments, real estate boards, citizen action committees, and the media all shed light on this problem.

Other Facilities

Colleges and universities make available to the members of their academic communities a wide variety of other facilities: athletic buildings and playing fields; meeting rooms, performing and exhibit spaces; parking lots and the grounds of the campus. While the use of some of these areas requires a formal request and the payment of a fee, other spaces are available to all at any time. Many of these facilities are an integral part of extracurricular activities and will be touched upon more specifically in the sections that follow.

Services

Related to housing are the support services that the institution provides to the students and often also to its faculty and staff. Included in this category are food and retail services and medical care.

The traditional cafeteria dispensing institutional food has been transformed in recent years in response to conflicting pressures from local fast food restaurants, students' weight and health consciousness, and the financial constraints of the provider and consumer. Colleges and universities are offering greater variety and more flexible food plans. Many institutions have also responded to the difficulty of staffing and running their food service operations by contracting with outside catering firms. Some food services are provided solely for the students in their dormitories. Many cafeterias, food machines, and other concession stands, however, serve the whole academic community.

In addition to providing meal service, academic institutions may run a variety of retail operations to dispense books, food, equipment, and household goods. The scale of these operations often depends upon the proximity of the institution to local retail stores. Local and national legislators have expressed increasing concern about the possible unfair competition that these stores present. The scope of their operations and their tax status may be reexamined in coming years.

Additional services offered at each campus reflect their particular demographic and geographic situation. Child-care and day camps for children of staff and students are available at many campuses. Transportation systems exist when campuses are large and spread out (The University of Michigan, Ann Arbor; Harvard University, Cambridge).

Medical care is a major service provided to students and very often also to faculty and staff. Again, the scope of medical care programs varies. If the institution has a medical school, the health care services are often incorporated into the teaching hospital. Some institutions provide health maintenance care to their students and staff by establishing their own or using independent health maintenance organizations (HMOs). At the very least, academic institutions make provisions for emergency, in-patient, and ambulatory care by maintaining some services and staff on their campus and establishing relationships with nearby hospitals and doctors.

Services: Documentation

Published directories and reports that outline the services available to the students and staff may also provide evidence of the volume of their use. When services are contracted out, the institution holds only the records of contract negotiations. The administrative records are held by the con-tracting company, but as few of these have long-term value this is not a problem, and possibly a benefit since the the contractor must care for and manage them.

If an institution runs its own health care facility, the creation and main-tenance of individual patient records are an integral part of its operation. Medical facilities normally retain their own patient records, but archi-vists may be called upon to provide archival and records management advice. The retention of patient care records is regulated by state law according to standards established by the state departments of public health. Recommended retention periods differ greatly from state to state: Arkansas requires retention until 10 years following the known death of the patient or 99 years from the creation of the record; North Carolina requires retention for only 3 years following the creation of the record. Official patient care files include notes made by doctors and nurses as well as test results and records of visits and procedures. More specific advice about patient care records is available from the department of health in each state and the publications issued by hospital administra-tors (see Bibliography).

Extracurricular Activities

The term extracurricular encompasses all of the activities — social, religious, athletic, political, and cultural — that engage students outside of the classroom. These can range from activities highly controlled by the faculty and administration to informal activities totally controlled by the students.

Once again, while this section emphasizes students, it is important to remember that faculty and staff are also participants in extracurricular activities. Choral societies, jazz bands, and orchestras often include people from all parts of the academic community, and the lanes of the swimming pool and the baseball fields are filled by staff and faculty as well as students.

Governance and Activism

Students are involved in the governance of their institution in two different ways: they participate in university governance (e.g., serve on governing boards and faculty committees) and administer the student government. The role of students in university governance is treated in the chapter *Sustain the Institution.*

College and university administrators sanction student government and delineate its areas of responsibility and authority to make rules, judge infractions, and administer its affairs. The university has additional control over student government in that it generally allocates space and funds for these activities. While the actual power and effectiveness of student governments vary, in recent years students have appeared increasingly apathetic about these activities. Fewer students vote in student elections, and few are interested in running for office. It may be that because colleges and universities have provided students with a greater opportunity to exercise their leadership within the governance of the institution, the role of student government is perceived as less important. Students may also be choosing to exercise their leadership within their housing units and clubs and in political and social activities.

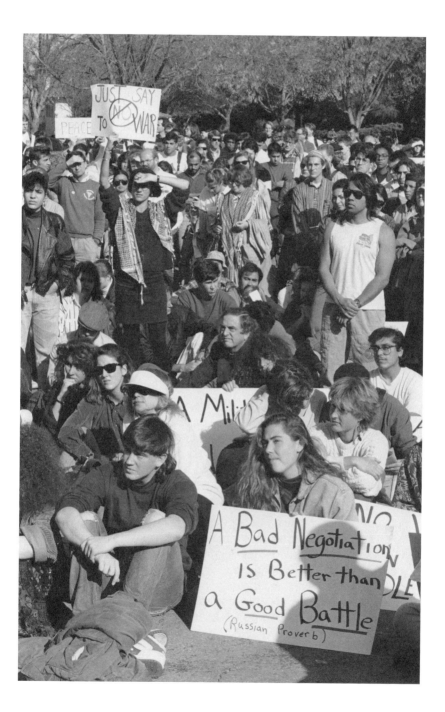

Students participate in activities relating to social and political issues that arise both on their campuses and in the local, national, and world communities. Recently students have been perceived to be less active and concerned than their 1960s counterparts; but, although the issues may be different and the scale somewhat smaller, students still engage in social and political action. Some activism is focused on specific problems at their own institutions (racial prejudice, institutional support of businesses in South Africa), while other activities address societal issues (environmental pollution, gay rights, racial equality, animal rights).

While ad hoc political and social activism varies according to the issues of the day and the mood of the campus, ongoing student organizations provide a forum for participating in societal issues. Young Republicans, Students for a Democratic Society, and the Sierra Club may be represented by groups on college campuses but may not be officially approved or supported by the institution.

Governance and Activism: Documentation

Student governments generate records in the course of holding elections and administering their business. The constitution and bylaws clarify their structure and purposes, while agendas and minutes provide a sense of the scope of activities and actions taken. In addition, campus newspapers report on elections and actions taken. Finally, the office that oversees these activities, most likely the officer in charge of student affairs, can provide evidence of institutional policies and oversight.

It is much more difficult to document activist organizations. While some of these organizations maintain some records, many operate quite informally and leave little evidence. Student handbooks may list such organizations and even include names of the officers and the purpose of the groups, but many organizations remain quite invisible until they become involved with a particular issue or campaign. Often newspaper accounts, posters, handouts, photographic records, institutional disciplinary records, or police reports are the only available evidence of these activities, unless participants are interviewed or asked deliberately to record their experiences. In order to document adequately major episodes of student unrest, as witnessed in the late 1960s and early 1970s and more recently with anti-apartheid and anti-war protests, a conscious effort on the part of archivists and other members of the institution may be required.

Performing Arts

Performing arts activities are usually available to some degree within the college curriculum. Students may earn credit as they choreograph and perform dances, write and act in plays, and compose and participate in musical presentations. Many of these same pursuits are available to students outside the classroom in formal and informal activities. Utilizing dance studios, concert halls, and theaters, students participate in institutionally sponsored noncredit activities such as choral societies, orchestras, and student drama groups. Faculty members generally serve as advisors and leaders of these activities which are supported with institutional funds. Often the staff of the institution and members of local communities participate in these groups. Performances are generally open to the public, thereby providing a further opportunity to involve the community with the campus.

In addition to structured programs, students undertake informal performing arts activities. They practice their instruments and study technique individually, and they form groups to play classical, jazz, or rock music. Dance and theater students assemble groups both to study technique and to perform works by students. While some of these activities may result in formal performances, often the focus is on the practice and group experience rather than formal presentation.

Performing Arts: Documentation

Theater programs, posters, photographs, and newspaper reviews are generally produced for formal performances. The more prominent and better funded groups may issue recordings, films, and videos of their performances. Performing arts departments may also have correspondence documenting the repertoire, expenses, and appearances of the groups. Some of these groups participate in regional and national competitions as well as concert tours, in which case itineraries and attendance figures for performances might be available. Some formal groups clearly have longer histories and more prominent reputations than others.

For these, programs, posters, recordings, films, and organizational papers can provide a more complete picture. For other organizations, a collection of programs may be the easiest way to keep track of the offerings: what was presented, when, and by whom. In addition, campus calendars issued separately or in the newspapers provide a synopsis of performing arts activities.

Unless informal practice and group ensembles result in performances, it is difficult to gather evidence of these activities. When reservations are required for use of practice rooms and dance studios, sign-up logs may provide a sense of the number of individuals and groups engaged in these activities. The volume of chamber music parts borrowed from the music library may yield some information about informal musical ensembles. But these are clearly inefficient records, and the reality is that these activities will remain poorly documented.

Publications and Broadcast Media

A number of campus newspapers vie for the title of the oldest continuing student publication (often awarded to the *Yale News*, first issued 28 January 1878). While others started much more recently, almost every campus has a proliferation of newspapers and literary magazines as well as a radio and television station. Colleges and universities support these efforts by providing funds, facilities, and equipment. In addition to these officially supported publications and broadcast efforts, students initiate independent publications. Some of these "underground" journals survive for many years, while others, appearing irregularly, are short-lived.

Publications and radio and television stations provide opportunities for students interested in communications media to gain experience and test their abilities. Students utilize their organizational and engineering expertise, writing and speaking skills, and artistic talents to communicate with the campus community and often the surrounding community as well. Editorials and articles are vehicles to comment on school policy and larger social concerns and to influence opinion.

The legal relationship between the institution and student-run publications and broadcast media is delicate and often difficult. While institutions may be disturbed by some of the content of these publications, the First and Fourteenth Amendments of the Constitution provide protection for students. Although neither the First nor the Fourteenth

Amendment applies to private institutions, educational policy and societal pressures encourage private institutions to adhere to these standards. Both private and public institutions are obligated to abide by federal laws, such as the copyright law, and state statutes governing libel and obscenity. The student press is, therefore, subject to the same laws that apply to individuals and organizations outside of academe.

Recent court rulings confirm that institutions may not impose administrative sanctions or disciplinary actions or remove funds in reaction to objectionable material. Student publications cannot, therefore, be restricted or censored simply because the faculty or administration finds material objectionable. Disciplinary actions and restrictions can be imposed, however, when the content of the publications threatens to disrupt the institution or infringe on the rights of other students.

Publications and Broadcast Media: Documentation

Student publications, especially campus newspapers, are an important source of information about students and campus activities. Even when inaccuracies, outrageous opinions, and marginal writing skills are taken into account, campus papers and other periodicals provide insight into the students' points of view and their experiences. Copies of all publications should be collected and preserved. Keeping track of both the long-term and short-lived publications is often a challenge, but worth the effort to ensure the completeness of the collection.

Radio and television broadcasts are also valuable sources of information, but they pose preservation problems. Many radio and television stations do not record broadcasts, or, if they do, tapes may not be kept for more than a short period. Because campus stations broadcast campus events (athletic competitions, concerts, and special lectures), they can be a source of important documentation. Not all programs broadcast by the radio and television stations need be preserved. Published schedules will provide a sense of the programming and the staff. Archivists may want to monitor the schedule and request that tapes be made and preserved of events deemed to be of considerable interest or importance.

Religion

The church steeples that occupy a prominent place on American college and university campuses attest to the central role that religion played in the formative years of higher education. Even though the enhanced presence of public institutions and society's shifting attitudes have altered the place of religion on the campus, religion remains an important factor.

The law regulating the place of religion at academic campuses differs for private and public institutions. The First Amendment of the Constitution protects religious practice by prohibiting governments from establishing official religions and by protecting the right of the individual citizen to exercise free religious choice without the interference of governments. For public academic institutions, this means that they can neither establish an official religion nor prohibit the free exercise of religion on their campuses. Private institutions, however, can establish one religion as central to their campus and prohibit the free exercise of any but that religion. Religious life at private and public institutions therefore can be quite different.

There are at present 817 institutions of higher education affiliated with religious groups: 57% Protestant or smaller Christian denominations, 42% Roman Catholic, and 1% Jewish. Although these institutions theoretically can restrict the practice of other religions, in actuality they recognize religious pluralism. Required attendance at religious services is now rare, while observance by other religious groups is generally tolerated.

Many private institutions have never had any religious affiliation. Current practice generally supports free choice by providing facilities and staff to oversee diverse religious activities. One or more chaplains may be present on the staff to direct the religious activities of the predominant religious groups and facilitate observance by others.

Federal statutes suggest that at public institutions religion should be available to the community on a basis similar to all other extracurricular activities. Space may be allocated for religious activities in the student center; larger institutions may have a separate building. Such a religious center is generally directed by a lay coordinator rather than an ordained member of the clergy. The facilities and services provided by the institution are supplemented by independent denominational centers and churches located near the campus.

Religion:
Documentation

Documenting religion at academic institutions presents the same difficulties as documenting religion in any setting. Evidence is available of the presence of religion on the campus, but little evidence exists of the spiritual life of the individual.

Institutional and student directories list the religious facilities and staff present on the campus, and local telephone company yellow pages and other community directories provide information about churches, synagogues, and mosques in the area. The chaplains or coordinators that oversee religious programs may have records of their services and activities and also their relationships with the rest of the academic institution and the outside community. Records of denominational centers and churches located near the campuses may contain information about the participation of students, faculty, and staff.

At institutions with a religious affiliation, religious activities are more central and integrated into the life of the college and therefore generate a variety of valuable documentation. Records of the chaplain as well as those of student religious groups document the scope of their activities. Texts of sermons and programs of worship record the messages conveyed to the congregation and the participation of the academic community in religious services.

Service

Extracurricular service activities form part of the college's public service mission and may also reflect the values brought to the institution from its religious background. These activities are discussed in greater detail under the function *provide public service*. This section emphasizes the issues that are particularly relevant to the student experience.

Colleges and universities increasingly have adopted a more explicit policy of encouraging their students to participate in service activities both to emphasize the value of such endeavors and to provide "real life" educational experiences. Institutional ties to local school systems, community social welfare programs, and churches provide an opportunity for students to participate in diverse programs: teaching literacy classes, tutoring high school students, staffing soup kitchens, cleaning up local parks, making toys for hospitalized children at Christmas, and teaching courses in prisons. Fraternities, sororities, and other housing units generally engage in some sort of service activity. Student groups, such as service clubs, and individual students respond to specific needs and find ways of making contributions.

Service: Documentation

Service activities have a long history at academic institutions, but often remain relatively invisible as the work is conducted away from the campus. Occasionally college newspapers or magazines feature a story on a specific student service activity, but generally, such efforts are pursued quietly by the groups and individuals engaged in them.

Institutions may publish a guide to service activities that includes a statement of the institution's service philosophy and lists opportunities for students to participate. Those student organizations that engage in service activities may keep some records about their projects, including the number of students who participated, the services offered, and a sense of who benefited from their activities. Administrative offices that coordinate these efforts may have some records reflecting the types of projects undertaken and the ways in which students participate. Service fraternities and groups could be encouraged to gather or create written and visual documentation of particular projects.

Social

There are many, including Kurt Vonnegut, who say that social activities — meeting people, establishing friendships, dating — are what college is really all about. "I learned the joke at the core of American self-improvement: knowledge was so much junk to be processed one way or another at great universities. The real treasure the great universities offered was a lifelong membership in a respected artificial extended family" (*Bluebeard: A Novel*, New York: Delacorte Press, 1987, p. 184).

Although only a few friendships may endure when students leave college, all interactions contribute to the emotional and intellectual growth that is part of their college experience. Dealing with fellow students in living situations, classrooms, playing fields, and social encounters provides lessons about human behavior and social conduct. Students do become part of "an extended family" that forms the backdrop for their lives and provides social and often professional contacts as well.

Institutions set the stage for social activities by providing facilities, such as student centers and meeting rooms in dormitories, and establishing rules for the use of these facilities and for the conduct of their students. The strict rules that formerly governed almost every facet of students' lives were severely altered when the concept of *in loco parentis* was replaced by a relationship governed by constitutional and contractual provisions. While some regulations concerning firearms, explosives, and drugs can be justified to protect the safety of the students and the institution, on the whole, students must be treated as adults whose freedoms and privacy must be respected. Institutions are particularly concerned about the misuse of alcohol and drugs because of both the health risks to their students and the potential liability to the institution. In states where "the host" (in this case the college) is responsible for damages caused by intoxicated guests, the institution can be held liable for the conduct of its students.

In earlier days colleges could try to control the sexual activities of their students by creating separate living arrangements and controlling the visiting hours of guests. Now, the sexual conduct of students has become their own responsibility; visiting hours restrictions can only be justified to protect the privacy of the residents and to create an atmosphere that permits study and quiet. Once again, current law creates a situation in which the college is balancing the institution's concerns for its students with the threat of liability suits. Often, education, persuasion, and peer pressure are the only means by which colleges can influence the behavior of their students.

Independent of the administration, students direct their social activities both in formal ways, through clubs and programmed activities, and by more informal means. Single-sex and more recently coed clubs have a considerable history at academic institutions. While fraternities and sororities fulfill some of these same social functions, clubs that are not used as residences take on a deliberate role as social centers. At some institutions, particularly the Ivy League schools, these social clubs initiate contacts that can prove valuable throughout the professional careers of their members.

Each school has its own traditions: the gathering places and events that afford particular human qualities and an atmosphere to that institution. The local eating establishments provide a place to gather and share the various edible and inedible specialties of the house. Holiday gatherings,

spring rituals, and homecoming events furnish a focus for college traditions. Mountain Day at Elmira College, hoop rolling events at Bryn Mawr and Wellesley Colleges, and Dragon Day at Cornell all lend a particular character to those institutions. Whether they are called pranks, hacks, or just jokes, students enliven the campus and cause anxiety among college administrators by disrupting events in sometimes clever (usually unmalicious) ways. MIT's famed "hackers" have placed a cow on the main dome of the campus, inflated a balloon on the 50-yard line during a Harvard/ Yale football game, and welded a "Brass Rat" (the MIT school ring) on the finger of the John Harvard statue in Harvard Yard.

To describe the informal contacts of students is to describe the everyday conduct of each student. The relationships — hostile, friendly, polite, romantic — span the full range of human emotions and experiences and vary for every student. Each graduate need only reflect on his or her own academic career to recall the perils and rewards of these encounters. With a little luck and a large amount of awkward travail, the student emerges a more mature social creature.

Social: Documentation

The published rules and regulations for the conduct of students and the use of institutional facilities establish the structure and attitudes that control social activities. College handbooks, student guides, and yearbooks suggest the range of activities and the regulations that control them. Bulletin boards (both electronic and cork) are filled with announcements of coming events, and campus publications carry reports and visual evidence of parties, pranks, and proms. As discussed at the beginning of this section, however, little documentation exists to record the bulk of these interactions. Visual records are important, as they convey the mood and provide some evidence about social groupings, events, gathering places, and mores.

Special efforts may have to be made to document particular events, especially campus traditions that would otherwise be recorded only through oral tradition. Pranksters and hackers are rumored to maintain careful documentation of their accomplishments, and sufficient cajoling with promises of confidentiality (at least until they graduate) may be sufficient to acquire these records.

Sports

Newspaper and magazine stories bombard the public with news about intercollegiate athletic activities. TV and radio announcers comment on the competitions and the latest scandals in collegiate athletics. For much of the public, sports at colleges and universities are synonymous with NCAA football and basketball competitions, and one might be led to conclude that all of these activities are scandal-ridden and profit-making.

The true picture of athletic programs at colleges and universities is considerably different. College athletics actually comprise many layers of activities — intercollegiate, intramural, and individual sports. With the current value placed on physical fitness and health, many students are involved in athletics in one way or another. The proportion of students participating in intramural and individual athletics is significantly higher than those who are intercollegiate athletes. Students on athletic scholarships may be the most visible, but the overall importance of the athletic program is the impact it has on the majority of the members of the academic community.

The different facets of athletics reflect the many, often conflicting, motivations behind sports programs. While the physical and mental well-being of the students has generally been a factor, athletic programs also respond to pressures to build "team players" and to enhance institutional prestige through competitive achievements. Because intercollegiate athletics can bring not only prestige but also substantial revenues, academic institutions are motivated to engage in these programs.

Intercollegiate

Intercollegiate competition has been a part of the American academic scene since the mid-nineteenth century when crew, baseball, and football were the major sports. By the late nineteenth century, the violence of football games, questions about eligibility of players, and financial scandals motivated college presidents and legislators to call for reform. To respond to these concerns, the National Collegiate Athletic Association (NCAA) was established in 1905 and remains the primary authority governing intercollegiate athletics. Other coordinating athletic associations do exist, such as the National Association of Intercollegiate Athletics and the National Junior College Athletic Association. For four-year institutions, however, the NCAA, with a membership of 845, remains the dominant force.

The NCAA has authority to establish standards to maintain the level of athletic competition, establish eligibility standards for regional and national athletic events sponsored by NCAA, formulate and publish rules of play for intercollegiate sports, and preserve intercollegiate athletic records. It sponsors championships in twenty-one sports. Individual institutions are directed by the NCAA to establish their own eligibility rules to ensure that their athletes comply with satisfactory standards of scholarship, sportsmanship, and amateurism.

Institutions that want to compete in intercollegiate athletics must join an athletic association and comply with its rules. The NCAA separates its member institutions into three divisions based on the number of male and female varsity teams that an institution supports, the size of its stadiums, its paid attendance, and the number of contests per sport. Division I and II institutions recruit student-athletes and award athletic scholarships, while Division III institutions provide no special recruiting or financial treatment for student-athletes. Division I and II institutions fund intercollegiate athletics primarily from the revenues generated from the program itself, while Division III colleges fund athletics from institutional funds in a fashion similar to any other department at the school. As of September 1991 there were 295 members of Division I, 222 members of Division II, and 328 members of Division III. Within the NCAA and the other athletic associations, institutions with similar programs come together to form conferences to structure their athletic competitions (Big Ten, etc.).

The NCAA judges the eligibility of institutions for membership and can impose sanctions for rule infractions. In fall 1991, thirty-four institutions were under NCAA sanctions for recruiting, scholarship, eligibility, and other violations and had received penalties which excluded them from postseason play, barred coaches from recruiting and competition, and limited television appearances.

Scandals and concerns about the appropriate place of intercollegiate athletics in higher education are not new. Once again, college presidents and legislators are calling for reforms and threatening federal regulations. Although alumni, boards of trustees, and the general public may have concerns, they remain eager to watch the competitions. The profits and prestige attached to success in competition encourage the continuation of intercollegiate athletics. Reform will be difficult. College athletics are affected by the same societal values and problems that permeate professional athletics and other sectors of our culture.

Intercollegiate:
Documentation

In this study, athletics are described as part of the function *foster socialization*; however, intercollegiate athletic programs have ramifications that link these activities and their documentation to that of several other functions: recruiting of college athletes affects the admission process (*confer credentials*); the revenues that accrue from competitions affect finances (*sustain the institution*); the public spectacle of the games can have implications for the relations with local and national communities (*provide public service*); and, it can be argued, athletic competitions perpetuate cultural traditions (*promote culture*). Therefore, the documentary issues have implications in many areas.

The documentation of intercollegiate athletics is voluminous, and the size of the archival collection will reflect, in large measure, the importance of the program at an institution. Some campuses that have significant intercollegiate athletic programs are now considering establishing sports archives both to reflect the value that the institution places on these activities and to respond to the growing research trend in sports history.

Policy issues, including financial, athletic, and educational, are documented in the administrative records of the governing board, senior officers, alumni association, and athletic director. Negotiations with athletic associations and records of controversies and suspensions appear both in the administrative files of the college and in the records of the association.

College, local, and national media report on events, and carry results of games and feature stories about the players and coaches. Campus news and athletic offices generate news releases and capture the events in pictures and video. Published souvenir programs and reports chronicle the games and accomplishments of the college teams. Information on participants and achievements of individual athletes and teams is valued by athletic departments, public relations offices, historical researchers, and individual athletes and fans. While the national athletic associations maintain some statistics, a fuller statistical record should be maintained by the institution. Souvenir programs, films, videos, and still photos supplement the statistics and document the teams and events more fully.

The NCAA maintains a "National Statistics Service" for member institutions in the sports of football, men's and women's basketball, baseball, and women's softball. The service publishes weekly and annual statistical reports for each of these sports and maintains the original reports submitted to it by each member institution. Further information can be obtained by contacting the Statistics Service at the NCAA (6201 College Boulevard, Overland Park, KS 66211-2422, telephone 913-339-1906).

Intramural and Club Sports

Institutions encourage broad participation in competitive athletics by providing facilities, equipment, and officials to oversee intramural and club sports. Intramural sports foster on-campus competitive activities among baseball, softball, volleyball, and touch football teams. At many institutions, a high percentage of the undergraduates and a fair proportion of the faculty and staff participate. Financial support for intramural activities varies, but the costs may be defrayed by a combination of institutional funds and student fees. Club sports include a more diverse range of athletic competition (bowling, frisbee, rowing, cross-country skiing, squash, and tennis) and provide an opportunity to improve athletic skills and to compete against clubs at other institutions. Students generally make up at least 50% of a club team, but staff and faculty can be members as well. To a greater extent the club teams are expected to support their own activities.

Intramural and Club Sports: Documentation

Although a full documentation of these athletic activities may not be possible or desirable, it is valuable to gather some information about the extent of these activities and the accomplishments of the teams. Campus newspapers may cover selected competitions. Athletic department records may provide a sense of the number of teams and their schedules, but may not have full information about participants, games actually played, or results. The teams themselves may maintain these records and may be the only source of statistical and visual documentation.

Individual and Informal Groups

The runners, swimmers, bicyclists, tennis, squash, basketball, and frisbee players who pursue their sports activities on their own probably encompass the largest sector of the academic community. Individual athletic activity is governed by personal fitness goals and schedules. Groups of students from housing units may spend afternoons playing frisbee; colleagues at work may become squash partners; runners and swimmers may do their laps before classes, at lunch, or before they go home.

Extensive athletic facilities are often in heavy demand by commuting and residential students and staff alike. Often, athletic use cards must be purchased and courts reserved for tennis, squash, and pick-up basketball games. Beyond those details, however, the individuals are on their own.

Individual and Informal Groups: Documentation

Annual reports of directors of athletics may contain estimates of the number of people who use the athletic facilities and carry out their own practice. These figures are, most likely, less than accurate, but they do indicate the extent of the participation and the types of activities. A full record of individual participation is not required, but some information about these activities, both written and visual, provides evidence about the use of the athletic facilities, the institution's attitude toward the importance of sports in promoting the health and well-being of the community, and the interest in such activities of the students, staff, and faculty.

Bibliography

Guide to the Retention and Preservation of Records with Destruction Schedules. 6th Hospital edition. Oak Brook, Ill.: Records Control Inc. and the Hospital Financial Management Association, 1981.

Schlereth, Thomas J. *The University of Notre Dame: A Portrait of Its History and Campus.* Notre Dame, Ind.: University of Notre Dame Press, 1976.

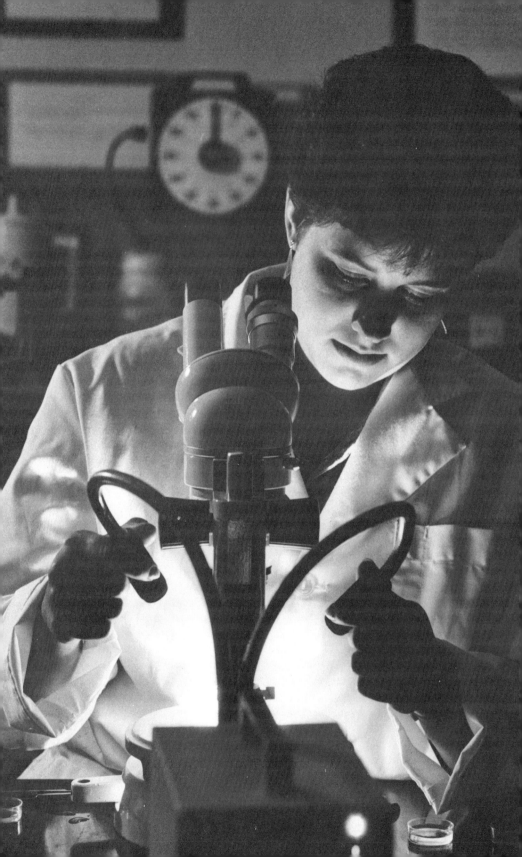

Conduct Research

The Role of Research

The rise of research to its central role at institutions of higher education is tied to the educational reforms of the mid-nineteenth century that called for more specialized knowledge, advanced study, and practical training. As the curriculum moved away from traditional classical subjects, faculty members with advanced training in specialized topics were required to meet the needs of the new elective system. Advanced training was understood to be acquired through original investigations carried out during studies following the bachelor's degree.

Graduate schools originally undertook research as part of their function to train researchers, but now the research function is driven by additional internal and external factors. Research is a major element in the evaluation and promotion of the faculty and contributes significantly to the financial well-being and prestige of the institution. In the absence of agreement on standards to measure teaching performance, research is one of the main criteria used to evaluate faculty in all disciplines, not only at research universities, but at most academic institutions with the exception of the two-year colleges. The peer review system provides evaluations of research required by academic institutions to judge their faculty. The particular nature of the institution and the discipline does, however, create variations in both the allocation of time and the value placed on research.

Research is a pawn in the continuing struggle among academic institutions for recognition. Schools vie to bring acknowledged published scholars and promising graduate students to their campuses. The successful institutions thereby acquire both prestige and research dollars.

Pressures exerted from outside academic institutions by the professional disciplines and funding agencies also have a strong influence on academic research. Disciplinary communities not only serve an evaluative function but also affect research programs through their professional consensus on desirable areas of research. As publishers of professional journals, conveners of meetings, and reviewers of the literature, professional societies and disciplinary colleagues stimulate research in those areas deemed currently of interest. It has been argued that this system makes it difficult for those working on the fringes of disciplines or in new areas to get their work accepted and published (see Bibliography, Root-Bernstein).

Funding agencies — governments, industry, and private foundations — affect the selection of research topics by allocating money for specific areas of research (e.g., diseases such as cancer or AIDS, economic conditions in Third World countries, or the impact of technology on historical records). The selection of specific topics by funding sources can be motivated by societal concerns, industrial needs, or other current considerations.

These internal and external pressures create conflicts and tensions around the research process. One of the questions that receives a great deal of attention is the relationship between research and teaching. The proportion of time allocated for each activity, the weight placed on research in promotion and tenure decisions, and the relative value of the research process to the undergraduate and graduate curricula have generated arguments among students, faculty, administrators, legislators, and the general public. The literature on higher education remains divided on the issue of whether the two activities support or conflict with each other.

In truth, there may be no simple answer to this debate; the relationship between research and teaching may vary among the disciplines and also between undergraduate and graduate teaching and research activities. A faculty member engaged in cutting-edge investigations in polymer chemistry may use the knowledge gained immediately in graduate seminars but not in undergraduate teaching. In some disciplinary areas a faculty member can use the opportunity to teach a new course as a way to conduct research. Helen Vendler, a literary scholar, said, "I always, when I am preparing a book, teach a course in that author. I consider the teaching an invaluable preparation for writing" (Vendler, p. 13).

The teaching in this case is an integral part of the research process and is more likely to occur at the graduate than the undergraduate level. In either case, however, the research is part of the process of keeping up to date with scholarship in the discipline. Curriculum materials are a distillation of past research conducted by the instructor and other scholars. It generally takes some time for new research to be disseminated, proven, and accepted into the basic teachings.

Closely allied to these debates is the question of the impact of graduate and research programs on undergraduate education. A common complaint is that undergraduates at universities are cut off from the senior faculty and the research process. Some efforts have been made to address these concerns, but the problems remain.

Conflicts also arise around the selection of research problems. How much are researchers influenced by the needs of the educational programs at their academic institutions, the priorities of their disciplinary community, the availability of funding, the promise of publication, or even the possibility of a prize? The priorities of many funding agencies often conflict with the interests of individual researchers and the disciplines to pursue basic research not directed toward the solution of specific problems.

Additional conflicts arise among the institution, researcher, and funder over the ownership of the products of research: the intellectual property including patents and copyrights. Government, foundation, and corporate research grants specify the rights of the funder. Greatest care is often taken to clarify the ownership of patents and the rights to develop the inventions conceived during funded work, as there are potentially large profits to be made by the patent holder. While the government receives the rights to use inventions, it encourages academic institutions to license the patents to corporations and others who want to develop practical applications. There was some initial concern that when corporations fund research they would require that patents become their property, but the recent trend has been to assign ownership to the institution with the requirement that the corporation receive a nonexclusive license to develop the invention. Corporations pay royalties to the institution when they receive a license to use the patent, and these fees are then generally shared by the institution with the inventor(s).

In a similar fashion, the funder of a grant might claim the ownership of the copyrights to the final products, including software. Generally, however, the funder will only claim copyright to the specific "deliverable product" requested in sponsored research agreements (body of data, software, or apparatus). Otherwise, the copyrights generally become the property of the institution, which in turn can assign them to the authors.

General Documentary Issues

Documenting research poses several problems: the need to document the process (not just the administration and final products) of research; the dispersal of the records; the multi-format nature of the documentation; and the undocumented and intangible aspects of the research process, including the impact of the work. These problems are summarized in this general discussion and referred to specifically in the sections that follow.

Documenting Process

Documenting research necessitates recording a process that may take years to accomplish. Several activities that comprise research are easier to document than others: the results of the research are generally widely available in published form; and the management of research activities is captured in financial and personnel records that track the administrative aspects of the work, especially if a project receives financial support of any kind. But the research process itself is more difficult to document: the framing of the research question; the conceptualization of the means to gather and analyze the information required; the assignment of responsibility to research staff; and the actual sequence of discovery, analysis, and work are harder to capture. Some of these activities are mental processes that are acted upon but not recorded. Evidence of other activities is buried in masses of data. The style of the individual researcher and the methods dictated by the discipline also create great variations in the evidence of the research process.

For many research projects, the final published products and a summary administrative record are sufficient documentation. When, however, the decision is made to document a specific research effort more fully, the records of the process itself are also required.

Dispersal of Documentation

The collaborative nature of some of the work, the peripatetic nature of researchers, and the funding of research by outside agencies create documentary problems by dispersing research records.

Collaborative or team research is increasingly accepted as an effective means to assemble the diverse knowledge, skills, and manpower required to address complex problems. While most common in the sciences and engineering, researchers in the social sciences and even the humanities collaborate as well. Members of a research team can be colleagues at the same institution or individuals from many academic campuses, or even from government and industry. Electronic mail networks, telephones, and facsimile machines greatly assist communication among distant collaborators, but create a documentary nightmare.

Academic research centers have proliferated in recent years to facilitate inter-, multi-, and crossdisciplinary collaborative research. Yale University's Program on Non-Profit Organizations brings anthropologists, economists, historians, legal scholars, and philosophers together to study philanthropy. The Program in World Hunger at Brown University employs historical geographers, agronomists, economists, sociologists, anthropologists, physicians, and nutritionists to examine the prevalence and persistence of hunger, study the trends in the developing world that will affect hunger, and propose methods to prevent hunger.

Collaborations are also established around the use of equipment that is only available at specific facilities due to its cost, size, and complexity. Large teams, often comprised of researchers from many institutions, conduct experiments at the particle accelerator at CERN in Switzerland and the Magnet Laboratory at MIT. These teams, often from several disciplinary areas, design and conduct an experiment, interpret data, and publish findings. In each case, the records of research are dispersed among all of the participants.

Dispersal of research records is also caused by the peripatetic nature of researchers who work in many locations: campus offices, laboratories and research centers at their own institutions and where they visit, as well as their offices at home. Some research records are therefore merged with personal and professional files maintained in individuals' offices and homes, while others will be found at the laboratories and centers where projects are carried out.

When research is supported by outside funding (government, industry, and private foundations), the records are dispersed among at least three locations: the funding source holds the records of the decision to fund the project; the college or university office that manages outside funding holds the administrative records documenting the award, negotiations, and reports to the funder; and the researchers (the principal investigator and other members of the staff) hold the records documenting the formulation of the project and the actual conduct of the work as well as the final products. If the work was carried out with colleagues at other institutions or using equipment at other sites, the record is further dispersed.

For collaborative and funded research, coordination is required to ensure the preservation of the separate parts of the documentary record. A dispersed record is the shared responsibility of archivists at many institutions. Collaborative development of records retention plans and discussions about the documentation of specific projects can establish cooperative plans to guarantee the retention of records by the appropriate institution. (See Bibliography, American Institute of Physics.)

Multiformats

Documenting research requires dealing with many forms of materials, some of them fragile, transient, and difficult to preserve. The sources or data that researchers study include periodicals and books, bones and teeth, scores and sound recordings, rocks and ice samples, prints and textiles. Researchers gather the artifacts themselves or reproductions of these objects in photographs, films, or digitized images. Data of all kinds are increasingly created, assembled, and analyzed in machine-readable form. The reporting of research results and communication among collaborators rely on electronic mail systems and the creation and dissemination of information in machine-readable form. The section on the research process that follows explores the problems associated with the retention of data. The general point to be made here is that multiformat collections require the shared expertise of many curators — librarians, museum curators, data archivists, and archivists — to select and preserve the records.

Undocumented and
Intangible Elements

Moments of insight when a problem is conceptualized, when the method is formulated to solve the problem, and when an answer is found are the key events in the research process. Most often, however, these are mental activities that are acted upon but unfortunately not recorded. The process of discovery, the actual sequence of events, the decisions made, and the participation of other researchers and staff members in the intellectual and physical work are of great interest to the practitioners themselves as well as historical researchers, but they are often poorly documented. The practice of maintaining chronological research notes is a thing of the past except for some disciplines such as chemistry, and for researchers who carry out field work, such as anthropologists and archeologists. A visual record (photographs, films, or video) can provide considerable evidence of the facilities and staff used during a project, the availability of equipment, and the interaction of the project staff. When the decision is made to document a specific project more fully, oral histories or other efforts may be required to record what would otherwise be the undocumented aspects of the research.

Minimum vs. Fuller Documentation

Every research project need not be fully documented. Efforts should be made, however, to capture information that provides a minimum record about research at the institution. For many projects, a bibliographic record of the final products or the published products themselves (see *Dissemination of Research Results: Documentation,* page 132) and the administrative files maintained by the senior officer for research and the office that manages research grants (see *Funding: Documentation,* page 130) supply this minimum record of research activities. The files in a grants office should contain much of the following information for funded projects: grant proposal; letter of award; negotiations and communications with the funding agency; information about equipment purchased and travel; copies of progress and final reports. Financial and personnel records are generally maintained separately and do not need to be included as part of this minimum record. Some campuses may also publish annual descriptions of current research or include a list of faculty publications in the annual report of the president. These lists are especially important to capture a record of research that was carried out without financial support.

Selecting those projects that deserve fuller documentation either because they were great successes or failures or because they serve as examples of more typical research requires advice from members of the faculty and administration. At any given time there may be hundreds or even thousands of research activities in progress at a college or university. Some of these may be projects of limited duration while others may be part of a long-term evolutionary investigation. In any case, only a few of them deserve to be documented in depth. A regular review of research efforts with disciplinary committees or individuals can be used to identify projects currently under way or just completed that merit fuller documentation. Criteria should include the significance of the work not only to the disciplinary community, but to the institution as well. Research that generates significant undergraduate or graduate theses or stimulates new course work would be of particular interest. The documentation of these selected projects should provide a more complete understanding and therefore requires records of the research process. (Additional guidance on the selection process is presented in the *Institutional Documentation Plan*.)

The Research Process

The discipline-specific literature on research reinforces the differences in the process of inquiry in science and technology, the social sciences, and the humanities. However, although the scale of the enterprise, the facilities and sources, and the final products differ, there are common elements in the sequence of events and the goals of the research process.

Any attempt to examine research in a general way, however, presents several problems. First, the literature on the research process is strongest in science and technology. The visibility and scale of science and technology and the value placed on them by modern society have meant that research in these disciplines has been examined more than in others. The literature on research in other disciplines is less analytic and more heavily devoted to descriptions of research methods. In the following presentation, while other disciplines are discussed, scientific and technological research are often presented as examples, as they offer the clearest and best understood cases.

Second, it is important to keep in mind the emotional component of the research activity. The analytic discussion of the research process that follows masks the personal motivations that draw faculty and graduate students to research. For most academics, the primary motivating factor is the pleasure they derive from the process of conducting research — the excitement of being engaged with ideas and satisfying an intellectual curiosity. The discovery of new source materials or a problem to solve; the search process to gather information; and the pleasure and pain of synthesizing, analyzing, and presenting the work all involve not only the intellectual skills but also the emotions of the researcher. It is a creative process from the selection of the question to be pursued to recording the findings. The labor can last years and be a lonely pursuit. The public presentation of the results is filled with joy, pride, and apprehension. It is the intellectual stimulation that keeps each researcher committed to the process.

Finally, the discussion of research as a sequential process belies the often fragmented task that it actually is. It is not neat, it is not orderly. Results can be obtained by trial and error, and failures may occur more frequently than successes. The process can be protracted, with periods of teaching and administrative responsibilities forcing delays and disruptions.

The following, then, is an idealized presentation. The experiences of individual researchers demonstrate the vagaries of research and reveal the motivations that keep people engaged in this process.

Framing the Research Problem

Research is a process of asking questions — questions about phenomena, sources, or current interpretations:

What causes cancer?

How did the English language evolve?

Can this body of documents help me reinterpret an author, a social phenomenon, or an event in history?

How did the symphonic form evolve?

What caused the great crash of 1929?

Does the evolution of the horse help explain the theory of the distribution of species?

Why do some so-called primitive tribes engage in ritual tattooing?

By what process did James Joyce create Finnegans Wake?

Is a new hybrid form of corn well adapted to grow in tropical climates?

The questions that researchers ask and the way in which these relate to the questions asked by others yield an understanding of the continuing cycle of the research process. The cycle can be seen in both the sequence of questions researchers ask throughout their own work and the sequence of questions or type of research problems pursued within disciplines.

Individual researchers form questions against a background of accumulated knowledge. Every researcher is heir to a body of traditions composed of sets of outstanding problems, theories, techniques, and information. Training and continuing scholarship suggest areas of inquiry that could add to the body of knowledge. Therefore, researchers approach their work like carpenters about to build a new house, bringing to the task a knowledge of materials and accepted methods and a belt full of tools. Past practice and skills inform the carpenter, but do not preclude the decision to deviate from past practice, invent a new tool or construction technique, or alter the nature of a structure.

The research question is derived, then, by defining a gap in existing knowledge or an inconsistency between accumulated knowledge and its explanation. In science and technology the question can be articulated as hypotheses about what an answer might be. In other disciplines the question may not be stated as explicitly. The research process is then devoted to the accumulation of sufficient evidence to validate one of the hypotheses and if possible to formulate a testable theory from the best hypothesis. Theories that have been sufficiently tested and validated can then be accepted as laws.

Part of a researcher's background knowledge is a general understanding of the accepted theories that guide research in a disciplinary area. The works of Darwin, Freud, Marx, Newton, Lévi-Strauss, Foucault, and Keynes provide the theoretical underpinnings to research in many disciplinary areas. These seminal writings and similar works are the products of theoretical or conceptual research that attempts to establish new definitions or theories. Conceptual and theoretical research problems generally focus on large questions: What is gravity? How do we explain the selection of species? How can human behavior be explained? How can we understand the rise and fall of nations? The importance of the theoretical or conceptual work is often described as revolutionary as it encourages new lines of questioning and often influences more than one discipline.

For example, the theory of structuralism was proposed by Roman Jakobson, a Slavic linguist, and the members of the Prague School of linguistics as a way to understand spoken language. Claude Lévi-Strauss, a French anthropologist, applied the theory to the study of human societies and thereby expanded and further defined it. The original theory, which suggested that the structure of language could be understood by examining the way it is segmented and ordered, was then used to support the analysis of human cultures through an examination of the way classifications and categories reveal the thought process. Historians, such as Robert Darnton, have recently applied Lévi-Strauss's anthropological approach to understand changes in society through history. Thus, structuralism, like the Darwinian theory of evolution by natural selection, is important because of its broad impact on thinking and research in many disciplines.

Theoretical foundations are incorporated into research activities through the methods and practices developed by each discipline. Research methodologies set the standards for accepted practice in a discipline by clarifying how data should be gathered, evaluated, and reported. Methodologies combine elements of craft with intellectual processes. Historical research methods establish procedures for the accumulation of evidence, the evaluation of historical documents, and the accepted practice for the use and citation of primary and secondary sources. The experimental methods used by scientists and engineers establish procedures to test and evaluate existing theories.

These research methods are then applied to solve specific types of problems. Robert Root-Bernstein has grouped these problem types in the following categories (Root-Bernstein, p. 61):

Type	Examples	Methods of Solution
Technique	How can we obtain data to fill gaps in our knowledge? How do we analyze data to determine if they are accurate?	Invention of instruments and methods of analysis and display
Evaluation	How adequate is a definition, theory, observation, or technique?	Invention of criteria for evaluation
Integration	Can two disparate theories or sets of data be integrated?	Reinterpretation and rethinking of existing concepts and theories
Extension	How many cases does a theory explain?	Prediction and testing
Comparison	When competing theories or data exist, which theory or data set is more useful?	Invention of criteria for comparison
Application	How can this observation, theory, or technique be used?	Knowledge of related unsolved problems; technological inventions; devising methods for acting on accumulated knowledge

While some research aims to test, refine, and extend existing theories, a great deal of research in all disciplines aims to enlarge the body of knowledge by describing or cataloging what exists, or by applying existing theories and techniques to new problems. The theoretical understanding of the structure of the genes of flies and bacteria led to the development of techniques that allow the "mapping" of these genes (the identification of individual markers on the gene that cause specific characteristics or mutations). The project to map the human genome is therefore an application of these earlier techniques. Similarly, quantitative history and the methods of the French School of historians offer research techniques to gather and evaluate historical evidence. The anthropologist in the field applies the structural theories of Claude Lévi-Strauss through the techniques developed to analyze the language and customs of specific cultural groups. The application of these techniques and research methods builds a body of evidence for each discipline by filling in gaps in knowledge. Thus, while the nature of the marriage ceremony in seventeenth-century Paris may be of little interest to an economist or political historian, the application of Lévi-Strauss's approach reveals that much can be learned about social structure through the use of his ideas. In this way, the sorts of problems and sources that are interesting and fruitful are redefined, new questions are posed, and new research is initiated.

Research entails the assembly and interpretation of data — historical documents or texts, observations or measurements of scientific or human phenomena, or artistic or cultural artifacts. Data by themselves do not yield answers to research problems; answers are only revealed when questions are applied and the evidence is analyzed and interpreted. More often than not, the questioning and analysis reveal new gaps or unexpected contradictions. New problems are generated, and the cycle of research in the discipline continues.

The type of research problems and style of work an individual pursues reflects, to a great extent, his or her personality. Textual analysts, observational astronomers, and others who undertake detailed work are likely to be very different from those who choose to pursue broad conceptual problems.

In addition to disciplinary background and personal style, the selection of a research problem also involves a series of practical concerns:

Does the evidence exist (manuscripts, published literature, or numerical scientific data) to address the research problem? Can the sources or data be obtained?

Can the research be carried out at the researcher's institution or is travel required to use libraries or to conduct field work in distant locations?

Do the techniques and equipment exist to pursue the research? Must equipment be built, acquired, or used at another site?

Is funding required to support the primary researcher and other staff members or pay for travel, services, or equipment?

Is the funding available from internal or external sources for research in this area?

What are the rewards of pursuing this line of research? How will the work be regarded within the institution and by colleagues in the discipline? Will it yield publications needed for promotion? Is there a possibility of a prize if the work is completed successfully?

How much competition is there to solve the problem? Has an established figure already "staked out" the field as his or her own? Is the research important enough to gain attention? Or is it so risky that tenure, promotion, or funding might be threatened?

Framing the Research Problem: Documentation

The process of conceptualizing and selecting research problems and formulating hypotheses is of great interest to those who study the research process, but unfortunately is rarely recorded. The process involves mental activities that are usually undocumented. Research notes, correspondence with colleagues, and grant proposals can capture the choice of the problem and the means to pursue the research, but most likely will not record the factors or the sequence of reasoning that led the researcher to the selection of the problem and the formulation of the hypothesis. Much can be inferred from a knowledge about the field and the types of research being pursued at any given time. For research projects that are to be documented more fully, an attempt can be made to recapture the mental process through oral history — although the accuracy of the reconstruction may be questionable.

Planning and Carrying Out the Work

Once the area of research is defined, researchers must plan the work. What information is needed to answer the questions or test the hypothesis? Does this information exist? How can it be created or gathered? What physical and intellectual tools are required to gather and analyze the information? What facilities are required? Where must the work be accomplished?

In the following idealized sequence of events, the research process is described as an orderly and logical set of activities. However, the discovery of unanticipated documents can, and usually does, force a researcher to reevaluate assumptions and even change or abandon a line of questioning. Other unanticipated events can also precipitate modifications in research plans: equipment can fail to operate properly or to give the desired results; or someone else can publish first. There are few absolute answers to research questions. No theory explains all phenomena, and if a theory fails a specific experimental test, it is still useful as it provides information about what failed.

The historical or literary researcher begins by identifying the primary and secondary sources to be examined and determines if the materials are housed in local collections or require travel to other libraries, archives, or museums. The sources are examined at their site or gathered by purchase of available materials or through the acquisition of photocopies. The researcher determines if existing literary and historical modes of analysis are to be employed or whether the study presents the opportunity to develop new analytic tools. A simple filing system is established or a software program employed to help organize the information as it is gathered. The work is accomplished in a campus office or frequently at the graduate student's or faculty member's home.

The anthropologist identifies the specific cultural groups to be studied and determines whether other groups will serve as controls and over what time period the observations of the groups are to be made. The research design specifies the activities to be observed in the field, the questions to be asked, and the statistical and analytical tools to be used to interpret the data. Again, manual and automated systems are established to organize the information as it is gathered and to facilitate the analysis. While the data gathering requires extensive time in the field, the analysis and writing is usually accomplished at the home campus.

The scientist or engineer determines if equipment exists to generate the data needed to verify the hypothesis. If not, the first step might be to design, build, and test apparatus required to produce and gather the information. If the desired data can be generated by an existing computer, the research may begin by writing the required computer programs. Scientists and engineers are not always able to acquire the equipment they need at their own institutions, as the size, cost, and complexity limit its availability to specialized installations (cyclotrons, telescopes). In this case, applications are made to travel to and use the equipment. The analysis of the data obtained from such activities can take years and can be carried out at the home institutions.

For observational scientists, such as astronomers and meteorologists, the required data may be obtained from an existing body of material held by a scientific data center such as the National Center for Atmospheric Research (NCAR) or the National Oceanographic and Atmospheric Administration (NOAA). In all cases scientists and engineers determine what existing theoretical assumptions are being made, what theories are being tested, and when new theories are required to explain phenomena and answer questions.

Planning and Carrying Out the Work: Documentation

The evidence of the work includes the administrative records and the research records themselves. Little evidence may exist of the formulation of the research plan, the design of the equipment and techniques used, the chronological sequence of the work, and the process of analysis and interpretation. If the researcher applied for funds to support the work, the application might contain evidence of the questions, rationale, and methods, while progress reports to funding agencies and working papers trace the accomplishments. Without records associated with the receipt of funding, documenting these activities is more difficult. Research carried out by an individual researcher without financial support generates few administrative records. Most research activities, however, generate data or informational files. Few researchers any longer maintain research notes to trace their intellectual progress; when such notes are available, they may exist in machine-readable form rather than in a notebook. Correspondence with colleagues and collaborators may shed some light on research activities, but most of these exchanges are now carried out by telephone or electronic mail.

For those projects chosen to be documented in greater detail, particular efforts must be made to gather (or, when necessary, encourage the creation of) a record of the research process. Grant proposals, progress reports, journals of the work process, and correspondence all contribute information. Assistance from the creators of the records, or researchers in the same discipline, and historical researchers may be needed to analyze and select the most relevant material from the data and the other records of the research process.

Data, Observational
and Experimental

The most voluminous record of the research process is often the data — reprints of articles, photocopies of manuscripts and published works, computer or card files of research notes, photographs of buildings or biological specimens, machine-readable raw and analyzed data, and objects of every variety. In making retention decisions, archivists must consider the potential reuse of the data by other investigators to continue, refine, and test research, and the long-term reuse for historical analysis of the research. One important guide in such decisions is the distinction between experimental and observational data.

Observational data are generated primarily by the scientific disciplines (including geology and astronomy), medicine, and the behavioral sciences, which study natural phenomena including weather systems, human disease and behavior, earthquakes, and comets. These data can be numerical (daily air and water temperatures from specific locations), descriptive (written notes on the social customs of an ethnic group), or visual (photographs of a solar eclipse). These data are time bound, since it is difficult if not impossible to recover observational data once the moment of the event has passed: measurements of the aftershocks of a specific earthquake cannot be reconstructed and recorded after the quake has ceased.

In contrast, experimental data are generated by experimentation, a process that can generally be repeated. Experimental data can be numerical (the distance a mannequin wearing a seat restraint is thrown forward in a test crash of an automobile), descriptive (reactions of automobile drivers and passengers to newly designed seat restraints), or visual (motion picture films of each test crash). It is theoretically possible to recover experimental data because experiments can be repeated as long as the experimental method and procedures are known. In this sense, literary, historical, and other similar research can be included in this category, as the data assembled — the documents and texts — can be reassembled.

The categories of observational and experimental data, however, often overlap and may not always be clearly distinguishable. An example of this is data gathered from testing ore samples for radioactive content. The experimental procedure used to test for radioactivity may be repeated, but because the specific samples of ore are distinctive, the data technically are unique and not reproducible. Practical considerations such as the high cost of some experimental procedures and the difficulty of gathering the documents may also lend greater value to some experimental data.

In evaluating data, especially observational data, the first consideration is the potential reuse by the disciplinary community. Researchers who generate observational data generally understand the continuing value of the information and place it at appropriate research centers where their colleagues expect to find it. Data on specific topics are gathered in central facilities, such as the National Geophysical and Solar-Terrestrial Data Center, or at the facility where the data were gathered, such as the Mt. Palomar Observatory or the center established at the Goddard Space Center to collect and service the data from the Hubble Space Telescope. The Centers for Disease Control retain epidemiological data, and the Smithsonian Institution collects anthropological and behavioral studies on film at its Human Studies Film Archives. Observational data are best located in such specialized centers where information can be selected, remanipulated, and used by specialists. The role of the archivist is to assist researchers in the proper placement of the data. Data collection and analysis can represent a sizable investment, often of taxpayers' money. Particular care should be taken to ensure that observational data are placed at the appropriate center where they will be available for reuse. The *CODATA Directory of Data Sources for Science and Technology* provides worldwide referrals to help researchers and archivists locate appropriate centers.

Collections of artifacts and unique specimens pose similar problems. The objects are valuable both for the information they provide about the sources examined by the researcher and for their continuing investigations by others in the discipline. In many cases the artifacts are therefore best placed in a facility where they can receive appropriate curatorial care: a museum, botanical garden, or zoo.

Experimental data present very different problems. These data are less valuable for the continuation of the research by others in the same field, as they can usually be recovered by rerunning the experiment or gathering the information once again from the original sources. The way in which researchers gather and organize their data may reveal something about their research style and mode of thinking and may therefore be useful to historical researchers interested in the research process. But this individuality also makes the data difficult for anyone else to reuse.

When examining data records, historical researchers often focus on the methods used and choices made, rather than on the specific data. Although the data may not be of interest or comprehensible to historical researchers, the way in which they were gathered may indicate something about the research methods, the sequence of events, and the choices made by the researcher. The data may then provide some understanding of the options and choices, the quality of the equipment, the evidence the researcher considered, and, by analogy, the sources or data not considered.

Experimental data can be voluminous and rarely should be preserved in their entirety. For those individuals or research projects deemed to have sufficient value, examples can be retained to document the methods and sources used and sequence of events. Data files are frequently specialized and highly technical. Selection decisions require advice from the creator of the records or researchers in the same field. Additional advice is available from historians of the appropriate discipline. For science and technology, more detailed advice on the appraisal of experimental and observational data is available in *Appraising the Records of Modern Science and Technology: A Guide* (pp. 56–67).

One type of resource file that is as common in the sciences as in the humanities and social sciences is a reprint or information file in which an individual researcher or team gathers published (or near-print) material from many sources. Reprint or information files were once regarded as a useful way to evaluate the information available to and used by a given researcher. This is no longer the case. Knowledge of modern bibliographic tools and services provides sufficient evidence that researchers can easily locate and obtain the material they require. Published monographic and serial literature in all disciplines is located through automated and library networks, while library catalogs and published guides identify the availability of other sources.

Information files may be convenient for the researcher, but generally they do not fully reflect the information that was accessible and used. The physical presence of an item in an information file does not indicate if the item was deliberately sought, received unsolicited, read, or used. Footnotes in a published work are a better indication of the actual use of specific literature. Therefore, as a general rule these files should not be saved. The comprehensive nature of a particular information file, however, can make it of great value to a particular subject area. In this case, the file could be given to an appropriate library, department, or laboratory. In any case, it is useful to include a description of the general contents and organization of the file in the inventory to the appropriate manuscript or archival collection.

Staff

Research is an important activity for faculty and graduate students alike. Graduate education is designed, in part, to teach research skills, and the master's thesis and doctoral dissertation demonstrate that achievement by engaging the graduate student in an original project. A faculty member's research generally continues throughout his or her career.

The image of the researcher alone in an office or laboratory pursuing a project is still accurate for much of literary, historical, and social science research. Even scientists and engineers who conduct their research without financial support may still work alone. The only help available to these individuals may be a research assistant (often a graduate student available for library searches or laboratory work) or a clerical or editorial assistant. For collaborative research of all kinds and the majority of scientific and technological efforts, project leaders work as part of a multi-layered team comprising researchers, administrators, and technical assistants. The research staff is made up of graduate students, postdoctoral fellows, and research assistants, who are directed by the team leaders in the assembly and analysis of data. Technical assistance is often required to program and run computers or to build and operate other equipment. Administrative and secretarial staff manage financial, personnel, and reporting requirements as well as document preparation.

Staff:
Documentation

On the whole, the documentation of the personnel engaged in research activities resembles the records described in the general section on personnel (see page 189). Achieving a picture of the layers of personnel associated with a specific project, however, can sometimes be difficult. The list of authors of a published journal article, the acknowledgments at the opening of a book, and even a description of the staff in a final report to a funding agency do not provide detailed information about all of the participants in a research project or information on the accomplishments of each. For those projects to be documented fully, an effort should be made to ascertain more specific information about the staff.

Directories of laboratories or research centers provide evidence of the personnel and can provide information about who was associated with particular research efforts. The personnel records of a project can provide lists of the staff, job descriptions, and responsibilities for specific time periods. Grant proposals provide job descriptions and budgets for the categories of personnel. Clarification of the particular work accomplished by members of the team is extremely difficult unless each person maintained chronological research notes. For particularly significant projects, oral history interviews with the research and technical staff may be required to clarify the contribution of each staff member.

Funding

Acquisition of source materials; travel to archives, libraries, or field sites; purchase and operation of equipment; and the staff to carry out the work all require financial resources. Though some research is still carried out with little or no support, research has become increasingly dependent on funding. The critical question about funding may be not how much is required but when it is required. A great deal of research in the humanities, social sciences, and even the sciences can be launched without financial support, but some funds may eventually be required for travel, staff, or use of equipment such as computers to analyze data. In other areas, especially those scientific and technological disciplines that require teams of researchers and elaborate equipment, the research cannot even begin until funds are secured. Where research is dependent on support, funds are sought from the home institution and many outside sources.

Colleges and universities encourage research activities by expending their resources in several ways. Institutions support research by providing the facilities (libraries, laboratories, and research centers), materials (books, journals, and equipment), and staff (research assistants, technicians, and clerical staff) needed for these activities. Additional support comes through the allocation of time to be spent on teaching and research activities and the provision of paid sabbaticals. Finally, most universities have some funds that are awarded to members of the faculty and graduate students to support research projects. The amount of funds available for such purposes varies greatly and is frequently inadequate to support larger projects.

Up until the early part of this century, academic research was supported primarily by internal funds specifically raised and allocated by the universities for this purpose. By the 1920s those funds were supplemented by grants available from private foundations such as the Rockefeller, Macy, and Kellogg Foundations. The decision made by the federal government at the beginning of World War II to base research projects at academic institutions rather than in existing or new government laboratories transformed the nature of research in the United States, particularly in science and technology. The establishment of the National Science Foundation and later the arts and humanities endowments structured and encouraged federal support of academic research. In recent decades industry has joined private foundations and the government as a source of research support. The proportion of funds currently contributed by each of these sources to academic research is as follows:

Federal Government	60.8%
State and Local Governments	8.3%
Industry	6.6%
The Institution Itself	17.3%
Other (including Foundations)	6.9%

The Chronicle of Higher Education Almanac,
5 September 1990, p. 3.

The research priorities of the funders and the procedures established to apply for support have a considerable impact on the structure as well as the subject of research. Agencies announce the topical areas they are willing to support, the amount of funds they will grant, and the desired length of the projects (generally one to three years). In addition to grants, the government also uses the mechanism of contracts, in which the applicant responds to a request for a proposal (RFP) that generally calls for research leading to the preparation of a specific product (a software package, a body of data, a technical development, or a report on a policy issue). The grant and contract process structures academic research around specific fundable projects of short duration rather than research that is open-ended in time and topic. Research results that suggest a new line of work or modification of a process may have to be set aside in favor of accomplishing the specific objectives of the funded project. The competitive short-cycle process creates continuing pressures and uncertainty about the future. Changing research priorities by the granting agencies can terminate traditional sources of support. Successful researchers are measured not just by the quality of their final products but also by their ability to secure grant support.

The application and award process varies from the informal methods favored by many foundations to the lengthy applications required by the government. Foundation and industrial sources generally rely on their own staff to evaluate proposals and make award decisions. The government's elaborate peer review and decision-making process allows the federal agencies to fulfill their obligation to be accountable to Congress and the taxpayers.

Funding:
Documentation

The means of funding affects not only the conduct of research but also the documentation of those activities, since the records are dispersed among those who fund, administer, and carry out the projects. While the colleges and universities hold the administrative records and the records of the research process, the funding agencies have the responsibility for their own documentation. Some of the private foundations, such as the Rockefeller and Ford Foundations, have preserved records of their support of academic research in their archives. Government and corporate records have fared less well. The federal government does not have a uniform policy for the records of those agencies that provide research funds to higher education. The National Historical Publications and Records Commission (NHPRC), for instance, selects case files of unique grants funded by their records program for retention by the National Archives. Archivists can inquire about records of particular concern and describe their availability (or destruction) in their own finding aids.

Information should be gathered about how the institution supports research. The availability of internal funds and their allocation to specific individuals or projects are recorded in financial and policy documents. Summary information about the sources of external support, the sums acquired, and the projects supported are generally included in reports of the president, treasurer, or senior officer for research.

Ample detailed and summary financial records exist at colleges and universities for projects supported through grants and contracts. Even for research projects chosen to be documented fully, detailed financial records are not necessary; the budget information in the proposal, the opening and closing budget statements, and, when additional information is deemed desirable, the monthly budget statements provide sufficient information (see *Financial Reporting*, page 183, for additional information).

The funded research efforts generally encompass the larger projects and are often concentrated in the science and engineering areas. It is harder to document the funding of the smaller projects, the individual efforts of graduate students and faculty who carry out their work with little or no support.

Dissemination of Research Results

Dissemination of research takes place as a continuous process that includes informal discussions with colleagues, reports at conferences, circulation of working papers and drafts through on-line networks and paper copies, and, finally, formal publications. Through this process, researchers test, refine, and lay claim to their results.

Teaching serves an important dissemination function as research results are incorporated into existing curriculum and courses are designed to reflect significant new knowledge. Teaching materials are a valuable source to document the impact of research on the process of education and the evolution of specific disciplines. This process of transferring knowledge, bringing the information gathered during research to the students, is particularly important in fields that are in the process of rapid change, such as physics in the earlier part of the twentieth century and molecular biology during the last decade.

Master's theses and doctoral dissertations are the results of the research that graduate students complete to earn their degrees. Some of these products are reworked by their authors and published in books and journals.

The most visible and voluminous products of research are the journal articles, technical reports, and books that disseminate the results of research. Technical reports are often issued by the laboratory where the work was done. Otherwise the author negotiates the publication of the findings with a book publisher or journal editor. Publishers use the peer review system to evaluate the quality of the work, recommend revisions, and determine if the work merits publication.

Dissemination of Research Results: Documentation

It is important to understand the purpose of the published results in order to evaluate the role that this formal dissemination of findings plays in documenting research. The purpose of the research literature is two-fold: to communicate results and discoveries in order to expand knowledge and to stake a claim to the results. Much of the literature is written in a formal objective manner; for most disciplines, the literature is intended to present the findings in a rational sequence, not to offer a historical or chronological presentation of the research, nor to discuss or analyze the process of achieving the results. The published products, therefore, often have little to say about why the topic was chosen in the first place, the actual sequence of events, the tasks performed by each researcher, the trials and tribulations of obtaining financial resources and making machines operate, the false starts, modifications in methods, and other frustrations that appeared along the way. While a researcher might discuss some of these issues in a biography, the formal published literature is not intended to include such information. Manuscript and archival records that document the research process are required to answer these questions.

At universities where graduate students and faculty are constantly issuing the results of their research, it is not feasible to collect copies of all publications. Although a bibliographic record of these works would be extremely useful, even this may prove to be too time and space consuming. If another office on campus (such as the president, senior research officer, dean, news office, or library) maintains such lists, the archives could eventually obtain copies. For projects and individuals to be documented more fully, however, it is desirable to obtain a complete bibliography of published products and, if possible, copies of the publications.

Researchers can produce a sizable record as they draft, revise, and edit a publication, but such draft materials and edited page proofs rarely provide evidence of the substantive intellectual process. While the retention of these materials may be justified for literary and for particularly important scholarly works, where it is valuable to capture the writing and editorial process, as a general rule these records need not be retained.

Colleges and universities have a particular obligation to ensure the availability and retention of the works issued by their own institution. These publications include theses and dissertations as well as technical reports issued by their laboratories and proceedings of conferences held at the institution. Provision should be made for these records of campus research activities (and in the case of the theses, the conferring of degrees) to be preserved in appropriate units of the institution, reported in bibliographic databases, and made available through services such as University Microfilms.

Bibliography

American Institute of Physics Study of Multi-institutional Collaborations in High-energy Physics. (New York: American Institute of Physics, 1991).

Brim, John A., and David H. Spain. *Research Design in Anthropology: Paradigms and Pragmatics in the Testing of Hypotheses.* New York: Holt, Rinehart and Winston, 1974.

Committee of Data for Science and Technology (CODATA). *CODATA Directory of Data Sources for Science and Technology.* Paris: CODATA Secretariat, 1977–.

Geiger, Roger. *To Advance Knowledge: The Growth of American Research Universities, 1900–1940.* New York: Oxford University Press, 1986.

Goldstein, Martin, and Inge F. Goldstein. *How We Know: An Exploration of the Scientific Process.* New York: Plenum Press, 1978.

Haas, Joan K., Helen Willa Samuels, and Barbara Trippel Simmons. *Appraising the Records of Modern Science and Technology: A Guide.* Cambridge: Massachusetts Institute of Technology (distributed by the Society of American Archivists), 1985.

Root-Bernstein, Robert. *Discovering.* Cambridge: Harvard University Press, 1989.

Vendler, Helen, quoted in "Balancing Teaching and Writing." *On Teaching and Learning. The Journal of the Harvard-Danforth Center.* (January 1987): 10–16.

Sustain
the Institution

General Documentary Issues

Every institution must manage
finances, facilities, and people in order to sustain itself: to ensure that
it continues to operate and carry out its mission. Although colleges and
universities in the nineteenth century were administered primarily by
the president and the trustees, the size, expense, and complexities of
modern colleges and universities require a sizable professional and support staff. The voluminous published literature on the administration of
academic institutions attests to the emphasis that is now placed on effective management. This chapter examines the major administrative areas:
governance, funding, staffing, and the physical plant of colleges and
universities. While some management activities are quite similar to
those of very different types of institutions, colleges and universities
do have unique practices.

Affecting all internal administrative activities are significant external
factors. Federal, state, and local governments; accrediting organizations;
religious institutions; professional societies; and labor unions — all have
an impact on academic institutions through funding, regulations, and
influence. Colleges and universities are also affected by changes in technology and communications systems and in the very nature and structure of modern institutions. A discussion of the influence of some of
these factors on all aspects of the *sustain* function precedes the sections
on governance, finances, personnel, and physical plant.

Throughout these discussions both the administrative and the historical
value of the documentation are considered. When evaluating records,
archivists assess both the immediate and long-term administrative, fiscal, and legal needs of the institution and the potential for reuse of the
material by historical researchers. Because such a high proportion of the
records of long-term administrative value are concentrated in this function, administrative considerations are emphasized. The evaluation of
long-term historical use, however, must also be kept in mind.

Legal Environment

The most pervasive external influence on colleges and universities is the complex legal environment in which they operate. Legal issues affect every aspect of higher education and therefore the documentation of these institutions as well. Until the middle of the twentieth century, higher education was for the most part self-regulated. The United States Constitution does not mention higher education, which was left to the control of the states and private citizens. Federal and state governments as well as the judiciary allowed academic traditions and consensual agreement to regulate colleges and universities. As late as the 1950s, federal policy prohibited the government from exercising control over the educational process of academic institutions. And yet, one of the most dominant influences in recent years has been the increasing role of federal, state, and local governments in the regulation of colleges and universities.

The federal government exercises control through its power to spend, tax, regulate commerce, and enforce civil rights. Government regulation of higher education affects private as well as public institutions. Public institutions, but not private ones, are subject to the provisions of the U.S. Constitution; however, governments retain the ability to control both public and private colleges and universities through their regulatory powers.

The more dominant role of the government in higher education and the increased attention to legal considerations came about through greater dependence on federal and state funds and the government's emphasis on social programs. The search for additional funds to run research projects, support students, and build facilities brought academic institutions out of their autonomy and into contact with government sponsors. Receipt of funds from government agencies obligates institutions to comply with regulations and reporting requirements. Through the granting of these funds, governments influence an institution's academic programs and its administrative practices.

Some regulations are specifically targeted to control academic institutions, but colleges and universities are also subject to general regulations governing minimum salary and wages, retirement age, access for the physically handicapped, etc. Higher education, as well as other institutions in society, is subject to laws and regulations that address a variety

136

of social issues, such as the civil rights of individual citizens and the environment. Academic institutions are subject to the regulations of multiple government authorities, including Health and Human Services, the Veterans Administration, and the Office of Education, as well as comparable offices within each state. The 23 April 1990 *Federal Register* listed forty-one new rules issued by nine agencies that affected higher education (*Chronicle of Higher Education*, 6 June 1990, p. A24). Each set of regulations imposes costs (raising minimum salaries, building ramps for the physically handicapped, etc.) and obligates institutions to create and maintain records of their compliance. Administrators have voiced great concern about the influence and expense that regulations impose upon them. Particular concern is voiced about those regulations, such as affirmative action, that impinge on the institution's ability to select students and faculty.

As burdensome as the regulatory environment is, there are additional factors that shape the legal atmosphere. In the past, litigation involving academic institutions was generally confined to contract disputes, labor negotiations, landlord-tenant disagreements, tax questions, zoning changes, and accidents that occurred on the campus. More recently, however, colleges and universities are being sued in their academic capacities. The recognition of students' rights as consumers introduced the possibility of litigation over rates of tuition, grades, the award of degrees, and campus security. Faculty denied promotion or tenure are increasingly using litigation as a recourse.

To protect themselves from litigation and further control by government agencies and the courts, academic institutions are stressing institutional self-regulation. Internal policies, procedures, rules, and regulations are now more explicit and encompassing. Internal grievance procedures are viewed as alternatives for faculty, students, and staff to prevent litigation and outside regulation.

Many of these legal issues have a direct bearing on the creation, maintenance, retention, and use of records. In some instances, policies governing records may be mandated by external factors. In other cases, the pressures of the legal environment create an implied obligation that may lead an institution to impose even stricter control over records than required by external sources.

Some federal and state regulations impose specific records requirements. This discussion cannot deal comprehensively with all regulations, as the requirements differ from state to state, and for private and public institutions. The published regulations provide detailed information on records requirements, and additional advice may be available from the officers on campus who oversee compliance. The affirmative action and student financial aid officers; registrar; and senior staff in the personnel, financial, and grants offices should all understand the regulations that govern their areas. The institution's auditor may be one of the people with a comprehensive knowledge of the records needed to comply with government regulations. State archives might also be a valuable source of information, especially for records covered by state laws.

Laws, regulations, and legal considerations affect records in the following ways:

Creation: Some federal and state regulations mandate the creation of specific records. Affirmative action requirements call for the documentation of search procedures and candidates interviewed and regular reports on the composition (by sex, race, etc.) of the faculty and staff. Federal research grants require the submission of periodic progress reports as well as final technical and financial reports.

Access: Federal and state regulations can mandate access or prohibit access to specific records. The Family Education Rights and Privacy Act (FERPA), also known as the Buckley amendment, guarantees access by students to their academic records while it prohibits unauthorized access by others. Privacy law, generally established by the states, is particularly important for the provisions on access to personnel records. In many states, privacy is defined as a personal right that ceases at death; therefore, records of deceased individuals can be considered unrestricted and available for research. State privacy laws differ, however, and must be verified. State "sunshine" laws may mandate access to specific records created by state institutions. In Ohio, for instance, salary information and the minutes of the governing board of each campus in the state system are open records. On occasion, public colleges and universities have petitioned the state to exempt specific records (e.g., minutes of boards that review human subject research and search committee records) from mandatory access provisions.

Retention: Government agencies stipulate the length of time that records needed for audit and legal reporting purposes must be retained. Student financial aid regulations obligate the institution to maintain records of students receiving aid until five years following the date on which the student repaid, cancelled, or assigned the loan. Financial records of federally funded research projects must be held by the institution until the federal agency assigned to that institution for audit purposes has completed its work. Specific provisions of government agencies and grant and contract awards must be verified to confirm retention requirements.

In addition to these considerations, institutions must retain sufficient documentation to protect themselves in areas of possible litigation, when legal actions are pending, and, in some cases, when legal action has been completed. An institution also has legal obligations to its employees and donors, among others, to create and maintain adequate records. Staff members need proof of employment to receive social security or medicare benefits. In accepting funds and physical property from donors, an institution enters into a contractual obligation to fulfill the donor's wishes. Records of the conditions under which gifts were accepted and the commitments made by the institution to the donor must be retained so that gifts can be properly administered.

Interconnected Documentation

Funding patterns and regulations create ties among academic institutions, foundations, corporations, governments, and other regulatory organizations such as accrediting bodies and professional societies. The documentation of the interaction among these organizations is located both at the academic institution and at the external bodies. The report and background materials gathered by the academic institution in preparation for reaccreditation are held by the college; the accrediting body holds the records of the deliberations and decisions concerning the reaccreditation of each campus. The college or university has the proposal requesting funds for a research project, and if the award is made, the records of the research process and the final reports; the granting agency, however, holds the records relating to the decision to make the award.

The division of the records reflects the separate responsibilities of each institution, and both should maintain their own records of long-term value. In selecting and describing records, however, it is useful for archivists to recognize the availability of related documentation at other institutions. Coordinated retention of interconnected records can be ensured if institutions work together to establish records policies and share information about their holdings.

Bulk and Duplication

While we await the "paperless office," academic institutions continue to create and maintain a huge quantity of paper documentation. Depending on the topic, presidents send copies of their correspondence to many individuals, including the head of the development office, the vice presidents, and the heads of schools. Five copies of drop/add course forms are created and filed by the registrar, department, advisor, bursar, and student. Supervisors, departments, colleges, and the central personnel office all have files on the same employee. Classrooms and offices are converted to storage rooms for filing cabinets.

Thus, for the archivist, the problem is not just the volume of material created but also the duplication of that information around the campus. Communication and reporting requirements encourage the distribution of multiple copies. In the absence of the broad application of the concept of a record copy in contrast to informational copies, many offices receive, file, and maintain copies. Prior planning is needed to ensure the logical but minimum distribution of duplicate information and the preservation of but one copy of the records of long-term value.

Many of the techniques that address the problems of bulk and duplication are drawn from records management practices (see page 146). Of particular relevance are filing and retention guidelines, which encourage the document's creator to identify the record copy and ensure that it is preserved as needed; informational copies can be destroyed by offices as soon as possible. Dealing with these issues while the records are active minimizes the problem of duplication.

Automation

While paper documentation still flourishes, automation continues to affect every facet of academic institutions, including the way information is created, disseminated, and preserved. The place of computers in teaching and research is discussed in *Convey Knowledge* and *Conduct Research*. This section deals specifically with computers in administrative areas.

In a recent study of the effect of computers on academic administration (*Making Computers Work for Administrators*), James Powell follows an imaginary college president through an average day. The president uses computers at home and in the office and conference room to check the calendar for the day's events; set up new meetings; draft letters, journal articles, and speeches; analyze past, current, and projected enrollment and budgetary figures; and communicate with colleagues on and off campus through an electronic mail network. As the costs for powerful computer systems have decreased, even the smallest campuses use electronic technology in administrative offices. Computers affect the way work is done, the way communication takes place, and the way in which records are created and retained.

Computers are currently used in the following ways:

Control: Automated databases are used to track and manage information for every facet of the institution: the admission, matriculation, and graduation of students; the receipt, commitment, and expenditure of funds; the assignment of class space for teaching; the payment of personnel; the solicitation and receipt of contributions from alumni; the receipt, cataloging, and loan of books; etc.

Analyze: The information contained in the databases is used by managers of the institution to project and analyze trends and to create models to support administrative decision making. Admissions' and registrars' databases are analyzed to determine future recruiting, enrollment, and housing decisions. Financial databases are analyzed to support budgetary and fund-raising decisions.

Produce: The capabilities of computers alter both who produces documents and how they are prepared. The ease of creating, altering, and producing correspondence, reports, and publications has changed the work pattern of almost every member of the academic institution, thereby redistributing the secretarial function.

Word processors facilitate the production of correspondence and reports; computers generate tables, charts, and other visual materials; and CAD (computer aided design) systems are now used to create and alter architectural renderings.

Communicate: Electronic networks facilitate communication among individuals on campus and at other institutions. Although first used primarily as a substitute for the telephone, electronic networks now distribute lengthy and substantive correspondence, drafts, working papers, final reports, and other publications.

Changes in computer technology affect the administrative structures that oversee these activities as well as who uses the technology and for what purposes. In the last thirty years, the one or two mainframe computers devoted to administration and research have been superseded by numerous smaller, more powerful machines. The environment that is now emerging is an academic institution interconnected through many layers of computer networks: campuswide mainframe computers; school, department, or other area mini- and microcomputer networks; and the personal computers of the faculty, students, and staff. These campus networks are in turn connected to national and international research and education computer networks.

These linked networks facilitate communication and access to the information needed by all members of the institution. In this distributed system, databases can be developed locally and still be accessible to other members of the institution. Development and use of databases can be shared by many offices: the student information database is used and altered by academic departments, student financial aid, and the bursar's office, as well as the registrar.

The evolution of computer technology has also affected which personnel are involved in the administration and use of the equipment. The first mainframe computers were run by a few experts, and users channeled their inquiries through a specialized staff. The simplicity and low cost of microcomputers has put the technology in the hands of staff at all levels. Faculty and supervisors perform their own secretarial tasks, while support staff, who in many cases have considerable technological expertise, are taking on new roles and responsibilities. Databases (e.g., student information, purchasing) are accessible to all staff who need to use and update the information.

The automated environment presents the archivist with considerable challenges. Indicative of the problem is the absence of any substantive discussion about the long-term preservation and reuse of machine-readable information in the voluminous literature on automation in the academic setting. On the rare occasion when the topic arises, the focus is on such issues as privacy, confidentiality, and the ownership of information. The consideration of long-term problems is dismissed with statements like "As relatively inexpensive record and playback optical discs become available, far more information will be stored much more compactly. Preservation of material will also become a less critical problem" (*Campus of the Future*, p. 85). Designers and users of automated systems must be reminded that information in automated form, as in paper, has continuing administrative, legal, fiscal, and historical value and therefore must be preserved and made accessible to the institution. The answer, however, is not to store all of the information in machine-readable form. Rather, as with paper records, selection decisions must be addressed as records are created and used.

What documentary problems are presented by the varied uses of computers?

Control: Managing informational and transactional databases presents similar problems to handling these records in paper form. A considerable proportion of the information must be created in an orderly fashion, retained until no longer of administrative and legal value, and then destroyed. Other databases (e.g., student, personnel, and alumni) contain information of long-term value, and in this case, the design and operation of the system must ensure that information needed for long-term purposes is entered and retained. For example, retaining prior employment information when updating the alumni database to reflect job changes yields a full record of where the institution's graduates worked, their job mobility, and length of employment. Such information can be useful both for fund raising and to analyze career paths of graduates. Using databases to track information over time is complicated by the fact that large databases are "archived" (as the systems people say) periodically: that is, portions of the database are removed from on-line systems and retained on machine-readable tapes or discs. Over time, some data elements in the newer portions of the database may be redefined or new elements added. Changes in hardware and software further compound the problems of integrating older and newer portions. Therefore, searching the entire database becomes increasingly difficult.

Analyze: The use of computers for analytic purposes has tangible and less tangible aspects. Institutions rely on computers to analyze large bodies of data and produce regular reports, projections, and analyses that are used to support planning and operations. Monthly, quarterly, or yearly reports are generally used and retained by administrative officers. In addition, administrators, staff, and faculty download information from the main campus systems into their local networks or personal computers to carry out analyses as needed. A department head projects the need for future staff and facilities by examining portions of the student information database supplemented by local information on courses offered, faculty on leave, and student assistantships. The development office projects the outcome of the capital campaign by analyzing the commitments of prospective donors and the potential effects of altered rules on tax deductions for charitable contributions. Some of the results of these analyses and projections may enter the record through memos, correspondence, and reports, but documenting how and when administrators and faculty use this type of computer analysis as part of making decisions and how access to the information affects those decisions is more difficult.

Produce: The most direct evidence of the use of computers is the correspondence, publications, and reports produced using these machines. The ability to trace the evolution of a document through its draft, comment, and editing stages has been diminished by the ease of altering machine-readable records on-line. Draft documents can be transmitted between collaborators who make modifications and add comments. If users fail to print and retain interim versions of a document, however, the evolutionary record is lost. Drafts would normally not be saved, but for important policy and literary records, the loss of drafts reduces the possibility of understanding the process.

Communication: The use of electronic mail networks, bulletin boards, conferencing capabilities, and other interactive systems to perform routine tasks, communicate with colleagues, and disseminate formal and informal research reports is difficult to capture. Unless individual users save their communications or an automatic system is set in place to select and preserve a portion of the machine-readable file, the use and impact of electronic networks on the community are currently very hard to document. Additional research is required by archivists and systems designers to determine if it is possible to preserve these interactive systems.

Professionals in all sectors are struggling with the problems of electronic records. Archivists and records managers are developing conceptual solutions to promote the orderly creation, maintenance, and reuse of relational databases (student information, personnel, and business systems), but considerable obstacles — technical and preservation — inhibit the ability to carry out these plans. The messages sent via electronic communication systems (internal and external electronic communication networks) are even more problematic: in addition to the technical problems that must be solved to capture and retain information from these unstructured machine-readable files, there are behavioral problems as well. The communities that use these networks appear to value the immediate and transitory nature of the communication and the privacy that the systems afford them. To date, they have resisted efforts to capture and preserve their interactions.

The literature developed by archivists outlining standards and procedures for electronic records in other settings will generally be useful to college and university archivists (see Bibliography). One of the most important recommendations is that archivists be involved with systems designers and administrators as automated systems are set up. In this way, archivists will have a say about what data are to be gathered and preserved in the system; ensure that retained data remain usable in the future by urging that automated systems (hardware, software, and data structure) permit future data migration and transportability; ensure that the system documentation (the technical documentation of the data structure and content values represented in the data) is also retained and updated if necessary; and ensure that procedures have been developed to recopy archival datasets onto new tape stock every five years (to be sure that information is not lost) and rewind them every year (to prevent tapes from shrinking and loss from data print-through) and that data sets are reconfigured when hardware or software changes.

To achieve these aims, archivists should work with data administrators, systems designers, and owners of data. The data administrators, in particular the data security officers who carry the responsibility for protecting and maintaining information in machine-readable form, can serve as strong allies because their concerns are very similar to those of the archivist.

The evaluation of an automated database requires asking separate questions about the value of the information and the form in which the information should be preserved. Some data may have long-term value but can be maintained in computer output microfiche or as a paper printout if the information does not need to be remanipulated to be useful. If further analysis and remanipulation of the data are likely to be required for future administrative or historical research, it would be desirable to maintain the information in machine-readable form. (See Bibliography for information on retaining data files in machine-readable form.)

Long-term preservation and use of data files require environmentally controlled housing, access to appropriate hardware and software, and the expertise to handle tapes and use the data with various application programs. Lacking such expertise and equipment, archivists should establish cooperative arrangements with their administrative or research computing centers. Under such circumstances, special care must be taken to ensure long-term access, security, and preservation of the information.

Records Management

Whether records management programs are administered as part of an archival program or separately, archivists can use records management skills to address the problems created by administrative records. Among the most useful techniques are planning and analysis before records are created, systematic filing procedures, and records retention schedules. While analysis and planning are imperative for machine-readable records, they are also extremely useful to help records creators and archivists manage paper files. Prior analysis helps to ensure that offices create and retain appropriate information and that it is managed effectively for as long as it must be retained.

Both administrative offices and the archives benefit greatly if files are created and maintained in an orderly fashion. Filing systems establish logical structures for office files by introducing useful principles such as filing housekeeping and records of other routine operations separate from operational and policy materials (sources that document the primary responsibilities of the office) so that the former can be easily removed and destroyed; dividing files into discrete chronological groupings so that they can be separated and stored at regular intervals; and labeling folders with meaningful headings. Well-maintained files accompanied by lists of filing headings can have a considerable positive impact on the archives. Records received in an orderly condition need less rearrangement and weeding, and the lists generated by the office can be used as the inventory to the collection.

Many college and university records management and archival programs use schedules to control the retention and destruction of records. While some institutions use schedules just to control routine transactional records such as purchase orders, others use schedules to control the full breadth of academic and administrative records. Such schedules provide considerable assistance by clarifying and assigning responsibility for the record copy of the document to one office and by specifying the period of retention for the record and non-record copies. The schedules, properly authorized by the appropriate officials, provide legal protection for the institution, facilitate administrative activities by ensuring the availability of relevant information, guarantee that records without long-term value are destroyed as rapidly as possible, and support the archival retention of records of long-term value.

Intangible Aspects

The availability of massive quantities of information in paper and automated files masks the fact that many aspects of administrative activities are poorly documented and difficult to capture. For example, the governance section that follows describes the informal decision-making process that takes place in the halls and dining rooms. The final decision may be recorded, but how and why the choice was made is not likely to be documented.

It is also hard to capture in a tangible form the administrative style and ambiance of the institution — now referred to as its "corporate culture." What is the style of the president? What factors influence the way that crucial decisions are made and who is involved? Such questions may only be answered if the members of the administration are willing to supplement the existing record through oral histories.

Governance

This section examines the structures, processes, and multiple actors that administer institutions of higher education. In essence the question is who controls the institution: who makes the decisions, how are they made, and how are they carried out? Both external and internal bodies govern colleges and universities.

External Governance

Founding and Incorporation

The most fundamental outside influence on the governance of higher education is exercised by the power of governments to establish public and private institutions and control them through laws, regulations, and statewide governing boards. With the exception of the few early institutions that were chartered by the English crown, all public and private institutions receive their legal authority from a state government through incorporation or licensing (an administrative procedure generally conducted by the secretary of state) or the process of granting a charter (a legislative act). The provisions in the charter, license, or documents of incorporation define the nature of the institution and the authority and responsibilities of the trustees to govern it. The trustees in turn adopt bylaws to specify details about their authority, membership, and rules of governance. State governments play a continuing role through their power to fund, regulate, and oversee academic institutions. The sections on finances and personnel, especially, explore this role in greater depth.

Founding and Incorporation: Documentation

Evidence of the legal foundation of the institution is critical for administrative and historical purposes. Copies of the founding documents exist at the college, but the originals and the records of the administrative or legislative processes are held by the state and controlled through state records laws. The records could include petitions to incorporate, license applications, bills submitted to the legislature, and associated reports of legislative committees as well as the final engrossed act. In the case of the legislative process, charters are finally published in the acts of the state. College archivists should determine what records exist and where they reside and, when appropriate, obtain copies of these records for preservation at the college or university.

Statewide Governing Boards

State boards have existed in different forms since the early nineteenth century, but in the last few decades there has been an increasing emphasis on statewide coordination of education. In the 1950s–70s, state governing boards were established to oversee the public multicampus "systems" of higher education (two-year colleges, state colleges, and comprehensive universities) that proliferated in the postwar period.

The 1972 amendments to the (U.S.) Higher Education Act of 1965 required that all states receiving aid to higher education must establish statewide boards to coordinate and plan the activities of their colleges and universities. These boards were required to represent all higher education in the state, and therefore they include representatives of private as well as public institutions. Three different types of statewide boards exist: advisory (primarily planning and informational functions); coordinating (prepare and maintain master plan, review and recommend budget, and approve new degree programs); and consolidated governing boards (distribute budget, control programs, and exercise authority over personnel). These statewide boards stand between the state legislature and the trustees of the individual institutions.

The 1982 Carnegie Foundation report entitled *The Control of the Campus* claims that statewide boards have "changed the governance structure of higher education. America's colleges and universities are no longer viewed as wholly independent institutions. Instead, they have become 'units' in a 'statewide system'" (p. 39). The report discusses the dangers to academic institutions created by external decision making that is driven by budget and efficiency concerns. (Some statewide boards determine the student-faculty ratio and evaluate and eliminate academic programs.) The Carnegie report stresses the importance of the internal governance structure of each campus as the needed counterbalance to these external forces.

Statewide Governing Boards: Documentation

While administrators of colleges and universities have records of their communications with statewide governing boards, the minutes, correspondence, and reports of the board are under the control of the state records managers and archivists. College and university archivists should know where the records are generated and preserved and what types of information they contain, and they should secure reference copies of statewide planning, statistical, and other key reports as needed. The archival records of governing boards should be housed and administered by the state archives or another appropriate repository designated to care for the systemwide records. If deficiencies exist in the long-term care of the records of governing boards, college and university archivists within the state should persuade the appropriate agency to rectify the situation.

Accrediting Organizations

The tension between external and internal control is a continuing theme in higher education. Fearing increased control by the government, colleges and universities stress the desirability of self-regulation. A critical part of this process is the accreditation of colleges and universities.

The proliferation of colleges and universities in the late nineteenth and early twentieth centuries created problems that demonstrated the need for standards. High schools needed to determine how to prepare their students for specific college programs; foreign institutions offering advanced studies needed to evaluate the validity of degrees from American institutions; and government and private organizations needed to judge which institutions qualified for receipt of awards. In 1910 the Federal Bureau of Education attempted to respond to these needs by developing a ranked list of colleges and universities. Concerns about the government's role in this evaluative process led to the development of a regional and professional system of accreditation in which colleges and universities voluntarily agree to a review by their peers. The government's role is now limited to the approval of the accrediting agencies.

By 1982 the Division of Eligibility and Agency Evaluation in the United States Office of Education had approved six regional and·fifty-eight specialized accrediting associations. While accreditation was first seen as a means to establish standards, over the years it evolved into a process of encouraging, stimulating, and evaluating educational institutions. Accreditation teams from the regional and professional organizations evaluate broad areas of the institution including administration, management, curriculum, qualifications of the faculty, admissions policies, and resources including library collections.

Graduate and specialized programs are accredited by professional organizations: American Bar Association, American Dental Association, National Association of Schools of Music, American Library Association, etc. These accrediting bodies often venture beyond the evaluative process used by the regional associations and tend, to a greater extent, to establish standards for the curriculum and minimum competency for graduates. This larger role for external bodies, which may involve establishing teaching requirements, student-teacher ratios, length of academic programs, and teaching loads, creates concern for the integrity of academic campuses.

Accrediting Organizations: Documentation

Colleges and universities generate considerable documentation to prepare for and achieve the reaccreditation of their institutions. Voluminous studies and background materials are submitted to the regional or professional association; in addition, the officers and committees charged by the college to prepare the studies might have correspondence and working files. The college or university subsequently receives a copy of the reaccreditation report and recommendations.

Accreditation records should be preserved for at least two reasons. First, reaccreditation is a cyclical phenomenon (every ten years for the institution as a whole). Therefore, the records inform the administration of the process used by the institution to accomplish previous accreditations. Second, the reports and background materials provide valuable analyses about the institution. In addition to general administrative and academic information, each reaccreditation review involves in-depth studies of specific programs; areas for special studies are agreed upon with the accreditation association and could include the undergraduate curriculum, the library, or the funding of the institution. While some of the findings are presented in the report to the accrediting association, the files of those who assembled the report may provide additional information.

The accrediting bodies themselves generate and collect records during each reaccreditation process, and while the retention practices of the accreditation associations vary, a considerable volume of material is preserved. Some accrediting bodies utilize external archival repositories to preserve their records including their accreditation materials (the American Library Association records are housed at the University of Illinois at Urbana-Champaign), while other bodies maintain their own "archives." Generally, accrediting organizations assume that institutions maintain their own reaccreditation self-studies and reports. Some associations keep only the most recent reports for their reference purposes; others keep past reports on microfilm only. The accrediting bodies do keep the evaluative reports submitted by their review teams and the formal correspondence between the school and the associations that reflect the selection of the review team, the topics to be studied, and the logistics of the visit and review.

The information gathered about each institution is protected by an agreement of confidentiality between the institution and the association. The information that an accrediting body can release without the institution's permission is limited and generally consists of the following: the date the college or university received its initial accreditation; the nature of the most recent on-site evaluation and the status of the action on that review; the date and nature of the next scheduled evaluation; and a list of the degrees that are accredited. The reports submitted to accrediting bodies and their reports to colleges and universities are confidential, but the associations encourage the institutions to release and publicize them. While the records held by the accrediting bodies are confidential, the associations are generally willing to make material available for research with the permission of the school. It is therefore possible for the institution and researchers to make use of the records held by accrediting organizations.

College and university archivists should know something about the records policies of the regional and professional associations that accredit their institutions: the records these groups maintain and what their access policy is for representatives of the institution and for researchers.

Internal Governance

With the award of a charter, the college or university becomes a corporation responsible for the management of the institution. Legal responsibility rests with the corporate board, which appoints the president and has final approval over the policies of the institution. As in other corporations, the president establishes an administrative structure to carry out the mandate of the board. What sets the governance of academic institutions apart from other organizations is, among other things, the diversity of the participants in governance and the shared and multileveled nature of the decision-making process. In the nineteenth and early twentieth centuries, governance of colleges and universities was carried out largely by the president and the board. During the twentieth century, however, there has been a diffusion of decision making: faculty, students, and staff participate through their representative bodies, administrative and academic positions, and standing and ad hoc committees.

The growing acceptance of a specialized faculty and a departmental structure to organize the disciplines shifted the governance of academic issues from the president and board to the faculty and their departments. While the faculty exercise considerable authority over academic matters, their role in administrative areas is often more consultative. Campus-wide senates and standing and ad hoc committees provide a means for the faculty to oversee academic policy and programs and to ensure that they play an advisory role in administrative decisions that touch on academic issues, such as curriculum and admissions.

Governance is therefore a balancing act among the governing board, administrative officers, faculty, students, staff, and other interested internal and external parties. Governance ultimately encompasses the management of both academic and administrative matters: this section, however, focuses only on administrative concerns; academic issues are discussed in *Convey Knowledge*.

General Documentary Issues for Internal Governance

Two seemingly contradictory problems impede the documentation of internal governance. On the one hand the governing boards, committees, and administrative offices produce a voluminous record, and a high proportion of the records of decision-making bodies are of long-term value. On the other hand, despite its size, the record is deceptive. The minutes, correspondence, and reports record the officials involved, the decisions, and, to some extent, a sense of the deliberations and process. What is often not documented, however, is the role that individuals play and factors within and outside the official process that actually influence decisions. These undocumented aspects are often only ascertained by understanding the manner in which the institution is managed.

Each academic institution has its own style, which is shaped by many factors: the personality of the president; the traditional management style of the institution — participatory or autocratic; the physical configuration of the campus(es) and the managerial relationship between the parts of the institution; the pace of activity at the institution; the presence of staff and faculty unions; and the alliances and animosities among faculty members, departments, and administrators.

How this "corporate culture" of the institution affects the governance and decision-making process is difficult to document. Official records usually capture only the final decision and some sense of the process, and without additional documentation many of the factors and the individuals involved in that decision remain unknown. Although a detailed investigation of every decision is clearly not needed, for major decisions, such as the acceptance of a new core curriculum or a change in the academic calendar, an oral history should be obtained to supplement the written documentation in order to record the details of the process and the individuals that influenced the decision.

Internal Governing Boards

Since the nineteenth century, governing boards of private institutions were recognized by the state as the independent corporate body that held ultimate responsibility for the property and control of the school. Public governing boards were given the same authority as a means to protect academic freedom and distance the institution from interference from the short-term political interests of the state. These governing bodies are called board of governors, managers, trustees, overseers, fellows, or the corporation. The bylaws of the institution not only define the nature and purpose of the school but also the operation, membership, and rules of the governing boards. Responsibilities differ, but generally the board has ultimate authority to confer degrees; hold title to property; choose the chief executive officer (president or chancellor); authorize or abolish departments, colleges, and programs; borrow money and approve financial affairs; and control the use of the university seal and name.

The size, composition, method of appointment, length of term, and frequency of meetings of the boards vary. Members can be appointed, or elected through a public political election, by the alumni association or other relevant organization, or by the board itself. (The latter process is known as a self-perpetuating board.) Boards may also have ex officio members (the governor of the Commonwealth of Massachusetts is an ex officio member of MIT's Corporation) as well as representatives of the faculty and the student body. Boards generally conduct their work through committees of which the most prevalent and important deal with finances (investments, development, and budget), educational policy, and property.

Bylaws of the Board of Trustees
Clark University, Worcester, Massachusetts
1962

Article I. Name and Purpose
The Corporation shall be known as
"Trustees of Clark University."

Its purpose shall be to establish and maintain
in the City of Worcester
an institution for the promotion of education and investigation in
science, literature and art,
to be called Clark University.

Subject to the Charter, any amendments thereto,
and the laws of the Commonwealth of Massachusetts,
the members of the Corporation
shall have the power to manage and control
Clark University in all its departments.

In the twentieth century, the role of internal governing boards was transformed as the growth of academic institutions created the need for an increasingly specialized and professional staff to administer the finances, personnel, physical plant, and other support services of the institution. As responsibility for daily administration shifted to the president and the professional staff and control of academic matters was ceded to the faculty, governing bodies relinquished their role as the overseer of routine administrative matters. Their focus of concern shifted to other responsibilities such as the oversight of policy and planning, fund raising, and monitoring the educational quality of the institution.

Internal Governing Boards: Documentation

The main record produced by the governing board is the minutes of its meetings. The style of the minutes varies depending on the institution, the secretary, and the wishes of the chairman, but in recent years they have tended to be generally brief and sketchy, recording decisions with little indication of the deliberations. Extensive minutes containing debates and discussions are treasured by historical researchers but increasingly shunned by lawyers and boards with busy agendas.

Additional background information can be ascertained, however, from the supporting papers that accompany each set of minutes. These documents include published materials, position papers, data, correspondence, and whatever information is deemed necessary to prepare board members to discuss and decide on agenda items. The supporting papers include reports prepared by the faculty and administrators that must be approved by the board (budgets, lists of students qualified to receive degrees, proposals for revision of the curriculum, a new benefit package).

In addition to the minutes and supporting papers, correspondence between senior officials and board members provides information about meetings and special projects. Some of this interaction appears in the files of the secretary or clerk of the board; other relevant correspondence may be found in the records of many senior officers.

Each of the board's committees has its own set of minutes, supporting papers, and correspondence. Generally one member of the administration is assigned to work with a committee (the treasurer works with the investment committee), and that office as well as the board office should have sets of the committee's records. When individual members of the board take on specific responsibilities (chair the search committee for a new president, head a fund-raising effort), their personal papers may contain additional information about board activities.

Access policies to board records differ markedly between private and public institutions. Private institutions have discretion over access to their governing records and often establish a restricted period and a procedure for requests for access. Public institutions may be mandated by state law to open their governing records to all who request to see them, and some even publish the proceedings of their board.

The records of governing boards are generally regarded as vital and are required to fulfill legal and administrative obligations. Therefore, particular care must be taken to ensure their proper maintenance. Minutes, accompanied by a full set of supporting papers, should be preserved. When possible, a microfilm or other security copy should be made of these records and stored in a secure off-site facility.

The archives should obtain the full set of records from the office responsible for the board's activities as well as related materials maintained by senior officers. Consideration should also be given to acquiring records from individual board members that supplement the official record assembled at the school.

Once an official set of board records is preserved, some attention should be paid to the copies held by the members of the board. Colleges and universities should advise the board members about the disposition of their official papers. When an institution restricts access to these papers, members should be told to destroy duplicate board materials when no longer needed and to give their unique board materials to the institution. If they donate their papers to another institution, they should first remove or destroy restricted board records.

The Administration of Governance

Under the leadership of the president, an internal governance structure is established to assign responsibility, clarify decision-making authority, and manage all aspects of the institution. Organization charts, studied closely by managers and archivists, record the hierarchical structure established to achieve these purposes. The administrative structure of each institution reflects both the size, scope, and complexity of the institution and the management style of the senior administrators. While several areas of responsibility may be merged into one office in a smaller institution, specialized offices are needed for each area at the larger schools. Multiple layers of the hierarchy are often required to manage the larger and multicampus universities.

Each administrative organization is therefore configured to manage a diverse set of activities or programmatic areas including academic, business, student services, and development functions. To understand the current structure of a given institution and the allocation of responsibilities, it is useful to examine the programmatic elements and trace how they are grouped and assigned. The National Center for Higher Education Management Systems publishes *Program Classification Structure*, "a set of categories and related definitions which allows its users to examine the operations of a post-secondary education institution." Such a knowledge of the activities provides understanding of the changing titles, responsibilities, and administrative structures.

An organization chart clarifies the assignment of responsibility and reporting lines but does not provide information about the balance of authority among the parts of the institution or specify the actual allocation of responsibility and power to each unit. Each institution retains certain governance responsibilities for the central administrative offices while it permits the individual units leeway to govern themselves in other ways. Establishing an equilibrium between the central and decentralized administration is a delicate task: the need to share expensive technology (computer systems) and adhere to uniform policies (government regulations and personnel policies) argues for central control; the individual research and curriculum needs of the departments and schools argue for decentralization. The way in which the parts of an institution interact is defined to a great extent by the policies, rules, and regulations that establish the procedural guides: personnel policies define the authority of the individual units to hire, fire, and reward employees; procedures for budget preparation and approval control the implementation of new programs; research policies affirm the right of faculty members to choose their areas of study. Again, the size and history of the institution heavily influence how the equilibrium is established.

Another factor that remains somewhat unclear from the organization chart is the superimposed structure of faculty and student committees that play a role in governance. The responsibility of such committees ranges from an oversight or advisory role in administrative areas such as university investments to a policy role for curriculum and other academic issues. Faculty committees set policy for curriculum and academic standards, but administrative offices carry out those policies. Students have a say in housing, extracurricular, and curriculum issues, but the faculty and administrative officers must approve and then carry out the decisions. The need to coordinate all of the actors that have a hand in advising or overseeing decisions remains a constant problem in academic governance.

Finally, there are the layers of personnel who bring that organization chart to life. The administrative officers — presidents, deans, vice presidents, department heads, and other directors of units — have the responsibility to establish policy and make decisions in the areas assigned to them. The senior administration must coordinate the many players, promote communication and coordination among the parts, and provide the overall direction and policies for the institution.

The individuals who serve in these administrative capacities are drawn from two different communities. The senior officers of the academic areas — the provost, deans, and department heads — are generally members of the faculty; the administrative officers — vice presidents for finance, operations, and planning — more often come from the professional or business world of individuals trained in these areas. Twentieth-century academic presidents are generally academics who have moved into the world of administration.

Below the level of the senior officers is an administrative and senior support staff whose roles remain less visible than those of their bosses. They often draft policies and procedures and oversee their implementation, but little evidence may exist of the contribution these individuals make to the governance process.

The increasing funds spent on academic administration encourage state legislators and disgruntled faculty to accuse administrators of perpetuating themselves for their own sakes. Administrators are needed, however, to manage specific areas of the institution. This discussion of the administration of governance therefore continues in the specific sections that follow on the management of finances, personnel, and the physical plant.

The Administration of Governance: Documentation

The composite picture that results from examining not only the organizational chart but also the dynamics of how the organization is realized in actual operation is complex but vital to an understanding of how the institution governs itself. Administrators, faculty members, historical researchers, and archivists alike need to comprehend how the organization functions.

The documentation starts with the organization chart — the document itself and materials that shed light on how the organization was structured and how and why it changed over time. Generally, such deliberations are part of the records of senior administrative officers. Published manuals of policies and procedures indicate the authority assigned to each part of the organization and the communication among the units. These policies have continuing value to the administration and staff who need to understand the rules under which the institution operated at any given time. All published versions of policies and procedures should be preserved. On occasion, particularly important policies are reviewed and revised by a committee or senior officers. The records of these deliberations shed light on the evolution and changes of institutional policies.

As governance and decision-making responsibilities are dispersed, so too are the records. Most important are the records of the senior officers: president, vice presidents, deans, and department heads, who administer major sectors of the institution and formulate policies and procedures for their areas. Their records always comprise a central portion of an archives. For all levels of the administration, the documentary emphasis is on decision making — the formulation of policies and procedures, the process of starting and ending programs, the selection of staff, and the establishment of goals. Administrative files should be sought that chronicle how and why the decisions are made, how they are implemented, and, when possible, the implications and ramifications of these decisions.

For some of the key offices (president, provost, etc.), a more detailed understanding of the administrative staff is desirable. The names and titles of the staff members may be learned from directories, but internal documents or interviews may be required to ascertain the assignment of responsibilities and the tasks performed.

Since the process of making decisions is also often poorly documented, oral history can be used to supplement the existing records in two ways. For a general understanding of the governance of the institution, oral histories can be obtained from members of the administration and faculty during their tenure or as they are about to leave the institution. Assurances of restrictions on the use of these interviews for some time following their tenure may encourage participation. During or immediately following major studies or reexaminations of the institution (reaccreditation, scandals or controversies, curriculum reform, retrenchment), oral history projects can document the process and individuals involved and explore the undocumented pressures and influences that shaped the conclusions and the decisions.

Administrative records, particularly those that capture the process by which decisions are made and the evidence about specific decisions, have important continuing legal and administrative value to the institution and to historical researchers as well. By actively working with administrative officers, the archivist can ensure the creation, maintenance, and transfer of the valuable policy records of the institution, while enhancing the visibility and services of the archives. Archivists facilitate their own work and promote preservation by providing retention guidelines and filing recommendations so that officers can organize these records in a logical fashion, separate housekeeping and routine materials from policy records, and establish chronological breaks to facilitate regular transfer.

Regular contact must also be maintained with committee chairs. Records of schoolwide committees (faculty senates, committees on curriculum or discipline) and committees that have a similar responsibility for units of the institution (separate colleges and departments) are critical. Some standing committees have a permanent home (the chairman of the department or the dean for student affairs), in which case the minutes and other records are created and cared for by the staff of that office. The responsibility for other committees, especially those that involve the faculty, may rotate regularly, with the staff of the new faculty chair assuming the responsibility for the creation and care of the records. Older records may be moved from the former chair to the new one or be retained by the previous chairs. The archivist could recommend that although the chairmanship moves, a permanent secretariat be established for committees.

Finally, there are ad hoc committees appointed by the institution or a unit to make recommendations about a specific problem (termination of a program, school calendar, housing of undergraduates). For major studies, a staff may be established to research and write the report and maintain the files. More often, the regular staff of the faculty member or administrative officer in charge of the committee assumes these responsibilities. When ad hoc committees are established, the archivist should contact the chair to provide assistance in setting up the records, ask that the records be transferred to the archives at the conclusion, and offer research services and background information that may be available in the archives. When the committee concludes its work, the archivist should obtain its report immediately and remind the chair that its other records should also be transferred to the archives.

Active involvement by archivists with administrators and committees renders service to the institution and promotes the visibility of the archives while ensuring the preservation of vital records of the governance process.

Finances

"Follow the money" was the advice offered during the Watergate investigation. An examination of finances also offers considerable evidence about the nature of modern institutions of higher education. Monetary considerations are integral to almost every activity. The documentation of acquiring, managing, and expending resources is probably the most voluminous record at any institution and therefore problematic for administrators and archivists alike. The volume masks the potential managerial, legal, and historical value of a small portion of this information to the institution and researchers. This section explores where the money comes from and how it is managed and suggests which financial records have long-term value.

Sources of Revenue

Colleges and universities, like all institutions in the nonprofit sector, are under constant pressure to generate revenue from the few sources available to them: tuition and fees; sales and services; endowment; governments (appropriations and grants); and gifts from foundations, corporations, and individuals. Institutions have more control over some sources, such as tuition, than others, such as government funding and gifts. They engage in a constant struggle to control costs and to maintain a regular flow of revenue to the institution.

The sources of revenue for public and private colleges and universities are now quite similar, but the proportion of revenue from the sources differs:

	Public	Private
Tuition	14.7%	39.6%
Appropriations:		
Federal	2.1%	0.6%
State	41.6%	0.9%
Local	3.3%	—
Government Grants and Contracts:		
Federal	8.3%	16.5%
State	2.1%	1.3%
Local	0.4%	0.7%
Private Gifts, Grants, and Contracts	3.3%	9.3%
Endowment Income	0.5%	5.2%
Sales and Services:		
Educational Activities	2.5%	2.2%
Auxiliary Enterprises	10.2%	10.9%
Hospitals	8.5%	8.6%
Other	2.6%	4.3%

The Chronicle of Higher Education Almanac,
5 September 1990, p. 25.

Tuition

Each year parents and students are inevitably unhappy when tuition figures are announced. Institutions are accused of raising costs beyond the inflation rate and placing too great a burden on students. In recent years, tuition charges have increased significantly (Boston University tuition rose 141% between 1968 and 1978) but often still represent a fraction of the actual educational costs.

Tuition remains a major source of regular unrestricted income, especially for private colleges and universities. For private institutions without endowment income and other income from gifts, tuition is the primary source of revenue. While it may appear that colleges exercise complete control over tuition, there are constraints: the tuition rate has significant ramifications on the number and type of applicants, the diversity of students admitted, and the ability of the institution to retain those students. Therefore, faculty as well as administrators are involved in deliberations about tuition.

Outside factors also influence tuition. States may control the tuition rates of their public institutions, often setting higher rates for out-of-state students. Recently, state legislators have argued that rates should rise so that students carry a greater share of the actual cost of their education. For public and private colleges and universities, a decisive factor is the availability of student financial aid from inside (scholarships, etc.) and outside (federal, state, and other grant and loan funds). Federal aid programs, especially the Office of Education, are among the largest sources of tuition support and therefore vital to students and institutions as providers of revenue.

State and Local Governments

State governments are generally the primary source of support for public colleges and universities and increasingly an important source of revenue for private institutions as well. In 1989/90 state governments spent $39.3 billion for higher education, which represents a 14.2% increase over 1987/88. The support comes to public institutions primarily as general appropriations. Methods of allocating revenues to the colleges vary among the states, but many use a formula based on enrollment figures. In some states, the legislature appropriates a lump sum to each institution, while in others the money is given to the statewide coordinating board which in turn allocates funds to each institution.

As private institutions faced increased financial pressures, they also turned to the states for assistance. Private schools argue that they actually save the states money, as they grant a significant portion of the degrees awarded but receive a very small share of the state's appropriation for higher education. The willingness to provide funds to private institutions is fostered, in part, by statewide boards which have the responsibility to coordinate the activities of all colleges and universities. The largest amount of state support to private colleges is in the form of student aid; state allocations for student financial aid increased approximately 30% in 1989/90. States also support private institutions by lending funds for construction and equipment and by granting the authority to issue tax-exempt bonds.

Federal Government

With few exceptions, such as Howard and Gallaudet Universities and the institutions run by the military services, the federal government has never assumed responsibility for the financial solvency of either private or public academic institutions. Funds are provided for specific purposes and not for general unrestricted ongoing support. Still, the federal government has a tremendous impact on the financing of higher education through its funding programs (student financial aid, grants, and contracts) and legislation (tax policies, etc.).

Student Financial Aid. The federal government channels money to colleges and universities through four hundred separate programs located in a diverse range of government agencies. More than half of this money is given to assist individuals to pay for their college education. Federal aid is available to veterans, the poor, and children of social security beneficiaries through about a dozen major and several dozen smaller grant programs. Financial aid to other students is transmitted through loan and fellowship programs.

Grant and Contract Funds. Other federal funds are given to colleges and universities to meet specific objectives of the government. To the greatest extent, these funds are awarded for research and development (R&D) and to support the facilities in which this work takes place. These funds cannot be relied upon as steady steams of unrestricted income but are instead competitive awards earmarked for restricted purposes. While some efforts have been made to distribute these funds to more institutions, 90% of federal R&D funds still go to about a hundred universities that specialize in research and graduate education.

For these institutions, federal funds have become a major means to support their research programs. Competitive awards and changing government priorities, however, always create uncertainty about the availability of these funds.

There are two types of costs associated with funded projects: direct and indirect. Direct costs include the charges that can be accurately associated with a specific project, including salaries and benefits, equipment, and services. At the same time, there are costs that the institution incurs that are less easily associated with any specific project but are tied to the general support of the campus. These indirect costs include administrative services (personnel administration, accounting, purchasing, etc.), the maintenance of buildings (heating, lighting, air conditioning, janitorial services, etc.), and the operation of the library. The total of indirect and direct costs is considered to be the best approximation of the true expense of the project to the institution.

For institutions that receive government funds for research, the indirect cost reimbursement represents an additional means of support. The indirect cost recovery rate for each institution is originally established through a negotiated process between one government agency and the school; the established rate is then applied to all federal grants and contracts. Concern expressed by the government about the impact of escalating indirect costs on granting programs has encouraged academic institutions to absorb some of these charges as a cost-sharing contribution.

Tax Policies and Legislation. The introduction to this chapter examines the regulatory and financial burdens placed on academic institutions by the federal government. At the same time, it must be recognized that the government also bestows a financial advantage on colleges and universities through the special status they are given in the tax code. Benefits accrue in four ways: the institution itself is exempt from income taxes; gifts given by individuals and corporations to the institution are generally tax deductible; scholarships, fellowships, and related benefits to students are generally exempt from taxation; and parents are entitled to a tax deduction for their dependents as long as they are full-time students. Changes in the law threaten to alter portions of these codes, but the basic provisions still prove advantageous to the institution itself, its students, and its benefactors.

Gifts

In 1990/91 colleges and universities received $10.2 billion in voluntary support:

Alumni/Alumnae	26%
Other Individuals	23%
Corporations	22%
Foundations	20%
Religious Organizations	2%
Other	7%

The Chronicle of Higher Education,
20 May 1992, p. A26.

Gift income is expended as current funds or added to the endowment. These funds also contribute to the ongoing support of the institution by funding research, scholarships, and the construction and renovation of buildings. The section below on the management of resources deals with the significant effort now devoted to gathering voluntary support.

Endowment

Large endowments have traditionally been associated with the older private institutions. Today, however, public and private institutions of all sizes are building significant endowments to ensure reliable steady sources of income. In 1989, 104 private and public institutions had endowments of more than $100 million, ranging from Harvard University's $4.5 billion to Cooper Union's $100 million.

Endowments consist of funds given by donors or allocated by the institution to be invested with a portion of the annual income expended for specified purposes or as part of the general fund. The principal of a true endowed fund is prohibited from being used; with quasi-endowed funds (funds set aside by the governing board to act as an endowment) and term endowments, the principal may be expended after a specified period.

More will be said about the process of building endowments. The point here is that income from endowments and tuition are generally the only sources of regular income that the institution controls. Therefore, increasing pressure is placed on the need to build, manage, and expend these funds wisely.

Other

Depending on the strengths of the academic institution, additional revenues may be obtained from any of the following:

Noncredit educational programs such as workshops, seminars, and conferences

Parking facilities, bookstores, housing, food, medical, and other auxiliary services

Rental of facilities such as athletic stadiums and concert halls

Consulting and research services to business and government

Licensing of patents developed by faculty

Investments in business enterprises and real estate

Proceeds from successful athletic teams.

Sources of Revenue: Documentation

The sections that follow on the management of resources deal more specifically with the documentation associated with efforts to acquire, manage, and expend resources. A continuing theme throughout is the need to document the following questions relating to sources of revenue:

Where and how does the institution obtain its revenue?

What proportion of the revenue is secured from each potential source?

What policies guide the decisions to acquire funds from each source?

What efforts are expended by the governing board and administration to secure the resources?

Administering Financial Resources

All colleges and universities have a legal and moral responsibility to administer their resources effectively. The cycle of financial management includes the need to acquire, enhance, budget, expend, and account for funds.

Acquiring Resources

Because the sources of income, as described above, are limited, funds must be solicited to guarantee a continuing flow of income for the institution. Different strategies are needed to ensure support from the different sources of revenue. State legislators and government officials are lobbied by college presidents, faculty, and members of the staff with particular responsibilities for government relations in order to promote adequate appropriations and favorable legislation. These lobbying efforts focus not only on the annual appropriations process of the state legislature but also on federal and state government reconsiderations of allocations for student financial aid, research, and construction, and on the adoption of regulations that have potential financial impact on academic institutions. At the same time, faculty and administrators prepare grant and contract proposals to acquire research funds from government agencies, foundations, and corporations.

The process of acquiring funds from individuals and organizations other than government sources through fund-raising activities has become a major enterprise for academic institutions. The earlier fund raising done by college presidents who sought out a few wealthy donors has been supplanted by the ongoing efforts of large professional staffs devoting their energies to acquiring significant funds from all available sources.

Annual Giving. In 1890, Yale University raised $11,015 from 385 donors in its first annual academic giving program; in 1990/91, it raised $132,416,904. Annual giving programs provide substantial sources of continuing income for academic institutions. As these efforts are focused in part on individual donors who are predominantly, but not exclusively, graduates of the institution, annual giving is often a joint enterprise of the development and alumni offices. Prominent graduates often act as voluntary chairmen, and numerous volunteers work with the professional staff at the institution to coordinate solicitation efforts. Larger fund-raising opportunities are coordinated with major reunions, significant events such as the retirement of a president, and memorials for prominent alumni or members of the faculty. Depending on the provisions associated with the gifts, funds raised from annual giving efforts can be expended as current income or added to the endowment.

Deferred Giving. Annual giving is primarily directed toward acquiring funds for current expenditures; deferred giving addresses the need to plan for the future. Donations mentioned in a will can always be revoked before the donor's death. Deferred giving provides an irrevocable gift to the institution in exchange for a guaranteed life income to the donor.

Because of its many advantages both to the institution and to donors, deferred giving has become a part of most fund-raising efforts. The donor and beneficiaries secure a regular income and tax advantages while freeing themselves from the burden of managing their own assets. The institution receives sizable irrevocable gifts that become part of the funds it can plan on in the future; in return the institution assumes the responsibility for managing these assets for the life of the donor. Institutions with sizable deferred giving programs establish their own offices to manage these funds, while others have a trust company carry out these responsibilities for them.

Capital Campaigns. From time to time, often at a major anniversary, an institution launches a capital campaign to generate sizable revenue over a concentrated period of time. A campaign sets a goal for the amount of money to be raised and the specific areas for which support is sought: general endowment, endowment of faculty positions, scholarships, new buildings.

Capital campaigns entail an enormous commitment and involve the institution's administration, alumni volunteers, consultants, and a sizable professional staff. Financial pressures have encouraged more institutions to launch campaigns ever more frequently and to set increasingly high goals. Stanford, Cornell, New York, and Boston Universities as well as the University of Pennsylvania have all recently announced capital campaign goals of $1 billion.

Foundation and Corporate Donors.
Foundations and corporations are increasingly solicited for the large
sums needed to endow faculty positions and scholarships, construct
buildings, and fund research. Several major foundations, including the
Andrew W. Mellon Foundation, the Pew Charitable Trust, and the
Rockefeller Foundation, have long traditions of supporting higher education. American colleges and universities have also benefited greatly from
the community foundations and trusts, such as the Cleveland Foundation and the New York Community Trust, that support institutions in
their geographical areas.

Corporate support of academic institutions is a newer phenomenon.
Until a 1953 New Jersey Supreme Court ruling, the law was unclear
about the right of corporations to give funds to academic institutions. In
deciding a suit brought against the A.P. Smith Manufacturing Company
for declaring its intent to give $1,500 to Princeton University, the state
judge ruled that corporations could make unrestricted gifts to higher
education. Business donations have increased greatly since that ruling
and since the liberalization of federal tax laws to permit corporations to
deduct such contributions.

In addition to the tax advantages and favorable publicity associated with
such donations, there are other benefits to the corporate sector. Endowment of faculty chairs, scholarships, and funding of research projects
promote the future availability of skilled professionals and new knowledge in their fields. When a chemical company endows a research
professorship in organic chemistry or an electronics company establishes
a research laboratory, both the institution and the company can benefit.

Concerns have been voiced by legislators and the public about the dangers of close ties between corporations and academe. University officials
are cautioned to scrutinize corporate requirements for exclusive use of
patents, delay in publication of research results, or other provisions that
might be construed as limiting academic freedom. The benefits and dangers of corporate giving will become clearer as academic institutions gain
more experience in accepting and using these funds. At present, the corporate sector, foreign and domestic, is viewed as a major source of new
revenue.

Acquiring Resources:
Documentation

The documentation of the process of acquiring resources includes evidence of lobbying activities, acquisition of research grants (see *Conduct Research*), and fund raising.

Some evidence of lobbying efforts exists in the form of correspondence from college presidents, senior officers, staff, and faculty with federal and state officials. Records of meetings and discussions with legislators are harder to capture. Additional documentation exists in the files of the legislators, committee chairmen, and other government officials who are the targets. Examples of lobbying activities are of interest, as they document the effort by colleges and universities both to control the positive and negative impact of government on their institutions and to influence appropriations and the outcome of particular legislation.

Fund-raising activities present several documentary challenges. First, the process of planning and carrying out fund-raising activities produces voluminous documentation. Second, a portion of this record has considerable long-term legal and administrative value to the institution. And finally, current and historical records of development activities are a primary source of information about potential donors.

Policy decisions that shape fund-raising programs, the implementation of policy, and the results of fund-raising efforts all should be fully documented. The institution's policy on fund raising is made at the highest levels, generally by the governing board and senior administrators. They determine both development goals and what funds the institution will expend to gather and manage these assets. The records of the governing board and particularly the minutes of fund-raising and investment committees as well as the correspondence files of senior officers provide valuable information.

Fund-raising activities are generally carried out by many offices and individuals including senior administrators, development and alumni officers, and volunteer alumni. The records are therefore dispersed and often duplicated. Development offices play a central role in formulating and carrying out fund-raising strategies. Gifts are acknowledged by the development office for the president; copies of letters are often filed by the president and treasurer as well as the development office. Filing and retention recommendations prepared by the archives can eliminate some of this duplication while ensuring the retention of a record.

Much information about the logistics of annual giving, capital campaigns, and other fund-raising efforts need not be preserved. What is required are records that reveal the basic strategy, staff, activities, and presentations. Development offices rely on information about past fund-raising activities and the giving record of individual donors to map future efforts. Administrative records of prior capital campaigns provide evidence of the structure and strategies of the efforts, the ceremonies that launched and concluded the campaigns, and the design of promotional literature. Sample literature and letters of solicitation, programs of events as well as publicity are valuable to future fund raisers and to those who study fund-raising activities. Summary information about the total funds received and the names, donations, and purposes of the larger funds are generally printed in the annual report of the treasurer.

The primary records of long-term legal and administrative value are the more detailed development and gift files that chronicle the solicitation of and donations from individuals, corporations, and foundations. Information in the development files includes biographical and corporate background data and assessments of net worth. Internal memoranda chronicle the deliberations about amounts to be solicited and the suggested purposes of the gifts, while the correspondence records the contacts and negotiations with potential donors. Memos to the file are generally prepared to record meetings with donors. Because of the highly confidential nature of these files, they are maintained by development offices, rather than an archives, for as long as they are needed.

While the development office notes and acknowledges gifts, legal, administrative, and historical considerations suggest that the official gift records be maintained by the office responsible for the receipt of property (generally the treasurer's office) or the archives. Large gifts, especially restricted ones such as a fund for an endowed professorship, require long-term access to information about the donations to ensure that their terms are properly fulfilled. The official gift records or register of gifts includes the name of donor(s) and relevant biographical background (class affiliation, location of donor, and next of kin); amount and date of donation; type of fund established (e.g., endowment, term endowment); restrictions on the use of the fund or income and identification of the party that placed the restriction (e.g., donor, governing board); limitations on investments that can be made with the donation;

and references to formal acceptance or other actions taken by the governing board with respect to the donation. This information is supplemented and further clarified by supporting material including correspondence, wills, deeds of gift, conveyances, or other legal documents. All of this information is needed as proof of receipt and guidance for ongoing compliance with the requirements of the gift.

The development and treasurer's offices increasingly store information on individual, foundation, and corporate donors in machine-readable form. The development office relies on these data to determine the appropriate time to ask and the amount to seek from their prospects and to track contacts and receipt of gifts.

Development activities require considerable information about potential donors. Researchers assigned to fund-raising activities use published and automated databases to gather background data. As many prospects are graduates or other individuals associated with the institution, an archives is also a potential supplier of information:

> *Yes, Robert Smith did row with the 1937 championship crew and therefore might be willing to support the construction of a boat house.*

> *No, the Reed Library is so named by tradition and not by an endowed gift, and therefore funds can be accepted with the proviso that the name be changed.*

An archives, therefore, supports fund-raising activities both as advisor and holder of records and as supplier of information about donors and previous fund-raising activities.

Managing Resources

Colleges and universities once had a simple stewardship responsibility for their resources that entailed collecting and dispersing revenues. Now those responsibilities have expanded to include the active management of resources to promote maximum growth through sound investments, effective allocation through budgeting, and proper accounting of expenditures.

Investment Management. Investment policies are formulated and overseen by an investment committee of the governing board. Unlike the investment policies of institutions in the for-profit sphere, those of colleges and universities are formulated in an environment where both current and future income are required but where the institution is exempt from income and capital gains taxation. Investment objectives are delineated in policies that stipulate the approved types and diversification of investments; the size of investment that may be made in any one company; the required size of the cash reserve; the appropriate use of capital gains or appreciation on investments (whether they are to be expended as income or reinvested); the level of risk the institution is willing to assume; and the institution's attitude on the social, moral, and ethical implications of its investments.

Within the limits imposed by the donor's wishes and the level of acceptable risk, institutions seek to obtain the greatest return possible on their investments. Some techniques have been adopted from the for-profit sector to further these goals. Typical investments include bonds, stocks, mutual funds, and real estate.

Each fund is tracked and reported separately, but for more efficient and effective management, they are consolidated into investment pools whenever legally possible (see *Fund Accounting*, page 184). The revenues that flow into the institution are grouped into three or more general categories that include endowment, plant, and current funds. Each general category is managed separately to realize the individual objectives of that fund. Plant and current funds, which are used to meet immediate objectives like construction schedules for new buildings and paying personnel, are invested to realize short-term gains. Endowment funds, however, are invested and managed to realize long-term benefits.

Institutions with sizable endowments have staff on campus to oversee investment management. These individuals work with outside consultants, bank trust officers, and mutual fund managers, among others, to obtain specific advice. Institutions with smaller endowments may rely solely on banks and consultants to provide these services. When outside firms are used for financial management, an officer of the school is designated to oversee these activities and ensure that the investment policies of the governing board are followed.

Investment Management:
Documentation. The adequate documentation of the investment process requires evidence of the policy and players that govern these activities, and of the results of their efforts. In addition to the governing board and its investment committee, evidence should be gathered about the senior officers and other advisors in the school and outside who influence the investment policy as well as their respective roles and responsibilities. It is also important to document how investment policies have changed and what factors influenced those changes.

The records of the investment committee of the governing board and the files of the senior officers who work with this group contain the fullest documentation of the institution's objectives and policies. The records documenting the implementation of policy decisions are produced by campus offices and off-site firms charged with investment responsibilities, thereby creating a large and possibly dispersed record. When an outside firm is used as the prime investment manager, the archivist can work with the on-campus advisor to see that adequate documentation is received and retained by the institution. Reports prepared by outside consultants are generally found in campus administrative records and should be retained as a reflection of the influences on investment policy.

The actual management of investments produces voluminous transactional records and extensive reports of the outcomes. While much of the transactional record is not of long-term value, records that demonstrate compliance with a donor's wishes must be retained. The published reports of the president and treasurer contain information on the results of investment management: summary information on the rise or fall of the endowment, the rate of return on investments, and the changing value of each fund. Published reports may also provide information on the institution's portfolio: the holdings and yield and changes in the investments over time. If this detailed information is not included in published reports, the records of the investment committee and officers in charge could supply this information. At some institutions such information may be restricted, while at state institutions it could be a public document.

Budget. Once the anticipated annual resources are calculated, the institution allocates those funds through a budgetary process to teaching, research, and administrative activities. The formulation of the budget is the means by which the institution translates its objectives into a detailed operating plan. Once the budget is approved, an ongoing monitoring process checks whether the actual resources and expenditures match the budget figures. Shortfalls in revenue, caused by failure to receive anticipated state revenue or tuition and fees, necessitate modifications in budget allocations. Other revisions may be caused by supplementary requests from units. Therefore, the approved or opening budget is a record of the funds anticipated and authorized for each unit or program at the school; the closing or actual budget records final income and expenditures.

The governing board oversees the process by which the budget is formulated and reviews and approves final recommendations. The chief executive officer, however, initiates the process by developing guidelines for the formulation of the budget with the officers responsible for this task, generally the chief financial and academic officers. These guidelines establish the ground rules by delineating the period of the budget (e.g., one or two years); the calendar for preparing, submitting, and reviewing requests; and the limitations on the requests. Budget preparation begins as much as a year or more before the start of the institution's fiscal year, which for many academic institutions runs from July 1 to June 30. Some public institutions have the same fiscal cycle as their state government.

Budget preparation differs at campuses that are decentralized rather than centralized, where the style is controlled rather than participatory, and where the state exercises considerable control over finances. The specific guidelines and techniques used may also differ based on the current financial condition and managerial style of the institution. Budget formulation procedures include the following methods:

> *Incremental:* uses the last budget and adds on for inflation and new programs

> *Open-ended:* asks each unit to submit a request that reflects its actual needs

> *Quota:* gives each unit a specific figure on which to base its budget

Alternative-level: asks each unit to prepare several budget proposals based on projections of a specified increase, decrease, or stable budget

Formula-base: uses enrollment figures or credit-hour production as a means to determine budget allocation

Program: uses planning objectives for programmatic areas as the method to determine operating budget

Zero-base: asks each unit to justify a budget assuming nothing about previous budgets and therefore starting from zero each year.

After guidelines for budget preparation are formulated by senior officers, they are distributed through supervisors to each unit head. The budget is then generally developed as a bottom-up procedure, with unit heads submitting requests for personnel, materials, and capital equipment to their supervisors, who formulate composites based on judgments and priorities for their departments. The requests are then sent on to the appropriate officials (e.g., the senior academic officer for the academic departments), where they are reviewed and often discussed with the department head during budget hearings. At the larger and multi-campus institutions, additional levels of review may exist. Senior officers must then evaluate all requests against institutional priorities and constraints and formulate a budget which the chief officer submits to the board for approval.

Each unit is notified of its authorized budget and receives detailed monthly accounting reports to aid in monitoring commitments and expenditures. Administrative officers receive monthly or quarterly reports to oversee the compliance of their units. Modifications for shortfalls, windfalls, and reallocation of resources are reflected in periodic budget reports. The closing or actual budget for the year reflects the final expenditures.

Budget: Documentation. The budget process involves three separate steps: formulation of budget guidelines and process; budget preparation, negotiation, and approval; and budget tracking. The records of each step in the process shed light on the other parts. Budget requests for each unit might appear to be useful annual statements of programmatic objectives. The institutional guidelines that shape each request, however, are needed to understand the constraints imposed on each unit head. A unit's request does not reflect its actual needs and objectives if the institutional guidelines mandated a zero-growth budget. A strategic planning document more accurately reflects current and future objectives.

The documentation of the budget process therefore consists of the budget guidelines and instructions for preparation; individual unit budget proposals; the authorized budget; periodic statements monitoring the budget throughout the year; and closing or actual budget.

Different documentary goals are appropriate for each part of the budget process. Copies of the budget guidelines and instructions are a vital key to the documentation and are generally found in the records of the chief financial officer. Evidence should also be gathered of the process and techniques used to formulate the budget as well as the individuals and committees who are involved. Harder to capture are the deliberations by the board and senior officers as they estimate the funds available, formulate the fiscal policy for the year, and structure the budget process.

The individual budget requests are generally found in both the records of the chief financial officer and the administrative records of the unit. At a large institution it may not be possible or desirable to retain individual requests, in which case those of some departments and units could be selected as examples of the budget preparation and negotiation process. An indication of the institution's priorities, however, can be gleaned when the budget requests are compared with the authorized budgets.

The authorized or opening budget reflects the funds allocated to each programmatic area of the institution. Budgets are constructed and tracked by individual numbered accounts, a system that is sometimes referred to as fund accounting (see *Fund Accounting*, page 184). Each account contains funds allocated for specific purposes: salaries, equipment, telephones, travel, etc.

Institutions use different reports to track the progress and record changes to the budget. Some institutions include budget information on the monthly accounting statements, while others keep this information separate. Periodic budget reports are distributed to each unit and supervisor, generally still as a paper document. For purposes of analysis by the board or administrative offices, budget information is frequently summarized or presented in different ways. The full budget, however, is maintained, altered, and tracked in machine-readable form. For reference and security purposes, many institutions produce not only monthly paper but also computer output microfiche (COM) reports. The closing or actual budget is reflected in a very summarized fashion in the published annual reports of the president and treasurer; it is more fully captured as a machine-readable file, COM, or paper report at the close of the fiscal year.

The authorized budget, its updates, and the closing figures for each account are crucial documents for the institution and the archives. In the section on financial reporting that follows, the budget records are discussed in relation to other key financial records. The budget is the most complete financial record of the institution from a programmatic point of view. Other records track the funds and report on the general financial health of the institution, but the budget is the document that provides the best evidence of the financial status of each educational and administrative program of the institution.

Space and preservation considerations suggest retaining a COM report to capture the opening and closing budgets as well as the periodic updates. Paper reports are too voluminous. The COM report also provides a picture in time while the automated database is constantly altered and updated.

The most complete and flexible record is the machine-readable file of the budget. Academic administrators value access to the automated file to analyze the successes and failures of their financial planning and to inform their future efforts by reference to historical trends. Future researchers will value the machine-readable file for similar purposes if the hardware and software permit the reuse of the data.

Financial Accounting

Money constantly flows in and out of an institution. Accounting functions assure that funds are received, recorded, allocated to the proper fund, and paid out for services rendered. The receipt and expenditure of these funds generate the voluminous transactional record dreaded by administrators and archivists alike. The purchase of pencils, the payment of staff, and the receipt of gifts and tuition payments all create duplicate records in the offices that initiate, process, and monitor the transactions.

Financial administration encompasses many activities, including a large number that are particularly devoted to maintaining records and generating reports. Financial offices receive, record, and, when appropriate, acknowledge all income including gifts, endowment income, tuition and fees, repayment of loans, charges for housing, government grants, sales of goods; deposit income into banks and reconcile bank statements; establish accounts and monitor funds added to and expended from each account; and pay bills for supplies, equipment, and services, verifying the authority to make such expenditures.

The number of offices assigned these responsibilities and the titles of the officers in charge vary with the size of the institution. Small colleges subsume many of these functions within just one or two offices, while larger universities establish separate offices for the diverse tasks. The following are among the more common financial titles and associated responsibilities:

Vice President for Business and Finance: general responsibility for administering all business and financial operations, including financial management, budget preparation and control, investment and bank relations

Treasurer: responsible for financial administration and investments; budgetary control; custody of deeds, contracts, etc.; and the preparation of financial reports

Comptroller: provides general supervision for record-keeping and accounting operations for all financial transactions

Bursar: at a small college, performs the functions of a comptroller; at a larger institution, responsibilities are limited to the receipt of all income from tuition, fees, food services, and housing

Cashier: responsible for receiving cash, checks, and other income; depositing them in banks; and reconciling bank statements

Accounts Receivable Officer: responsible for collecting and recording all funds for services

Accounts Payable Officer: responsible for payment of all bills for supplies, equipment, and services.

The two organization charts taken from Asa Knowles, *Handbook of College and University Administration,* are examples of how financial activities are structured at large and small institutions.

*Organization of an Office of Finance
Adaptable to a Large or Medium-Sized College
or University*

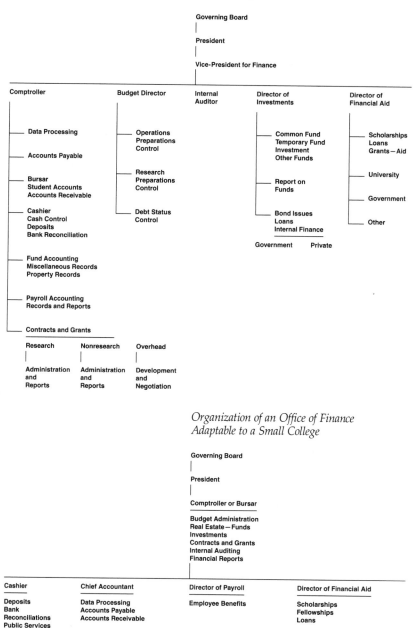

Governing Board

President

Vice-President for Finance

Comptroller

Budget Director

Internal Auditor

Director of Investments

Director of Financial Aid

— Data Processing

— Accounts Payable

— Bursar
Student Accounts
Accounts Receivable

— Cashier
Cash Control
Deposits
Bank Reconciliation

— Fund Accounting
Miscellaneous Records
Property Records

— Payroll Accounting
Records and Reports

— Contracts and Grants

Research | Nonresearch | Overhead

Administration and Reports | Administration and Reports | Development and Negotiation

— Operations
Preparations
Control

— Research
Preparations
Control

— Debt Status
Control

— Common Fund
Temporary Fund
Investment
Other Funds

— Report on
Funds

— Bond Issues
Loans
Internal Finance

Government   Private

— Scholarships
Loans
Grants — Aid

— University

— Government

— Other

*Organization of an Office of Finance
Adaptable to a Small College*

Governing Board

President

Comptroller or Bursar

Budget Administration
Real Estate — Funds
Investments
Contracts and Grants
Internal Auditing
Financial Reports

Cashier

Deposits
Bank
Reconciliations
Public Services

Chief Accountant

Data Processing
Accounts Payable
Accounts Receivable

Director of Payroll

Employee Benefits

Director of Financial Aid

Scholarships
Fellowships
Loans

181

Financial Accounting:
Documentation

Transactional financial records, which track the payment of individual bills and the receipt of income from students, donors, and others, on the whole are of short-term value. The problem for administrators and archivists alike is to coordinate the creation, retention, and destruction of this highly duplicative and often decentralized record. The challenge is to ensure the retention of an official copy (called the record copy) of a document for as long (but only as long) as it is needed and to encourage the destruction of all reference copies as soon as they no longer have administrative value. Reference copies are needed to assist offices in the administration of their responsibilities; official copies are maintained to comply with government audits, institutional claims, and other legal requirements. Once these administrative and legal needs are fulfilled, the records should be destroyed as rapidly as possible to minimize storage costs.

Records management retention schedules are an ideal way to control these records and provide useful guidance to the administrative staff of the institution. Such a schedule should designate the holder of the record copy and the length of time the record and reference copies should be retained, but one uniform schedule cannot suffice for all institutions because state law and the variations of private and public institutions require individual adjustments. Schedules must be established to meet the legal requirements imposed by state and federal regulations. State records schedules (both general schedules and those specifically prepared for institutions of higher education) can be used or adapted by many public institutions. To ensure the acceptance and legality of records schedules, archivists and records managers must work with and receive approval from the senior financial officers, auditor, and legal counsel of their institution.

As financial accounting systems are increasingly being transformed from paper-based to machine-readable form, provisions must be made to incorporate records management controls in the automated systems. For security and preservation, provisions also should be made to back up and maintain technical documentation for the automated system and produce a computer output microfiche version of the database at specified intervals. As technologies evolve, the back-up systems for computer databases will most likely change.

As few of these records will ever be held by an archives, in this area archivists serve primarily as advisors rather than curators. An understanding of the offices responsible for these tasks and their relationship to other financial responsibilities permits the archivist to work with the offices, establish records schedules, and separate the records of short-term value from those few that eventually come to the archives. It is important, however, to document the changing structure and methods by which the institution carries out its financial accounting. Annual reports of the president and treasurer, organization charts and policy, procedural and forms manuals provide basic information about financial operations. The administrative records of the officer in charge of financial administration also provide evidence of the structure and activities in this area.

Financial Reporting

Financial operations generate mountains of machine-readable data and paper records that are used by institutions in a variety of ways. Transactional data track the individual payment of bills and receipt of funds, but these data are also summed up, analyzed, and incorporated into financial reports to fulfill managerial and legal requirements. Formal reports, such as the published annual report of the treasurer, fulfill obligations to external communities. A variety of internal reports are designed to support management activities by monitoring and analyzing expenditures and receipts. Now, with the ability to download and manipulate parts of large databases, individuals with access to machine-readable financial information can shape their own reports as needed.

A variety of professional and governmental bodies control the collection and reporting of financial data by issuing standards for colleges and universities. The Financial Accounting Standards Board (FASB) and the Governmental Accounting Standards Board (GASB) issue accounting standards that are interpreted and adapted for the college and university community by the National Association of College and University Business Officers (NACUBO). Additional uniformity of financial reporting has been encouraged by the National Center for Education Statistics (NCES), which issues annually the Higher Education General Information Survey (HEGIS) on finances. Colleges and universities regularly submit information on their financial conditions and operations for inclusion in publications issued by NCES and other organizations. The purpose behind the uniform reports and standards is to respond to the pressures for credible financial accounting to outside communities — both government agencies and private citizens — and to enable analysis among academic institutions.

Adherence to the standards, however, does not imply a uniformity in financial operations at all academic institutions. While the type of information gathered and reported is similar, each institution has its own idiosyncratic way of managing its financial operations.

Academic institutions and businesses prepare financial reports for different purposes. Business annual reports are intended to inform stockholders about profits and losses, but colleges and universities have no comparable single indicator of their success or failure. Instead academic financial reports monitor the management of financial resources and the fulfillment of a stewardship responsibility for their revenues.

Fund Accounting. Colleges and universities are given funds not to make a profit but to provide services. Revenues come to academic institutions designated for specific purposes and with requirements tied to their management. The focus of accounting activities at academic institutions is therefore to monitor the proper administration of revenues. For this reason academic institutions use the principles and practices of fund accounting.

In a fund accounting system, revenues are classified, managed, and reported to reflect the objectives and restrictions specified by the donor. A separate account is established for each fund and reports are made regularly to ensure that the fund is continuously administered in accordance with the goals and limitations imposed by the donor. Separate funds with similar characteristics and requirements are grouped into a few large fund categories to facilitate financial management and reporting. The number and names of these fund categories vary but generally include current, loan, endowment and funds acting as endowment, annuity and life income, plant, and agency funds.

Chart of Accounts and General Ledger. Institutions issue many reports, but the most comprehensive records, and the ones that serve as the source for all others, are the chart of accounts and the general ledger. These records reflect the principles of fund accounting, as each fund is listed and reported separately; fund accounting provides the structure and rationale for the institution's financial reports.

The chart of accounts is a dictionary. Each account number in the chart of accounts is defined by the name of the account and its supervisor, restrictions, purposes, and other attributes. Account numbers also serve as a linking tool in much the same fashion as our social security numbers (whether we like it or not) serve as an identification that provides access to information about each of us in a variety of databases. Each citizen has a name, birthday, and address, but it is the social security number that serves as the unique identifier. Account numbers serve a similar function as they are the access point to the chart and all other financial reports.

Code numbers are assigned for all revenue and expenditure accounts including funds for petty cash, deferred assets, current construction, accounts payable, research funds, and endowed professorships. The numbering system is organized in a logical way to reflect the organization of the institution and the fund groups into which the accounts are organized. A uniform system of subcodes for account numbers is generally used to reflect typical expenses (e.g., telephones, supplies, equipment, and travel).

The general ledger supplies the financial data for each account: the cumulative financial history for the fund accounts and the financial information on the current fiscal year for the budgeted accounts. Thus this record monitors the activity of each account by reporting the ongoing assets, liabilities, and balances.

All financial reports derive from these master records (the chart of accounts serving as the dictionary and the general ledger supplying current information), including monthly updates of accounts, periodic analysis of financial status, and final versions of the budget and treasurer's report. The information can be sorted in various ways (by account number, name of supervisor, academic or administrative unit, or type of expense such as travel) and issued at regular intervals or as needed to analyze specific areas. Supervisors receive monthly reports of all their accounts to track their expenditures and monitor their budgets. Monthly and quarterly analyses of the financial condition of the institution are prepared for the governing board and administrators. Finally, the published annual reports are produced from this same database.

Financial Reporting:
Documentation

Theoretically, if periodic copies of the chart of accounts and the general ledger are preserved in machine-readable form and can continue to be permuted as needed, no other financial reports would be needed. For practical purposes, however, other reports are useful for administrators and historical researchers alike.

The most readily available report is the annual published report of the treasurer. This is an important document that usually contains the following basic financial information:

> *Balance sheet, a summary financial statement of the status of all funds as of the close of the institution's fiscal year*
>
> *Statements on the revenues, expenditures, and changes in the current fund balances*
>
> *Summary of gifts received*
>
> *Summary of investments*
>
> *External auditor's annual report.*

Supplementary material and additional schedules provide explanations of accounting methods, definitions, and other interpretive material.

The treasurer's report reflects the principles of fund accounting by providing a summary of the fund accounts and a status report for the individual funds. It focuses on tracking the receipt of funds and their expenditure but usually does not report on the purposes and programs for which the funds are expended. The summary expenditure statement in the annual report provides total figures for all operating and programmatic areas but does not provide information about where each program gets its funds or details about how the programs allocate and expend their resources. For this information other reports are needed.

Budgets and periodic financial statements provide a detailed financial picture for each programmatic area (academic and administrative) of the institution, but budgets, on the whole, do not clarify what funds are used to support the programs. Some funds, of course, are explicitly designated for specific purposes such as the acquisition of library materials, scholarships for minority students, or a professorship in Victorian literature. Other funds are flexible: an endowed chair to be rotated among the departments at the discretion of the school, funds for graduate stipends to be used as needed. Unrestricted and general funds are allocated by the administration during the budget process. The most satisfactory way, therefore, to determine the source of support for each unit is to obtain a list of all revenue fund accounts organized by the unit to which they are assigned. Such a document provides a useful record of the way each programmatic area is funded.

The basic financial records of long-term value to the institution and to historical researchers as well, therefore, are the following:

The published treasurer's reports, for annual financial summary information

The chart of accounts and general ledger, for comprehensive financial information for each account

The authorized and actual budget, supplemented by periodic reports that record changes to the budget elements, for information about the financial operations of each programmatic area of the institution

A list of the revenue fund accounts listed by the unit to which they are assigned, for information about what funds are used to support those programmatic budgets.

As these financial reports are gathered, it is important to be sure that reports intended to be used together cover the same time periods. If the chart of accounts and general ledger are captured on the first of each month, then the budget or accounting reports should cover the same period.

The records discussed above provide fairly detailed information. Monthly or quarterly, a summary analysis of the financial condition of the institution is prepared for the governing board, and these reports become part of their records. These summary statements can be useful in addressing questions that require a general understanding rather than a detailed financial picture.

Auditing

Auditing is a process designed to ensure the proper management of financial resources. Current emphasis on the need to be accountable to students and parents as well as to state and federal governments has increased the pressure for both internal and external audits.

Institutions establish permanent internal auditing offices to provide continuous monitoring and analysis. Originally, auditing activities were limited to the review of financial accounting. Now, internal audits often examine operations to evaluate the efficiency and effectiveness of management, compliance with laws and regulations, adherence to internal and external policies, the accuracy and reliability of accounting data, the availability of appropriate records, and the maintenance of logical systems of record keeping.

As an extension of their concern for internal controls, auditors examine electronic data processing records to assess the availability and protection of information in machine-readable form. Particular attention is given to the proper programming, adequate technical documentation, and security of the automated systems.

Individual areas of an institution are audited on a periodic basis or when problems are perceived with compliance or management. During their work, the auditing staff carries out extensive research in the financial and administrative records of the unit and generates additional documentation through interviews and reports. The auditor's evaluations and recommendations are used by the administration to guide needed changes.

In addition to the permanent internal auditing office, once a year the governing board asks an external certified public accounting firm to evaluate the financial integrity of the institution. This auditing process pays particular attention to the effectiveness and reliability of the accounting and internal auditing procedures. The report of the external auditor is given to the governing board for evaluation.

Finally, external audits can be imposed on an institution by government agencies to monitor the proper use of federal and state funds. At public institutions, a state or federal auditor carries out this task. The government is now turning part of this auditing function over to academic institutions; it may require, for example, that the school assume auditing responsibility for its student financial aid funds.

Auditing:
Documentation

It is important to understand how the institution uses its auditing function to provide oversight of financial and managerial areas. The official external auditing report is contained in the records of the governing board. Additional information is available from the chief financial officer and the auditor's office to document auditing activities, their findings, and how their recommendations influenced the management of the institution.

The auditor also produces useful records. Internal auditing reports contain analyses of the financial management of the institution as a whole as well as of the specific units they examine. Records of external audits provide a summary analysis of the financial condition of the entire institution.

As the auditing process places a heavy emphasis on examining record-keeping practices, the work of the auditor is of particular importance to the archivist. The auditor examines, evaluates, and uses records and is therefore a key source of information about how records systems work, their relationship to other information, and their short- or long-term legal and administrative value. As an officer with oversight responsibility for record-keeping practices, the auditor's advice and approval strengthens records management and archival policies. The auditor is therefore a valuable ally of the archivist.

Personnel

Academe is a labor-intensive enterprise: about 80% of the operating budget of each college and university is expended on salaries. In many ways, managing the administrative and support staff (including student employees) resembles personnel operations in any other sector of society. The distinguishing characteristic of academic institutions is the administration of the faculty: the way they are hired, reviewed, granted sabbaticals, and awarded tenure. The presentation that follows deals first with issues that affect all employees and ends with separate sections on the staff and the faculty.

189

The terminology used to categorize employees differs among institutions, reflecting in part the divisions between professional and nonprofessional staff and the groups delineated by the bargaining groups of the labor unions. Where librarians and other staff are members of the faculty, they are often referred to as "nonteaching faculty." Some institutions use the terms administrative and academic staff to differentiate responsibilities. In the sections that follow, two general terms are used: faculty includes all employees holding tenure or nontenure track positions who are hired, evaluated, and promoted as faculty members; staff includes all other administrative, support, and maintenance personnel.

Personnel policy is shaped by four major factors: the institution as the employer, the employees (faculty and staff), the unions, and the government. Once again, the legal environment created by state and federal regulations sets the tone and controls these activities in many ways, including their documentation.

Government Regulations

Colleges and universities are subject to the same state and federal regulations that control employment practices of industrial and other work settings. Both public and private academic institutions must comply with a variety of state laws. In many cases, however, federal laws regulating employment practices preempt state law. The overlapping state and federal regulations governing employment practices can best be described as a quagmire. Federal regulations govern the following areas:

Discrimination on the Basis of
Race: Title VII (administered by the Equal Employment Opportunity Commission-EEOC) of the Civil Rights Act of 1964 (amended), and Executive Order 11246 (amended).
Sex: Title VII and Title IX of the Education Amendments of 1972, the Equal Pay Act, and Executive Order 11246.
Age: Age Discrimination in Employment Act of 1967 (amended).
Handicap: Rehabilitation Act of 1973.
Religion: Title VII and Executive Order 11246.
National Origin: Title VII and Executive Order 11246.
Aliens: Title VII and 42 U.S.C. sec. 1981.
Veterans: The Vietnam Era Veterans Readjustment Act of 1974 and 38 U.S.C. sec. 2012.

Fair Labor Practices: The Fair Labor Standards Act controls minimum wages, equal pay, overtime, and child labor.

Labor Relations: The Labor-Management Relations Act (LMRA) protects the rights of employees to organize and negotiate the terms of their employment. (More will be said about LMRA in the section *Labor Relations.*)

Retirement: The Employee Retirement Income Security Act of 1974 sets standards for the management of employee benefit plans.

Unemployment: Federal unemployment compensation laws require academic institutions to make contributions to state unemployment insurance plans.

Some additional discussion of discrimination regulations is warranted. William A. Kaplin, one of the most respected writers on the law of higher education, states, "The problem of employment discrimination is probably more heavily blanketed with overlapping statutory and regulatory requirements than any other area of post-secondary education law" (Kaplin, p. 119). Public and private institutions are subject to the laws enumerated above as well as to state laws on fair employment practices. Public institutions are also subject to the equal protection clause of the Fourteenth Amendment of the U.S. Constitution. Establishing personnel policy that complies with all of these requirements is complex, to say the least.

The authority of the government to enforce employment practices is embedded primarily in the provisions tied to federal aid programs. Institutions that accept money from the federal government are obliged to conform to civil rights requirements. Title VII of the Civil Rights Act of 1964, the most comprehensive of the federal discrimination laws, is administered by the Equal Employment Opportunities Commission (EEOC). Colleges and universities experience the impact of Title VII as they must establish and administer policies that conform to the regulations and report to the government to demonstrate compliance. Biennial reports are required by the EEOC to monitor recruiting and hiring practices.

The impact of Title VII has also been felt in ever increasing litigation. Among the areas that have been highly litigated are sexual harassment, sex-biased retirement plans, sex discrimination in pay, pregnancy disability benefits, confidentiality of faculty votes on personnel decisions, race discrimination, time limitations in filing Title VII claims, and religious and national origin discrimination.

While Title VII aims to eliminate discrimination in the future, affirmative action regulations attempt to rectify the effects of past discriminatory practices. Executive Orders 11246 and 11375, for instance, require that all federal contractors develop and adhere to affirmative action plans. Institutions are required to set goals and timetables for the hiring of specified minority groups. The goals are intended to be reasonable hiring targets, not rigid quotas. Colleges and universities are required to submit affirmative action plans and regular compliance reports to the Department of Labor. Administering affirmative action policies while balancing the requirements of Title VII and the equal protection clause of the Fourteenth Amendment of the U.S. Constitution has kept academic administrators, lawyers, and the courts busy interpreting the law. William Kaplin's *The Law of Higher Education* contains extended discussions of each of the laws cited above. Legal counsel, affirmative action officers, and personnel administrators can shed light on the implementation of these regulations by each campus.

Personnel Administration

The responsibility for the administration of employees is shared, at most institutions, among a centralized office and the individual schools, departments, and units. Centralized offices establish and oversee a coherent and uniform personnel policy. This coordination and oversight is particularly necessary in light of the regulatory and reporting requirements for affirmative action, equal pay and work provisions, and collective bargaining agreements. Centralized personnel services also ensure a uniformity of job descriptions, pay scales, and recruitment practices. Separate offices may exist in the central administration to oversee compliance with affirmative action, equal opportunity, and grievance procedures. Personnel officers in each unit disseminate and adapt institutional policy to their areas and respond more immediately to local needs.

The policies and programs that govern the relationship between employee and employer are generally delineated in personnel handbooks and policy manuals. These publications describe general policies on employment, hiring, and work conditions and specific practices governing leaves, pay, termination, and labor relations. Separate publications may be prepared for the faculty and the staff.

Embedded in these policies are the programs that the institution adopts to evaluate, promote, and provide training and development for their employees. Formal and informal evaluations are used to monitor the performance of staff, to reward achievements through promotions and salary increases, and to document and correct poor performance. Educational programs are provided to enhance employees' abilities and satisfaction. Training and development opportunities broaden general knowledge and provide the specific skills needed, for instance, to master a new technology. The evaluation and promotion of the faculty (discussed below) is quite different from that of the staff but is also delineated in published policy and procedure manuals.

Personnel Administration: Documentation

Personnel administration is heavily dependent on records. Both the institution and employees have long-term need for the information they contain. The institution requires personnel information to manage and pay its employees; to comply with government regulations to report on recruiting and hiring practices and on the current composition of the staff; and to analyze staffing patterns, payroll and benefit expenditures, and other employment issues to support future planning efforts. Employees require information to verify their past employment and to obtain their benefits.

Coordination and control of these records is complicated by the overlapping and duplicate nature of the information created in central and local personnel offices and by the maintenance of the information in both paper and machine-readable form. Personnel transaction forms and other relevant information about employees tend to be sent by the local unit to the central personnel office where actions are recorded and implemented. Duplicate copies of personnel transaction forms and other records may be filed in two or more offices; some of the information is also entered into a machine-readable database.

While some of the information is of long-term value to the institution, the employee, and historical researchers, there are problems associated with the use of personally identifiable records. Access and privacy restrictions should not alter a decision to retain records but must inform their administration. There is no federal privacy statute that controls personnel records; the Privacy Act of 1974 controls only the records of the federal government, but the act served as a model for the states that adopted their own privacy laws. "In the absence of a specific act, privacy issues will be judged by common law principles and by the holdings of courts in previously litigated cases" (Peterson and Peterson, p. 40). In light of this legal environment, institutions must delineate their own policy on access to personnel records. Such policies clarify employees' right to see and to amend their own records, control access by others, and define the information about employees that can be made public (e.g., the dates of employment, positions held.)

One of the basic premises of privacy law is that records cannot be reused for a purpose other than the intended one without the permission of the subject of the record. The Privacy Act of 1974, for instance, requires that individuals be informed of the principal purpose of recording any information about them and that their written permission is required for other uses. It is generally assumed that institutional and aggregate research is permitted without the consent of the subject. Biographical research by historical researchers in personnel files, however, is more problematic, as it involves the reuse of a personally identifiable record for a purpose other than its original one. Though privacy law differs from state to state, in general, privacy rights are considered to cease at death. Therefore, personnel files of deceased employees could be administered as unrestricted records.

The documentary goal for personnel administration must be to record sufficient information to understand the evolution and implementation of personnel policy; the composition and administration of the staff as an aggregate body over time; and the employment history of the individual members of the staff. In this way the needs of both the institution and the individual are accommodated.

Published manuals and handbooks offer a concise summary of personnel policies and practices. Each edition and revision of these publications should be preserved. To track the evolution of these policies and the factors that affect decisions on salary, benefits, affirmative action policies, and the size and composition of the staff, administrative files from the senior officers responsible for personnel are needed.

Records should then be sought to develop an aggregate picture of the staff including its demography: the types of jobs, pay scale, and composition of the employees at the institution. Job descriptions and salary ranges provide information on the changing skills needed to run the college and the amount of money paid for specific categories of employment. Detailed analyses of the composition of the staff might be available both in the annual report of the president and in compliance reports submitted to the government. The reports prepared for the EEOC, for instance, contain the following information: the number of employees enumerated by sex, race, and salary within the following categories: executive, administrative, and managerial; faculty; nonfaculty professionals; clericals and secretarial; technical and paraprofessionals; skilled craft; and service and maintenance. Copies of these reports should be preserved in administrators' files and then retained in the archives as a valuable summary analysis of the staff.

The annual report of the president and treasurer and the more detailed reports discussed in the section on financial records (above) provide information on the cost of salaries and benefits. For administrative and historical purposes, it is also valuable to preserve a record of the institution's benefits package. Since the benefits office prepares extensive printed material to inform new staff and to update employees, a published annual summary should be readily available. The benefits office should also be able to provide a summary of the options chosen by employees, and the total costs incurred by employees and the institution.

The annual telephone directory provides information about the people working at the institution, their titles and where they work, but additional information is required to meet the needs of the individual employee. Sufficient information must be retained to verify employment history and to award benefits to current and former employees (and beneficiaries). Personnel offices in the individual units often retain records on former employees to respond to questions from other employers, landlords, and banks.

Ultimately, however, the central personnel office retains the minimum information deemed necessary to fulfill the obligations of the institution to its employees, which should include the dates of employment, positions or job descriptions, and salary information.

Many personnel information systems rely on both paper and machine-readable records. While automated databases are increasingly useful, paper files are still required to verify specific personnel actions, especially on documents containing signatures. The long-term importance of personnel records requires particular attention to the question of the security and long-term preservation of machine-readable records. (See *Automation*, page 141.)

Records of search committees used to select administrators, faculty, and staff have value for the information they provide both about the candidates selected and about the process used. Search committees refer to the records of previous committees as they establish their own procedures.

Labor Relations

Labor relations involve those aspects of personnel administration in which the management of the institution and organized segments of the staff, represented by unions, negotiate conditions of employment. While some categories of nonacademic staff have been represented by unions since the 1930s, the unionization of the faculty is a more recent phenomenon. The presence of labor unions has altered the relationship between the administration and its employees and has affected the tone and style of personnel deliberations.

The laws controlling collective bargaining differ for public and private institutions. The National Labor Relations Act (NLRA) of 1935 (the Wagner Act) as amended by the Labor-Management Relations Act of 1947 (the Taft-Hartley Act) governs all collective bargaining activities in the private sector. In the early 1970s the National Labor Relations Board (NLRB) clarified that the Wagner Act applies to private nonprofit colleges and universities, and specifically to faculty members, as well. Collective bargaining in public institutions of higher education is controlled by state laws. At least one-half of the states have some sort of enabling legislation that permits employees of colleges and universities to join unions. Even where such legislation is not present, public employees have a constitutional right protected by the freedom of speech and association provisions of the First Amendment to organize and bargain collectively.

Segments of the academic workforce, clerical, maintenance, and faculty, are represented by separate unions. Therefore, many unions may exist at the same time at any given college or university. Nonacademic employees are most often organized by the American Federation of State, County, and Municipal Employees (AFSCME), Service Employees International Union, Teamsters Union, or a more specialized union such as the International Brotherhood of Electrical Workers. The three unions that most often organize faculty members are the National Education Association (NEA), the American Federation of Teachers (AFT), and the American Association of University Professors (AAUP).

Faculty and nonacademic staff alike unionize to strengthen their ability to bargain with the administration, especially in difficult economic times. Collective bargaining agreements generally specify hours of work, salary and wages, working conditions, promotion opportunities, and benefits. Job security is addressed through agreements on seniority, grievance, and termination procedures. Faculty bargaining also involves academic issues such as teaching loads, class sizes, and sabbaticals.

When members of the workforce declare that they want to bargain collectively, a secret ballot is held to certify a union to represent them. One of the most difficult issues that arise during this process is the consideration of the groups or the types of workers to be included in the bargaining unit. A bargaining group must have a "community of interest," and a general principle is that supervisors and nonsupervisors are not combined in the same union. In faculty unions, questions arise about the inclusion of part-time faculty, librarians, research staff, and faculty members acting as managers, such as department heads. Once the membership of the unit is established and the certification election has been successful, the union selected becomes the sole bargaining agent for all employees in the unit, whether or not the individual members join the union or wish to be represented.

Once the union is approved, bargaining teams are established for the institution and the employees with the understanding that both sides will "bargain in good faith." Issues are negotiated and mediation or arbitration can be used to overcome problems and avoid strikes. The outcome is a contract that specifies the terms of the agreement. When unions are new, contracts are often negotiated every year. For multiyear agreements, all provisions remain constant throughout the period with the exception of salaries, which can be renegotiated each year.

Academic collective bargaining is complicated by the role of the faculty in the governance of the institution. In industry, the demarcation between supervisors and employees is generally clear. In higher education, while faculty members are employees, their role in governance and administration also makes them managers. The question has been, therefore, how to evaluate the managerial responsibilities of the faculty to determine when they must be excluded from a bargaining unit.

In 1980, the U.S. Supreme Court dealt with these problems when it ruled that the faculty of Yeshiva University were managerial employees and thus were not covered by the Wagner Act (*NLRB* v. *Yeshiva University*). The Court ruled that the faculty are managers in that they "formulate and effectuate management policies by expressing and making operative the decisions of the employer." The Court added that "their authority in academic matters is absolute."

A very different view of the role of faculty was offered by Justice Brennan in the dissent: "The Court's conclusion that the faculty's professional interests are indistinguishable from those of the administration is bottomed on an idealized model of collegial decision making that is a vestige of the great medieval university" (100 S. Ct. 856 (1980), quoted in Kaplin, pp. 107–111).

The effect of the Yeshiva decision on faculty bargaining at other colleges and universities is still in question, as the faculty at Yeshiva University do have much greater managerial authority than is the case at other academic institutions. The decision seems to establish an exclusion only for "Yeshiva-like" faculty. Case-by-case decisions by the NLRB and additional court rulings should clarify the future of faculty collective bargaining.

Labor Relations: Documentation

The primary documentary problem for labor relations is the dispersal of the records among the administration, the employee bargaining group, the union, and each individual participant in the contract negotiation process. Each side is required to generate and retain the "bargaining history" from its point of view. This full record of the contract negotiations is necessary in the event of any future arbitration, when each side must clarify its perception of the intention of the contract.

Throughout the bargaining process, each team — administration and employees — meets separately to decide what offers to present to the other side. The deliberations in these caucus sessions are often not recorded. What is documented is the proposal the team decides to present for negotiation. Each negotiating team keeps copies of the proposals and separate minutes of the bargaining meetings. The most complete record of each side is usually maintained by the team spokesman, but each member of the negotiating team maintains a record of the negotiations as well. The union also receives and maintains a full record. The labor contract reflects the actual agreement achieved by the parties often after lengthy negotiations. For legal, administrative, and historical purposes, a more detailed record of the process of achieving that contract is required.

While a contract is active or negotiations are under way, both sides may be reluctant to place their records in the same repository. Even after the contract has expired, unions may choose to place their papers at repositories not affiliated with the institution. Appropriate assurances of restrictions on access might be used to encourage the preservation of both sides of the record. Contract negotiations could be used as an opportunity to coordinate and ensure the preservation of these records.

For a particularly vital (the first contract for a specific segment of the community) or difficult labor negotiation, oral history may be desirable to record additional information about the unionization of the campus.

Staff

The following personnel administration activities are relevant to most members of the staff:

Analyzing and Defining Jobs

The personnel process begins with the preparation of job descriptions that specify the activities and responsibilities for each position at the institution. The skills required and tasks to be performed are analyzed, the job is assigned a category (administrative, faculty, clerical, maintenance, etc.), and a salary range is established for the position. The job description is used first to screen and hire prospective candidates and then to evaluate employees once they are in the job. While some institutions write job descriptions for each position, others utilize a series of standard descriptions, which are matched as closely as possible to the responsibilities of specific situations.

Recruiting and Hiring

Once the appropriate officials have approved the job description and authorized the hiring of staff, a search can begin. Personnel departments generally coordinate the posting of jobs within the institution and advertising in the appropriate external publications to ensure compliance with affirmative action plans. Depending on the level of the position and the skills required, hiring decisions may be made by personnel officers and supervisors after screening candidates or by a more formal search committee process. Information required to make decisions is gathered in standard application forms and in letters and resumes submitted by the candidates.

Paying Staff

An institution balances several factors as it establishes a salary plan. Salaries must be competitive with those of other employers, especially in the immediate geographic area, to provide incentives and rewards for the staff, and remuneration must be equitable to comply with state and federal laws. At the same time, the institution must try to control personnel costs. The role of unions in negotiating salaries for one or more segments of the staff further complicates the process of establishing pay plans.

Academic institutions generally use a pay structure that establishes a range of pay for each job category. Each range can have a number of steps which the employee achieves through merit increases or rewards for length of service. Readjustments to the pay scales and equity reviews of current employees are conducted periodically to adjust for inflation and competitive job markets.

Benefits

Generous benefit packages were once considered an added incentive to attract and retain employees. Now, legal requirements, demands by unions, and expectations of employees have made benefit programs a significant given part of staff compensation.

Some benefits, such as social security, unemployment compensation, worker's compensation, and, in some states, disability insurance, are required by law. All other benefits are optional. Each institution chooses the types of benefits it offers to the staff as a whole or to specific segments of the staff and decides if the costs will be paid by the institution or shared with the employees. Major benefit programs generally include health care, life insurance, disability insurance, and retirement plans.

Academic institutions also provide benefits to their staff through their policies on vacations, holidays, sick and personal leaves; time and financial support to attend classes; scholarship programs for dependents; access to library, athletic, daycare, and arts facilities; faculty and staff club privileges; and payment of professional dues.

Staff:
Documentation

The documentation of the staff is generally covered in *Personnel Administration: Documentation*, page 194, where the documentary goals concentrate on the management of personnel records and the need to preserve information for legal and administrative purposes. There is, however, another aspect of personnel that is much more difficult to document: What is the experience of a worker at the institution? While personal and professional correspondence from members of the administration and faculty reveal something of their reactions to the institution, the staff remains virtually invisible. Where do these people come from? What is their experience of working at the institution? How are they affected by the college and how do they affect it? For maintenance, clerical, and even some administrative professional staff, there is virtually no record of their experience or their contribution to the institution. Telephone books list who they are and where they live, job descriptions give a formal statement of what they do, and photographs of work places may shed some light on the work environment and the interaction of the staff. A broader understanding, however, will require oral histories and other conscious efforts to capture the experiences of these important members of the community.

Faculty

The methods used to hire, promote, and dismiss members of the faculty differentiate them from the rest of staff. Faculty appointments have two main variables: appointments can be full- or part-time and nontenure or tenure track. A tenure track appointment requires the availability of a tenured position. If all of the positions allocated by an institution to a specific department are filled by tenured faculty, the department must hire the new faculty they require only into nontenure track jobs. More will be said below about the process of moving through the tenure track and the award of tenure. Faculty filling nontenure track positions are given full- or part-time appointments of varying duration. Some adjuncts, lecturers, and other temporary full-time instructors may remain at an institution for many years.

The proliferation of adjunct and other full-time nontenure track positions may be due in part to the current shortage of tenure track positions, the budgetary constraints of the institutions, or the growing need for professional school staff. Instructor and adjunct appointments are used extensively in medical, business, and other professional schools to hire clinicians and practitioners.

Tenure

From the late middle ages to the present day, faculty have sought intellectual, economic, and in early periods even physical protection from the church, the state, and the administration of their institution. In the middle ages, the *privilegia scholastica* gave the faculty immunity and autonomy from the power of the church and state. In modern times, protection and security are granted to the faculty through the principles of academic freedom and the practice of granting tenure.

Threatened by their lack of job security, in 1913 a group of faculty members organized the American Association of University Professors (AAUP) to establish "general principles respecting the tenure of the professional office and the legitimate ground for the dismissal of faculty." From 1915 on, AAUP has issued a series of policy documents and reports that have established the modern principles of academic freedom and tenure that now govern the procedures of most American academic institutions.

The most widely endorsed and influential of the AAUP documents is the 1940 statement *Academic Freedom and Tenure; Statement of Principles and Interpretive Comments*, which was issued "to promote public understanding and support of academic freedom and tenure and agreement upon procedures to assure them in colleges and universities....Tenure is a means to certain ends; specifically: (1) Freedom of teaching and research and of extramural activities and (2) a sufficient degree of economic security to make the profession attractive to men and women of ability." From the beginning the AAUP sought both the guarantees of academic freedom and the security of tenure. What is unique and important about the AAUP statements is the linking of these two separate concepts: tenure has become the means to ensure academic freedom.

The 1940 statement outlines the principles that underlie the process of granting tenure:

The Probationary Period: The probationary period assures the faculty member that a decision will be made about tenure at a specific time and commits the institution to make that decision. AAUP guidelines are that the probationary period is not to exceed seven years.

Causes of Dismissal: To safeguard the rights of a faculty member threatened with termination of a continuous appointment or dismissal for cause previous to the expiration of a term appointment, the reasons for the dismissal must be set forth in writing. A faculty committee and the governing board must hear the case, and the faculty member is assured representation by appropriate counsel and access to information about the case. The policy asserts the sole right of the faculty to make judgments about the merits of academic performance.

Years of Service: When faculty members move to other institutions, the total years of service in the profession are to be taken into consideration when determining their rank. Therefore, faculty members need not start afresh with each appointment.

Tenure and academic freedom became an accepted part of the American professoriate in the years following World War II and was solidified in the boom years of the 1960s, when colleges and universities wanted to attract and retain the best talent. In the 1970s, however, tenure came into question when decreasing enrollment and hard economic times forced college administrators and the public to question the practice of granting permanent appointments. A few institutions have abandoned the tenure system and now use contracts of specific durations for their faculty. Most four-year colleges and universities, however, retain the use of tenure.

Academic freedom continues to be a fundamental part of higher education that affords protection to all members of the faculty, tenured and nontenured alike. The concept has gained increased acceptance by the judicial system, which takes academic freedom "as a catch-all term to describe the legal rights and responsibilities of the teaching profession. ...The U.S. Supreme Court gave academic freedom constitutional status under the First Amendment freedoms of speech and association, the Fifth Amendment protection against self-incrimination, and the Fourteenth Amendment guarantee of due process" (Kaplin, pp. 180–181).

Recruiting and Hiring

Once a senior academic officer gives a department permission to hire new faculty or fill an existing vacancy, the department sets a search procedure in motion that can include a committee to screen and interview candidates and make a recommendation to the department head. Search committee members are generally drawn from the faculty of the department but could include faculty from other areas, especially for appointments to interdisciplinary programs.

Advertisements for the particular specialties sought are placed in the appropriate disciplinary journals and newsletters and general publications such as the *Chronicle of Higher Education*. Following the interview or review process, a recommendation is made to the department head, who forwards the name of the successful applicant to the appropriate senior official. The department and the college must then negotiate salary and a contract with the candidate and agree on such questions as course load and research facilities. If the appointment is to a tenure track position, agreement must also be reached on the length of the probationary period that precedes the decision on tenure and the criteria for promotion.

Promotion

The review and promotion of tenure and nontenure track faculty differ significantly. While nontenure track faculty are evaluated regularly, their rewards are limited to increases in salary and the possibility of a transfer to a tenure track position if and when one becomes available in their area of expertise. Tenure track faculty move through a continuous career path delineated by the ranks of the faculty: assistant, associate, and full professor.

Faculty progress through the ranks and up the salary scale through a combination of merit of performance and length of service. While some movement through the salary scale within a rank may be granted as a reward for length of service, movement between ranks is more dependent on the merit of that service. Institutional policies differ, including the rank at which tenure is awarded. Written policies and procedures stipulate when and how evaluations take place and the criteria on which faculty members are judged. Criteria for promotion generally include teaching effectiveness; research and publications; service to the department and the institution; professional service outside the institution; and community service.

Tenure track faculty members are evaluated for promotion to the next rank at agreed-upon times. The most elaborate review generally accompanies the decision regarding promotion from assistant to associate professor, as for most schools this review includes the decision to grant tenure. The candidate assembles a dossier for the committee charged with reviewing the case that includes biographical information; list of courses taught; student evaluations; list of internal and external professional and community service; funded research projects and names of sponsors; and copies of publications or citations. The committee and the candidate solicit evaluations and letters of support from faculty and administrators inside the institution and from colleagues at other institutions.

The committee reviews the dossier and makes a recommendation for or against promotion and tenure to the department. The tenured members of the department vote to affirm or deny the decision of the committee. The results of that vote are sent with the dossier and the department head's recommendation through the appropriate review procedure. A campuswide committee makes a final recommendation to the senior academic officer and the chief executive officer, and their recommendation is given to the governing board for final approval. At any stage the recommendation can be overturned. Final approval by the institution makes the individual a permanent tenured member of the faculty.

Another formal review, usually less extensive, takes place at the decision to promote a faculty member from associate to full professor. Again, internal and external evaluations are made of the work of the faculty member under review. If the university grants tenure at this point, however, the review increases in scope and importance. A negative recommendation at this review forces an associate professor without tenure to leave the institution. An associate professor with tenure can remain on the faculty at that rank.

Faculty: Documentation

The following discussion of documentation deals only with the personnel records of the faculty (hiring, evaluating, promoting, and granting tenure), not with the records of other faculty activities (teaching, research, and service), which are discussed in appropriate chapters (*Convey Knowledge*, *Conduct Research*, and *Provide Public Service*).

As is true for other employees, consideration must be given to documenting both the policies and procedures that govern their employment and the personnel history of each member of the faculty.

Published manuals that outline these policies and procedures generally delineate the sequence of events and parties that make and review promotion decisions. Information should also be included on the criteria for promotion, the process of preparing a dossier for review, and the grievance procedure. As these policies are made by the senior academic and administrative officers of the institution and appropriate representatives of the faculty, a more detailed record of how and why these policies came into being and changed may be found in their records.

Administrative files might also contain discussions about the general size, shape, and characteristics of the faculty: use of part-time and adjunct faculty; affirmative action goals for women and minorities; and goals for the proportion of tenured to nontenured faculty. Where the faculty is covered by a collective bargaining agreement, some of these issues may also be controlled by contract provisions.

Personnel information about each member of the faculty is generally available in three types of records:

Personnel Record: A central personnel office keeps track of the minimum information about the faculty as well as the rest of the staff. This information includes at least the dates of employment, positions held, and salary earned.

Department Personnel Record: In addition to the transactional information included in the first category, the departmental record generally contains considerable information that sheds light not only on personnel issues but also on academic and research matters. Correspondence with the department head tracks research and academic leaves (to teach at other institutions or serve in government posts), sabbaticals, annual reviews, salary negotiations, and promotions. The department file can provide information about annual course assignments, receipt of research funds, student evaluations, and administrative or committee assignments. Faculty may also be asked to submit curriculum vitae and bibliographies on a regular basis. Department personnel files are maintained for tenured and nontenured faculty alike and track the entire career of the faculty member at that institution.

Depending on the style of record keeping within the departments or units, this file can provide the most useful documentation of the faculty. This record, therefore, has long-term administrative value to the department and, once the faculty member has left the department, continuing historical value to the archives. Other offices — provost, schools, etc. — may also maintain files on individual faculty members, but these files tend not to be as complete as the departmental file.

Promotion and Tenure Record: This record is generally created and retained separately from the department file and captures the evaluation of faculty members at the one or two key points in their academic careers. In recent years, as the review process for tenure has become more elaborate, the documentation has become more extensive. Increasing litigation concerning tenure decisions has also made this a more problematic record. Therefore, this final category is discussed below at greater length.

The contents of the promotion and tenure file vary according to the procedure followed at each institution, but whatever this file contains, the volume and sensitive nature of its contents make it a problem. In addition to the dossier prepared by the candidate, the file may contain the minutes and recommendation of the committee charged to review the case as well as the deliberations of each committee and the department head or other individuals who subsequently pass judgment. Some committees prepare summaries of letters of evaluation, phone conversations, and their discussions. Individuals who review the file may leave informal notes on the candidate or the deliberations.

A distinction must be made between the files of individuals granted and denied tenure. The files for those faculty denied tenure must be kept for a legally authorized period (often seven years) in case the individual chooses to question the decision and sue the institution. Files of faculty granted tenure generally have a greater long-term value to the institution, and therefore the institution must weigh the benefits and risks of retaining them.

The present legal environment creates an uncertain atmosphere in which to make long-term decisions about promotion and tenure records. The growing number of suits by faculty members denied tenure makes institutions nervous about the contents and retention of these records. The

1990 U.S. Supreme Court ruling (*University of Pennsylvania* v. *Equal Employment Opportunity Commission*) questions the traditional belief that access by the courts to promotion and tenure records can be denied on the basis of academic freedom.

In establishing a policy on tenure records, therefore, the following are some of the key issues that must be considered:

Access: Controlling access to the records requires balancing the individual's right of privacy, the institution's need for confidentiality, and the public's interest. Institutional policies should specify who has access to the files and under what circumstances. Generally, these policies apply to active files and do not consider long-term issues. State institutions are governed by state records acts and freedom of information legislation that often guarantee access by individuals to their own records and may force the institution to make these and other records available to the press and other requesters. The need to protect the confidentiality of an individual is sometimes, but not always, taken as a reason to resist a freedom of information request. Further complicating these issues is the ruling in the *University of Pennsylvania* case, which forces academic institutions to comply with requests for tenure files, including confidential peer review letters, when subpoenaed as part of an employment discrimination investigation. While this ruling pertains specifically to discrimination suits, it is unclear if future decisions will make these records accessible for other reasons as well, and how these decisions will affect the peer review process. On the other hand, privacy is generally assumed to be a personal right that ceases at death. Therefore, following a lengthy restricted period (some institutions adopt the 72-year period used by the U.S. Census Bureau), the records could be opened for research.

Liability: While the files of faculty denied tenure represent a clear liability (as these are the individuals who may sue the institution), the files of the faculty awarded tenure can be a problem as well because they can be subpoenaed in a suit brought by an individual denied tenure. The recent Supreme Court ruling required the University of Pennsylvania to comply with a subpoena not only for the tenure file of the individual who was denied tenure but also for the files of five male faculty members granted tenure who the plaintiff believed to be no more qualified than herself.

Curatorial: Promotion and tenure files are voluminous even when actual publications are removed and only a bibliography retained. Space considerations must be part of the decision to retain these records, especially at institutions with a sizable faculty. Files can be weeded or converted to microfilm to reduce the bulk.

In light of all of these problems, it is useful to consider what value these records have. The faculty after all is a key component of the institution, and it seems desirable to retain information about them. But it should be determined whether the information in these files may be available more easily and in a less problematic form in another record.

What evidence is available in these files? Where else might it be available?

Biographical: The curriculum vita and description of teaching, research, publications, and outside pursuits only reflect the activities to the time of the evaluation, and such information is considered a publicly available record. Biographical information may be more readily available in the department, personnel office, or news office.

Peer Evaluations: The promotion and tenure review process relies heavily on the opinions of faculty in the same disciplinary area at other institutions as a means to assess the candidates' reputations in their profession. In the absence of reliable criteria to judge teaching quality, this peer review process takes on great weight. The letters of evaluation can provide an insight into a disciplinary community: evaluations of candidates solicit opinions not only on the quality of research and publications but also on the value of the line of research being pursued. One must ask, however, in light of recent court cases and the growing caution of individuals called upon to write evaluations, how open and honest are these letters? There are just as many who argue that these letters have been and continue to be extremely valuable as those who say that they have not been relied upon in years. The style of the individual asked for an opinion and even the style within the discipline may affect these letters. Whether evaluations are always honest or not, they do reflect the core of the promotion process and provide a potentially valuable look at the dynamics within a disciplinary community. Retaining the letters but removing the names of the writers denies future researchers a critical piece of knowledge. Summaries of the letters prepared by the review committee that include the names of the writers are a possible substitute for saving all of the letters.

Internal Evaluations — Students and Colleagues: Recommendations and evaluations are solicited both from graduate and undergraduate students and from colleagues. Again, there are questions about the value of these assessments, but they may provide the only evidence of students' reactions to a member of the faculty. If the faculty member has solicited all of the letters, clearly they will be complimentary. If the committee solicits additional letters, there may be a more mixed expression.

Process of Decision Making: For legal and managerial reasons, considerable attention has been focused on the process of making tenure decisions. While individual candidates might care most about seeing the record of the decisions made about them, administrators and researchers try to understand the process with respect to all candidates. The question is how revealing are the records about the decision-making process. How were the criteria for promotion applied to individual candidates? What factors or individuals influenced decisions? Do the minutes of the committees and the notes left in the file reveal this process? Is the record so revealing that it could be a liability to the institution?

In establishing a retention policy for these records, institutions must balance benefits and risks. Therefore, the decision must be shared by the administration, faculty, legal counsel, the curator of the records, and, when appropriate, state authorities and unions. Consideration must be given not only to the legal issues but also to the quality of the evidence in the files and the potential usefulness of the records. Full dossiers, evaluations drawn from a large professional community, and minutes or memos by the committee that track the process shed light on the four aspects of this process discussed above. Other promotion and tenure records might not be assembled or tracked as fully and carefully. An additional problem is locating one master copy of the file (probably that of the senior academic officer) while destroying all others.

If promotion and tenure records are to be retained, a policy should specify what records are to be kept in the file. Publications, for instance, could be given to the library and only a bibliography retained. A decision must be made whether to retain evaluations or just the summary prepared by the committee. Finally, the institution must agree on a long-term access policy to these records, which must, of course, conform to relevant laws.

Files that have been the subject of litigation, successful or not, should probably be retained as well as the court records and legal correspondence. Again, legal advice should be sought. Another source of information on grievances and litigation is the AAUP. Faculty members, whether members or not, contact the AAUP for advice. The AAUP maintains and preserves extensive files of their correspondence with faculty, especially with regard to the suits that they have advised and supported.

In summary, the basic records of the faculty are the minimum record maintained by the central personnel office and the departmental personnel file for each faculty member. The potential value and problems inherent in promotion and tenure records should be weighed to determine if any part of these records should be saved as well.

Physical Plant

The Campus as a
Physical Environment

Each year prospective college students and their parents tour college and university campuses to learn about academic programs, see their facilities, and "get a feel for the place." These outsiders are often more conscious of a school's ambience than the faculty, students, and staff who rapidly acclimatize themselves to their given environment. The architecture of the buildings, how they are sited and relate to one another, the open spaces or lack thereof, the views from one part of campus to another, and the vistas of the countryside or community beyond the campus all set the scene and to a large extent the tone of a campus.

The graduate school of the City University of New York, housed in a building on 42nd Street in Manhattan, provides an atmosphere very different from the sprawling prairie campus of the University of Illinois at Urbana-Champaign. The University of Chicago and the Illinois Institute of Technology (IIT) are neighboring campuses, but the Gothic buildings of the university and IIT's modern international school architecture create two very different moods. The similar teaching and research programs of the California and Massachusetts Institutes of Technology make them kindred schools, but the olive trees, running brooks, and small low buildings set on interior walkways with vistas of the hills beyond generate an entirely different ambience for the CalTech community from the one encountered at MIT with its massive structures set in an urban environment.

A campus plan and buildings are the physical embodiment of an educational mission, and studying a campus can reveal much about the history and philosophy of the institution. The relationship of buildings to one another suggests the desired interplay among the academic disciplines, students, faculty, and the outside world. The examination of specific building types or facilities over time, such as scientific laboratories or libraries, reveals changes in academic disciplines, teaching styles, and attitudes about service to the community. Studies of institutions designed specifically for women reveal gender-specific attitudes about education (see Bibliography, Horowitz).

More obviously, American college and university campuses offer considerable evidence of the history of planning, architecture, and landscape architecture. When Thomas Jefferson designed the campus for the University of Virginia, he justified the diversity of the buildings as a desire to provide the architecture students with specimens to study. Whether executed deliberately or not, many American campuses contain examples of the work of significant architects and planners. The following is a brief list of some of the most significant campus plans and buildings:

Campus Plans

John Trumbull	1792	Yale University
Joseph-Jacques Ramée	1813	Union College
Thomas Jefferson	1817	University of Virginia
Alexander Jackson Davis	1848	Virginia Military Institute
Frederick Law Olmsted	1866	University of California-Berkeley
	1867	Cornell University
	1886	Stanford University
Henry Ives Cobb	1893	University of Chicago
Charles Follen McKim	1894	Columbia University
Ralph Adams Cram	1902	Sweet Briar College
	1906–11	Princeton University
Cass Gilbert	1908	University of Minnesota-Minneapolis
Paul Philippe Cret	1908	University of Wisconsin-Madison
Charles Donagh Maginnis	1912	Boston College

Welles Bosworth	1913	Massachusetts Institute of Technology
John C.B. Moore & Robert S. Hutchins	1938	Goucher College
Frank Lloyd Wright	1938	Florida Southern College
Walter Gropius & Marcel Breuer, The Architects Collaborative	1939	Black Mountain College
Mies van der Rohe	1940	Illinois Institute of Technology
Paul Rudolph	1960	Tuskegee Institute
Edward Durell Stone	1961	State University of New York-Albany
Skidmore, Owings & Merrill	1956–62	U.S. Air Force Academy
Walter Netsch, Skidmore, Owings & Merrill	1963	University of Illinois at Chicago
John Carl Warnecke and Associates	1963	University of California-Santa Cruz

Buildings

Benjamin Henry Latrobe	1803	Old West Dickinson College
	1803	Nassau Hall Princeton University
Thomas Jefferson	1817–26	Original buildings University of Virginia
Henry Hobson Richardson	1880–84	Austin Hall Harvard University
Charles A. Coolidge, Shepley, Rutan & Coolidge	1892	Original buildings Stanford University
Ralph Adams Cram	1911–29	Chapel and graduate college Princeton University
Charles Zeller Klauder	1928–34	Cathedral of Learning University of Pittsburgh
Mies van der Rohe	1943–58	Original buildings Illinois Institute of Technology
Alvar Aalto	1947–48	Baker House Massachusetts Institute of Technology
Walter Gropius, The Architects Collaborative	1949	Graduate Center Harvard University

Marcel Breuer	1950	Co-operative Dormitory Vassar College
	1953–70	St. John's Abbey and university buildings St. John's University
Harrison & Abramovitz	1955	Inter-Faith Chapels Brandeis University
Eero Saarinen	1958–62	Morse and Stiles Colleges Yale University
José Luis Sert	1960–67	Charles River Campus Boston University
Le Corbusier	1961–64	Carpenter Center Harvard University
Louis Kahn	1963	Salk Institute
Frank Lloyd Wright	1964	Grady Gammage Auditorium Arizona State University
Walter Netsch, Skidmore Owings & Merrill	1965	Original buildings University of Illinois at Chicago
William Turnbull & Charles W. Moore	1973	Kresge College University of California-Santa Cruz
Frank Gehry	1981	Law School Loyola Marymount University
I.M. Pei	1984	Wiesner Building Massachusetts Institute of Technology

The campus, structures, and grounds are part of the legacy maintained and preserved by institutions of higher education. They are both a rich heritage and an expensive obligation. The tasks encompassed within the physical plant area include planning the campus as a whole and designing, building, and maintaining each structure and the grounds as well.

Campus Plans

Thomas Jefferson described his University of Virginia campus set around a three-sided mall as an "academical village." The coherent plan at Virginia is easier to discern than the plans of many modern sprawling universities that are more aptly described as collegiate cities. Some schools like the University of Virginia and Stanford have had coherent plans to guide the development of their campuses from the very beginning; some have imposed plans after years of random growth to bring coherence to the existing structures and order to future growth. Campus plans are updated and refined regularly to reflect changing short-, medium-, and long-range needs.

Jefferson's open quadrangle is one of several dominant schemes that have influenced campus planning. Although the open plan was extremely popular, the influence of Oxford and Cambridge stimulated the use of the closed quadrangle as the model for the ideal residential campus. The influence of Frederick Law Olmstead and the search for an appropriate model for the land-grant colleges initiated less formal and more park-like campus plans. The growth of the size of the campuses and the commuting patterns of students and staff encouraged plans that emphasized access to public transportation and the efficient flow of pedestrian and vehicular traffic. The importance of the automobile is reflected in campuses designed around ring roads and the attention paid to parking facilities.

Walking around academic campuses, one may not readily comprehend the physical arrangement that binds the structures together. Aerial photographs and architectural drawings reveal the patterns and relationships that have been established through a campus plan. From the seventeenth to the early twentieth century, campus plans were used not only to establish physical relationships but also to provide a unified design through the choice of architecture. In the years following World War II, campus planning moved away from the concept of a master unified plan that sought to control siting and design to more general plans that directed future growth. Modern campus planning focuses on the determination of land use and the reservation of sites for structures or open spaces, the relationship among structures, the flow of pedestrian and vehicular traffic, and the relationship of the campus to the surrounding community. With this type of planning, each new structure is sited as specified in the overall plan but has its own appropriate size, character, and architecture.

Campus planning was needed particularly in the 1960s and 1970s to coordinate development during a period of rapid growth. With few exceptions, such as the California system which is still building new campuses, the rate of adding new structures has slowed significantly. The focus of campus planning has shifted from controlling growth to redesigning campuses to make them more attractive, easier to get around, and safer. Landscaping, improvement of roads and parking facilities, walkways, lighting, and open areas are all being used to attract future students and make campuses more pleasant for the academic community and its neighbors. Wake Forest University in Winston-Salem,

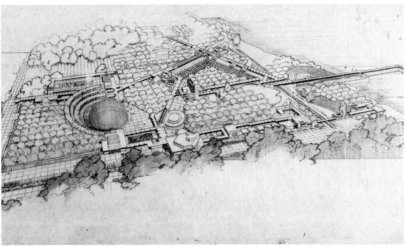

Campus plan for Florida Southern College
by Frank Lloyd Wright, 1942

Recent aerial photograph of
Florida Southern College

North Carolina, commissioned a new campus plan although there are no immediate plans to add new buildings. Instead, the new campus plan protects and enlarges open spaces, provides a new entryway for the campus by moving a major roadway, and adds plantings around the entire campus.

Campus planning requires considerable information not just about the buildings and grounds but also about the number of students, faculty, and staff; the residential and commuting patterns of those people; the development and demise of academic programs and administrative functions; and the changing status of the institution's sources of revenue. For this reason, the planning office often serves as a central source of information and may even publish a statistical factbook.

Buildings and Facilities

The very earliest buildings on American campuses housed classrooms, residential quarters for students and faculty, a library, and a chapel in one common structure. During the nineteenth century, individual structures and interior spaces were designed to meet the specialized needs of an academic department or function, such as the gym or the library. As disciplines and research methods changed, the single-use facilities were found to be difficult to re-adapt. The trend in the second half of the twentieth century has been to build structures that concentrate similar functions within one building and provide flexible interior spaces that can be easily redesigned as enrollments, disciplines, technology, and research methods change. Classroom buildings can be used for instruction by all disciplines; generic laboratory facilities are built to be re-adapted as equipment and research methods change.

At the same time, the limited funds available for new structures and the impact of the historic preservation movement have encouraged the renovation rather than the destruction of older buildings. Former chapels now serve as performing arts centers and audiovisual and computer facilities. As new libraries are built, the original structures are transformed into art galleries, information centers, or administrative offices.

The following sections explore the activities associated with the construction and renovation of buildings, space management, and the maintenance and repair of the facilities and grounds.

Planning, Erecting, and
Renovating Buildings

The commitment to erect a new structure sets a considerable process in motion involving the administration of the institution (fund raising and planning); administrators, faculty, staff, and students of the unit to be housed in the building; and outside architects, engineers, and contractors. Once funding is assured and the site identified, the requirements for the building must be defined by its future occupants in a document called a building program.

The program statement describes the academic, research, administrative, and social functions that are to be housed in the facility; the amount of space required for each; and the relationships among these activities. For example, proximity of offices, laboratories, and classrooms is important for scientific departments where the integrated use of these facilities is required. Libraries and archives require loading docks with easy access to the acquisition or processing areas. The estimated number of occupants, the technological and equipment needs (wiring and machinery), environmental and security controls, and hours of use of the facilities must all be specified. Campus engineers and planners add basic technical information to the building program to ensure that the facility fulfills general institutional needs for future growth, flexibility, proper maintenance, and compliance with technical and legal requirements (building codes, access by the handicapped, energy use standards). Campus planners address the need to integrate the new structure into the existing campus through its design and landscaping.

Architects and engineers may either be chosen through a design competition or selected from an invited list of firms. In some cases, the school may use one architectural firm for all of its renovations and building projects; a large institution may have an architect on its staff. A contract between the institution and the architect specifies the services to be rendered, payments, and relationships with subcontractors. A building committee or client team composed of university administrators (facilities, planning, engineering, and operations personnel), faculty, and other future occupants of the building is formed to oversee the design and construction process.

The first product the architect gives the client is a set of schematic designs that translates the building program into physical spaces. The schematic drawings suggest the spatial relationships among the parts, the allocation of amounts of space to specific functions, and the general design and siting of the building. Discussions with clients are used to refine the design, and the final schematics are presented with budget estimates and a schedule for design and construction.

Client approval of the schematic designs permits the architects and engineers to proceed with the design development during which the building is drawn in greater detail, and the uses of each area, whether occupied by people or equipment, are specified. The architect presents the client team with renderings (visualizations of the building), models, floor plans, building elevations, cross sections, specifications of the mechanical equipment, and cost estimates. Following the approval of these documents, the architect prepares construction documents that include the specific plans and construction information needed to guide the building of the facility. Cost estimates presented at this point are based on materials, equipment, and labor costs. Delays and modifications during construction may affect the final cost of the building.

From the construction documents, the architect and engineers prepare bid documents for the contractors needed to build the actual structure. The institution selects a general contractor or multiple contractors to carry out the structural, mechanical, and electrical work. Once final construction documents and procedures are approved, it is both difficult and expensive to make changes in the building. The architect and client team oversee the construction: inspect subcontractors' work, review materials, monitor schedules, and report on progress to the client. The architect and construction engineers are responsible for the inspection and approval of the building by the client. The contractor obtains for the client the appropriate certificates from public agencies and testing laboratories to authorize the occupancy of the building.

The architect delivers to the institution various documentation required to operate and maintain the building, including all guarantees and operating manuals for the equipment as well as the technical specifications and final approved set of drawings ("as-built" drawings), which record the final construction of the building and reflect all of the changes made through the process. These drawings must be presented in a reproducible form that can be used by the institution to repair, maintain, and in the future renovate the facility. Once the institution inspects and approves the building and receives the documentation it requires, final fees are paid and the institution takes ownership of the building.

A major renovation can entail almost as much effort as the construction of a new facility. Renovations are carried out to meet the needs of new programs and technologies and changing building codes. A renovation can also be undertaken to restore a historic structure, sometimes just the facade, to its original condition. If architectural and mechanical drawings are not available, renovation activities start with the production of plans of the existing structure. The rest of the planning and construction activities are much the same as the construction of a new facility.

Space Management

Obtaining additional space at most campuses may be more difficult than acquiring more funds or staff. Space is a carefully guarded scarce resource. Each institution conducts annual surveys to determine what space exists and how it is currently used. In this way space can be allocated as needed, and plans can be made to add space (acquire or build) when necessary. Knowledge of space utilization is also used to determine the size of future enrollments (is there sufficient dormitory and classroom space for additional students?), the expansion of academic programs (are laboratory or other specialized facilities available?), the disposal of property (can outmoded or underutilized facilities be sold or demolished?), and maintenance and energy costs (how many hours per week is each space used?). In addition, knowledge of the proportion of space allocated to teaching, research, and administration is used by the institution to calculate indirect cost rates for government contracts (see page 165).

Maintaining and Repairing
Structures and Grounds

Studies of space also provide the information needed to manage the cleaning, maintenance, and repair of the buildings. Facilities management includes routine cleaning, structural and mechanical repairs, and planned preventive maintenance. A legacy of aging buildings, the rapid increase in the number of buildings, poor construction techniques and materials, and high repair costs create an enormous maintenance and repair problem. In 1989 the American Association of Physical Plant Administrators estimated that $70 billion will be needed by colleges and universities in the coming years to correct deficiencies associated with deferred maintenance.

The types of custodial care, preventive maintenance, repair, and renovations required depend on many factors: age, size and number of buildings, extent of the grounds, and amount of use of the facilities and grounds. The use is affected both by the number of people assigned to the areas and by the number of hours each day and months each year that the campus is used. A commuting campus does not have resident students, but classrooms can be in use from 8 am to 10 pm. The size of the campus and its physical needs also determine whether the school hires its own maintenance and repair staff or contracts work out and whether it has its own power plant or buys utilities from local suppliers.

Physical Plant: Documentation

The campus, the buildings, and the grounds are constantly changing. The documentation of the physical plant must track the life cycle of the campus: plan, build, use, maintain, renovate, demolish.

Policies governing the physical plant are delineated in campus plans and facilities plans: the first controls the growth and configuration of the campus; the second specifies the proper maintenance and repair of the facilities. Campus and facilities plans have long-term administrative value to the offices that oversee the physical development and care of the institution; they also have historical value to the institution and to researchers in many disciplines. The records of the planning office provide more detailed information about the evolution of each planning document and building project. In addition, their records may provide considerable general and statistical information about the institution.

A composite record of campus facilities might be available in one of many forms. Some campuses publish an inventory of buildings that includes location, date of occupancy, architect, net square footage, benefactors, and current use. The planning or physical plant office generates annual space inventories that provide a useful quantification of the amount and use of all available space. The institution's insurance records or physical plant asset records will include a consolidated description of each structure.

The bulk of the documentation is generated tracking the life of each facility, be it a building, athletic field, or park. A considerable record is created during the planning and construction phase, but little of this material has long-term value. The building program remains an informative document, but ironically not necessarily about the building itself. The actual structure may differ markedly from what the client requested, but the program statement does provide a detailed description of particular academic or administrative activities and their perceived needs at a specific time.

The construction process generates voluminous sets of drawings, specification and construction documents, and progress reports that are maintained by the client, the architect, and the subcontractors. Architects and clients may take daily or weekly photographs to track the progress of a project and to document the use of appropriate materials. At the completion of the project, construction records are retained until legal requirements are fulfilled. Then, the bulk of construction records are generally destroyed. Exceptions are made for records of structures that are influential because of their design or construction. Architects and institutions might also have some interest in retaining the original renderings or models for their artistic or exhibit value. Selected construction photographs are particularly useful for exhibits at dedications and anniversaries of the building.

The record of the working life of the structure or facility starts when the architects and subcontractors transfer the technical specifications and final approved sets of drawings, or the as-builts, to the institution upon completion of the construction. A building file, generally maintained by the planning office or physical plant, should include the name (and name changes) or number of the building; the date of construction; original costs; names of architects and contractors; floor plans, with gross square footage and net assignable space; date, nature, and cost of major renovations and repairs; painting schedule; and projected timetable for major repairs such as machinery overhauls or roof replacement.

As long as an institution owns and uses land, buildings, and other facilities, the planning and physical plant staffs require access to information about these properties. The successive plans serve as reference points as campus and facilities plans are updated and revised. Information about individual structures is needed to maintain and repair buildings and to plan and carry out major renovations. Drawings allow contractors to locate the wiring and plumbing throughout a structure when they are in need of repair or replacement; drawings also identify non-loadbearing walls that can be removed during a renovation. Campus plans guide the long-term care and cultivation of the landscaping.

The master copies of these documents most likely reside in the planning and physical plant offices. The archives should ensure that these records are properly cared for both during the life of the facilities and after the institution has demolished or sold a property. The methods used to reproduce architectural drawings present long-term preservation problems that are compounded by their large size and the varying quality of the materials on which they are reproduced (the support materials). The chemicals in diazoprints cause them to yellow and fade, and blueprints may be unstable if they have not been properly washed. Long-term retention of architectural drawings generally requires a combination of proper housing of the drawings (flat files or rolled storage shelved horizontally under proper environmental controls), reformatting of unstable or fragile copies by photography or photocopying, and the production of an archival quality microform. (See Bibliography, Schrock and Lathrop.)

The archives can further ensure preservation of and access to these records by acquiring copies of campus and facilities plans as they are issued and maintaining a set of the architectural and mechanical drawings in microform (usually aperture cards) as a back-up security set for the institution. When a facility is sold or demolished, the archives should acquire the records from the planning and physical plant offices if they would normally be weeded or destroyed at that time. Working documents and technical information can be removed at this time, but a full set of the architectural drawings and site plans should be retained as a minimum record. For laboratory buildings or other structures that had a technical purpose, however, retaining some documentation that reveals the mechanical specifications, equipment, and facilities will be valued by historical researchers, especially historians of science and technology.

While drawings and specifications provide technical information about the construction and operation of facilities, these documents reveal little of the changing uses and atmosphere. A visual record is required to capture the life cycle: construction, uses, and demolition. Aerial photographs reveal the relationships among the structures, the flow of pedestrian and vehicular traffic, the changing landscape, and the physical relationship of the campus with the surrounding community. Photographs of the inside and outside of the individual structures bring the architectural drawings to life and show how the buildings were actually decorated and used.

Architects, news offices, and campus publications all create a voluminous visual record, as do students, visitors, and other amateur photographers. Archivists should seek this evidence and determine if the photos contribute to the documentation of the structures, the relationship of a structure with those around it, the landscaping, and the uses of the inside and outside of the facilities. The visual record must document not just the structures but the spaces in between, the formal parks and informal gathering places on the grounds. To capture this information over time may require that archives supplement the visual record through their own documentation projects or by asking the planning, physical plant, or news office to create the needed visual record.

Bibliography

General Documentary Issues

Finn, Chester E. *Scholars, Dollars and Bureaucrats*. Washington, D.C.: Brookings Institution, 1978.

Green, Kenneth C., and Steven W. Gilbert, eds. *Making Computers Work for Administrators*. San Francisco: Jossey-Bass Publishers, 1988. (Includes essay by James Powell.)

Hedstron, Margaret. *Archives and Manuscripts, Machine-readable Records*. Chicago: Society of American Archivists, 1984.

Information Resources for the Campus of the Future. *Campus of the Future: Conference on Information Resources* (Co-sponsored by OCLC and the Johnson Foundation). Dublin, Ohio: Online Computer Library Center, 1987.

Kaplin, William A. *The Law of Higher Education: A Comprehensive Guide to Legal Implications of Administrative Decision Making*. 2d ed. San Francisco: Jossey-Bass Publishers, 1985.

Management of Electronic Records: Issues and Guidelines, prepared by the Advisory Committee for the Co-ordination of Information Systems (ACCIS). New York: United Nations, 1990.

Managing Electronic Records. Washington, D.C.: National Archives and Records Administration, Office of Records Administration, 1990.

National Academy of Public Administration. *The Effects of Electronic Recordkeeping on the Historical Records of the U.S. Government: A Report for the National Archives and Records Administration*. Washington, D.C.: NAPA, 1989.

Peterson, Gary M., and Trudy Huskamp Peterson. *Archives and Manuscripts: Law*. Chicago: Society of American Archivists, 1985.

Special Media Records Project. A Strategic Plan for Managing and Preserving Electronic Records in New York State Government: Final Report of the Special Media Records Project. Albany: University of the State of New York, State Education Department, State Archives and Records Administration, 1988.

Governance

Collier, Douglas J. *Program Classification Structure*. 2d ed. Boulder, Colo.: National Center for Higher Education Management Systems, 1978.

The Control of the Campus: A Report on the Governance of Higher Education. Washington, D.C.: Carnegie Foundation for the Advancement of Teaching, 1982.

Knowles, Asa S., ed. *Handbook of College and University Administration*. Vol. 1, *General*. New York: McGraw-Hill, 1970.

Finances

Karol, Nathaniel H., and Sigmund G. Ginsburg. *Managing the Higher Education Enterprise*. New York: John Wiley & Sons, 1980.

Knowles, Asa S., ed. *Handbook of College and University Administration*. New York: McGraw-Hill, 1970. Charts on page 181 are reproduced with permission of McGraw-Hill, Inc.

Welzenbach, Lanora F., ed. *College and University Business Administration*. 4th ed. Washington, D.C.: NACUBO, 1982.

Personnel

American Association of University Professors. *Policy Documents and Reports*. Washington, D.C.: The Association, 1984.

Faculty Tenure: A Report and Recommendations by the Commission on Academic Tenure in Higher Education. San Francisco: Jossey-Bass Publishers, 1973. The essay by Walter P. Metzger, "Academic Tenure in America: A Historical Essay," is especially useful.

Finkelstein, Martin. *The American Academic Profession: A Synthesis of Social Scientific Inquiry since World War II*. Columbus: Ohio State University Press, 1984. Chapter 2, "The Emergence of the Modern Academic Role," provides a good history of the evolution of the modern faculty.

Fortunato, Ray T., and D. Geneva Waddell. *Personnel Administration in Higher Education*. San Francisco: Jossey-Bass Publishers, 1981.

Kaplin, William A. *The Law of Higher Education: A Comprehensive Guide to Legal Implications of Administrative Decision Making*. 2nd ed. San Francisco: Jossey-Bass Publishers, 1985.

Peterson, Gary M., and Trudy Huskamp Peterson. *Archives and Manuscripts: Law*. Chicago: Society of American Archivists, 1985.

Physical Plant

Ballast, David K. *Creative Records Management: A Guidebook for Architects, Engineers and Interior Designers*. Newton, Mass.: Practice Management Associates, Ltd., 1987.

"Campus Design," series of articles in *Landscape Architecture* 79, no. 10 (December 1989).

Dober, Richard P. *Campus Planning*. New York: Reinhold Publishing Corp., 1963.

Horowitz, Helen Lefkowitz. *Alma Mater: Design and Experience in the Women's Colleges from Their Nineteenth-century Beginnings to the 1930s*. New York: Alfred A. Knopf, 1984.

Lathrop, Alan. "The Provenance and Preservation of Architectural Records." *American Archivist* 49 (1980): 25–32.

Schrock, Nancy C. *Records in Architectural Offices*. 2d ed. Cambridge: Massachusetts Committee for the Preservation of Architectural Records, 1981.

Turner, Paul Venable. *Campus: An American Planning Tradition*. Cambridge: MIT Press, 1984.

Welzenbach, Lanora F., ed. *College and University Business Administration*. 4th ed. Washington, D.C.: NACUBO, 1982.

Provide
Public Service

*The three-part mission of teaching,
research, and service serves as the charter challenge for the University of
Nebraska-Lincoln....UNL is committed to the belief that knowledge gained in
the field and laboratory must be extended to the citizenry of the state. A large
part of this mission is concentrated in agricultural research and extension.
However, it is the general responsibility of UNL to make all of its programs and
resources available to the entire state through its public service efforts.*
> —University of Nebraska-Lincoln
> Catalog, 1986–87

*The University of Massachusetts at Boston
offers its community a multitude of educational opportunities, and brings the
benefits of a major public university to the people of metropolitan Boston and the
Commonwealth. The research of UMass/Boston's faculty contributes significantly
to the well-being of metropolitan Boston.*
> —University of Massachusetts-Boston
> Catalog, 1987–89

*The mission of Middlesex Community
College is to provide educational, occupational and cultural opportunities to
enrich the lives of people with varied backgrounds and needs from the cities and
towns of the Greater Middlesex Area....The College strives to improve the
quality of life in the community of which it is a part and to create a learning environment which will support, encourage, challenge and lead students to the
continuing discovery and development of their intellectual, occupational, personal, ethical-social, recreational and civic interests throughout life. Instructional
programs are based on assessed community needs with full accountability to the
College constituents.*
> —Middlesex Community College
> Academic Catalog, 1986–88

As a deliberate, continuing expression of the philosophy of its founders, New York University has created schools and programs to meet the evolving needs of the metropolitan community. As the city has developed, the University has developed. Although the University is independent of government — and is gift-supported rather than tax-supported — it is truly New York's university.

— The Mission of New York University, 1964

Public service is one of the three traditional missions assigned to institutions of higher education, but of the three, it is the most amorphous. Although its influence pervades higher education, pinpointing the many ways in which it manifests itself can be a challenge.

The concept of public service has been described as both too broad and too narrow. Almost all activities — teaching, research, and nearly everything else described in this volume — can be considered public service, as the shared goal is to prepare an informed citizenry for the benefit of society. Seen from the other end of the telescope, public service can be viewed as a narrow set of programs that are rendered to outside communities. For this discussion it is useful to focus on the broad intent and rationale as well as the specific means by which institutions carry out their public service mission.

The latent concept of colleges and universities serving society was made manifest with the passage of the Morrill (1862), Hatch (1887), and Smith-Lever (1914) Acts. Through these laws, institutions of higher education were directed to provide education and conduct research to meet the industrial and agricultural needs of the states. The legislation democratized the notion of who should receive an education, emphasized that curriculum and research efforts should be shaped to meet societal needs, and mandated that services be rendered through both campus and extension services. While at first these tasks were assigned only to the land grant institutions that were established and controlled by this legislation, by the early part of the twentieth century these values came to be accepted as the responsibility of all public and private colleges and universities. The greater dependence of private as well as public institutions on state and federal funds reinforces the obligation of higher education to respond to public needs. Public service provides benefits to many outside constituencies, but the institution benefits as well through support (financial, political, and moral), understanding, and good will.

Public service is best defined by focusing on who receives the service, as, no matter what the setting, the audience is primarily those individuals and groups who are not normally served by the institution. Public service activities are designed to meet the needs of external groups. With the audience as the focus, it is possible to examine how and why each institution designs and carries out its public service program.

Throughout this volume the caveat is offered that the size, location, and nature of an institution affect how its functions and activities manifest themselves. That caveat is especially true for public service. Community colleges, state and city universities, and private institutions respond to public service needs in very different ways. The "public" in each case differs, as does the obligation and means by which service is rendered. The publics who are served can be grouped into two categories: geographic or political communities; and disciplinary or professional communities.

The relationship between a college or university and its geographic communities — local, state, and national — varies significantly based upon the nature of the institution. Community colleges are public service institutions that develop their programs in direct response to the needs and concerns of the immediate geographic community. They serve as educational, cultural, social, and recreational centers for their communities. Local needs — of new immigrants for language and technical skills, of local employers for trained personnel, of the local government to solve economic and social problems — shape the community college's degree and non-degree academic and continuing education programs.

State and city universities also have strong ties to their geographic communities. The land grant schools provide the model for integrating public service into educational and research programs. The agricultural and industrial needs of the state influence both the academic programs on campus and the extension services offered to the citizens. When the land grant model was adopted by the city universities, the economic and social needs of the local citizens also came to be reflected in the institutions' programs. Schools in the western and the midwest states enlarged the land grant model into what became known as the "Wisconsin idea."

Charles Van Hise, president of the University of Wisconsin from 1904 to 1918, expressed the belief that the university should take an active part in improving society. The Wisconsin idea extended the public service of the university by establishing direct working relationships with state and local governments and by broadening the idea of extension services to include courses made available throughout the state in response to the varied needs of the citizens.

The relationship between private academic institutions and the communities they serve is not mandated by law but arises from the tradition of service accepted by higher education and the obligations incurred by the institutions as recipients of public and private funds. Social, moral, and financial obligations encourage private institutions to respond to local, state, and national communities. Private institutions, especially the research universities, often serve national communities even more than local ones. The federal government, businesses, and industry rely upon the training, research, and expert advice provided by these universities.

The relationship between professional communities and academic institutions has been touched on in other parts of this volume, especially in the chapter *Conduct Research*. For the public service area, the relevant ties are between the colleges and universities and professionals in business, industry, and government who use faculty and staff as consultants to obtain advice and expertise. By offering the knowledge developed at academic institutions to solve practical problems, the institution is viewed as providing a public service to society. Economists advise a government on restructuring the tax base, chemists advise industry on the development of a new drug, and historians advise a television producer on the script for a documentary. Academic institutions facilitate the transfer of knowledge by enabling and encouraging their faculty and staff to serve as consultants to outside agencies.

In recent years, new programs have evolved from these traditional activities and expanded the ways academic institutions provide public service. Building on the experience of offering advice to secondary educational institutions, colleges and universities have been asked by local school districts to take over the management of their elementary schools: Boston University (a private institution) now manages the school system of Chelsea, Massachusetts. On an even larger scale, foreign governments have asked American colleges and universities to help them establish similar educational institutions in their own countries: MIT was instrumental in establishing the Birla Institute of Technology and Science in India and the Ayra-Mehr University of Technology in Iran.

Ties to business and industry, traditionally limited to providing consultants, educational programs, and research services, have developed into full economic and research partnerships. These new arrangements are seen as mutually advantageous, as they bring new resources to academic institutions and promote the rapid transfer of scientific and technological research into new applications, products, and other commercial opportunities. These partnerships are viewed as public service activities because they aim to develop and apply science and technology to benefit society, strengthen the economy, and increase employment. Three examples of such research partnerships (drawn from Crosson, *Public Service in Higher Education*) follow:

Research Triangle Institute and Park

The Research Triangle is a nonprofit consortium established in 1959 with state support by the University of North Carolina, North Carolina State University, and Duke University to improve relationships between research-based industries and the universities. Private companies, professional associations, and university research projects rent space at the research park. The Research Triangle has become the model for state government support of the academic-industrial connection.

Center for Integrated Systems at Stanford University

Seventeen microelectronics firms have contributed $12 million to construct a new building and support research in electronics. The scientists and engineers at Stanford select the research projects; they are free to publish their findings, and they own the resulting patents. Stanford can award licenses to use the patents to any companies, whether or not they are members, but the royalties are shared with all the member companies. Unlike some of the other partnership arrangements, in this case the member companies are entitled to have their own scientists on site full-time.

Council for Chemical Research

The Council is an industry-wide effort that established a fund with contributions from chemical firms to provide grants to colleges and universities to support basic research of potential value to the industry; promote collaboration between academic institutions and the industry; encourage innovation; and promote the education of scientists and engineers.

Public service goals are often ambitious and lofty. The methods used to achieve them take on many guises, from formal policies and programs that encompass the entire institution to informal initiatives of individual faculty members or student organizations. The implementation of public service activities is somewhat similar to socialization (see the chapter *Foster Socialization*) in that the institution exercises control and sets the tone through the administrative structure and staff assigned to oversee these activities; the institutional policies on the use of staff, time, and facilities; the allocation of resources to fund public service programs; and the initiation of specific activities. Beyond that, and often independent of the formal programs of the institution, additional activities are undertaken by students, faculty, and staff acting as individuals and members of classes and clubs.

While some large and multicampus institutions have public service offices to coordinate their activities, other campuses assign the responsibility to their continuing education department or to a research institute with a public service mission. Many other institutions disperse the public service responsibility throughout the institution, placing particular emphasis on the role of the academic programs.

The funds allocated for campuswide and individual public service activities, and the institutional policies that control personnel and facilities act as additional controls. Many institutional policies encourage public service:

Promotion and tenure policies that call for service not only to the university but also to the external communities

Consulting policies that provide released paid time for the faculty (and often the staff as well) to work outside the institution for government, business, or cultural institutions

Research policies that encourage the establishment of centers on campus designed to meet the needs of government and industry, and the acceptance of research contracts and funds for these purposes

Patent policies that foster the licensing of patents to industry

Policies that consider the needs of outside communities — citizens, governments, industry, and professional groups — as academic and research programs are designed

Community outreach policies that encourage participation in campus activities (meetings and cultural events) by members of the local community, as well as community use of campus facilities (performing arts and recreational buildings) and campus grounds.

Technical assistance and continuing education programs will be discussed in greater detail as major examples of campuswide public service. Other institutional services, such as public radio, television stations, and health care facilities, are also important, but are not addressed in this study.

Less visible public service activities are those initiated by the faculty, students, and staff: the urban planning class that designs a community park as a term project; the faculty member who works with local town officers to automate the town's billing system; the staff group that knits afghans for a women's shelter; the numerous student groups that conduct literacy programs in prisons, tutor students in public schools, raise money for health and environmental concerns, and volunteer in local soup kitchens. Traditionally, these activities have been volunteer efforts initiated by faculty, students, or staff. But now there is growing pressure, exerted particularly by state legislatures, to require public service: undergraduates would be compelled to participate in community service activities, and professional students, especially legal and medical students, would be required to provide services for the poor. For now, however, these activities remain primarily motivated by the social, moral, and religious concerns of the individuals.

Technical Assistance

Academic institutions have always served as a repository of expert knowledge. Federal and state programs, such as the extension services created by the Smith-Lever Act, the experiment stations established by the Hatch Act, and the Wisconsin plan seek ways to make that expertise useful to the government, businesses, and citizens of the state. The Cooperative Extension Services, originally established to bring the latest agricultural knowledge and techniques to the American farmer, has broadened its purpose and been supplemented by other services directed at providing assistance to diverse groups. Technical assistance programs include consulting services provided by individual members of the faculty or staff to government, industry, cultural institutions, etc.; lending faculty or staff for more extended periods when a government or business needs particular expertise; and undertaking research to solve specific problems posed by a government or industry.

State institutions, especially the land grant schools, have always placed considerable emphasis on providing assistance to local and state governments. Expertise is sought by government officials to analyze policies; draft new legislation; provide testimony at hearings; and advise on particular problems such as repair of roads and bridges, improvement of public elementary schools, and provision of affordable housing. The states have utilized different mechanisms to facilitate these services. In some states, such as California and North Carolina, the governor has direct access to the universities and uses the faculty for policy studies. Other schools have established statewide centers or research institutes specifically geared to foster contacts with and provide services to the local and state government. In Pennsylvania the Legislative Office of Research Liaison (LORL) links the legislature with several public and private institutions in the state. Each campus assigns a member of the faculty to act as the institution's liaison. The legislature applies to these individuals for immediate answers to specific questions or for the initiation of research projects to address larger issues.

Private institutions have developed their own means of linking outside inquirers with the expertise sought. At MIT, the Industrial Liaison Program (ILP), established in 1948, serves as an example: corporations make annual contributions to the ILP for which they receive a variety of services including access to faculty members working in their areas of interest. At private and public institutions without an office to facilitate these contacts those outside the institution must rely on word of mouth recommendations from colleagues or references to the work of individuals in the published literature.

To encourage the faculty to work with government and industry, academic institutions establish policies that specify the amount of time that can be spent on consulting activities. Some campuses may have policies governing the acceptance of fees, involvement in secret projects, the assignment of patents and copyrights, and the ability of faculty to hold stock or managerial positions in companies that fund research at their institution.

An institution may utilize both policies and funding to encourage the faculty to participate in consulting and research projects that further their public service goals. Campus research centers that provide funding for specific types of research (agricultural research and technical assistance to state farmers; education, research, and advice for government officials; research and development of new technologies needed by industry) reinforce the institution's priorities and ensure their implementation.

Continuing Education and Training

Since the late nineteenth century, colleges and universities have become the prime providers of continuing and adult education. The extension services that provided demonstrations and workshops to citizens throughout the states on practical issues were enlarged and supplemented by classes designed to offer curricula in diverse topics to those not enrolled in formal degree programs. The inclusion of a university extension division by the University of Chicago in 1892 as part of its original mission, the funding of the university extension system in New York in 1891, and the broadening of the extension concept by Wisconsin in 1906 indicated that American universities were playing a major role in educating adult citizens. The G.I. Bill of Rights and the training and economic opportunity acts of the 1960s broadened the definition of the students to be educated and clearly tied the purpose of their continuing education to employment opportunities. The concept of continuing education is now often described as lifelong learning to recognize the desirability of acquiring new skills to function in a world of rapid changes.

Continuing education comprises two main areas. Credit programs are provided for individuals who need additional education to obtain employment, maintain certified standing, advance in their current positions, or change careers. The students in this category encompass all individuals who are unable to enroll in full-time degree programs, generally adults who are employed or who have family commitments. Although many students take only a few courses, others do earn bachelor's or advanced degrees. Noncredit programs are offered to fulfill the continuing educational needs of adults motivated to improve their own knowledge and skills. Some of these students wish to enhance their professional skills, but do not need credit to do so; others are retired people who wish to fill their leisure time with fruitful activities.

The continuing education programs of colleges and universities are generally delivered by a division or school established for this purpose. The faculty is drawn in part from the regular teaching staff of the institution, supplemented by instructors hired to teach specialized offerings. Additional workshops, seminars, and classes are presented by the professional schools to meet the need for current information and new skills.

The growing demand for continuing education has forced colleges and universities to evaluate their programs and methods of instruction in light of the different needs, skills, and interests of the consumers of this service. The shrinking pool of traditional college-age students and the need for colleges and universities to raise additional revenues have encouraged academic institutions to be responsive to continuing education students, who now exert a major influence on what is taught, how, when, and where.

The curriculum has expanded far beyond the original emphasis on agriculture, home economics, and engineering to encompass the liberal arts and professional education. The diverse methods employed to offer continuing education are another way institutions respond to the particular needs of their communities. The Wisconsin idea of providing education off campus led to the establishment of extension centers located conveniently throughout the state. Correspondence courses were among the early methods used to offer education to those who could not come to the classroom. While this service still exists, radio, television, and other media are now used to offer continuing education beyond the campus.

Pennsylvania State University's Division of Media and Learning Resources offers a good example. The correspondence courses begun in 1911 initiated Penn State's efforts at "distance learning." Radio broadcasts coordinated with lessons published in the state newspapers followed in the 1920s. Audiovisual services were added in the 1940s, educational television in 1964, and finally the first statewide cable television network for use in education was established in 1980. These resources are used by the Division to "provide services to the people, communities, business, industries and government bodies."

Documentation

For historical and political reasons, academic institutions need to capture a record of their efforts to serve outside communities. Pressures from legislators and taxpayers create a climate in which colleges and universities must demonstrate and justify their social value. Administrators and historical researchers have yet to assess fully the growing importance of academic public service activities. Scholars from many disciplines will need to evaluate the impact of these programs on higher education and their effect on society.

Continuing education presents documentary problems parallel to those described in the chapters *Convey Knowledge* and *Foster Socialization*. Compounding the general problems of acquiring an adequate record of teaching, learning, and social activities are the added difficulties presented by continuing education faculty and students who may often spend little time on the campus and lack strong ties to the institution. Additional problems are encountered as many activities take place away from the campus — for instance, when faculty and staff consult for business and government, and students receive continuing education in their homes by radio and television.

It is most important to document the goals, policies, funding decisions, and general management of public service activities. The offices, departments, or centers that deal with the administrative aspects of public service generate such records. These offices should also have evidence that provides an aggregate picture of the institution's public service activities: descriptions of the programs, services offered, number of people involved, and accomplishments.

The documentary problems arise in gathering a record of the implementation of these programs. Not all public service activities should be documented, but descriptions of major programs, their services and activities should be preserved (continuing education catalogues, brochures, and annual reports; descriptions of services designed for businesses, industry, and governments, and reports of these activities). Specific activities can be chosen for fuller documentation either because they were great successes or failures or because they represent the norm. While some of the curriculum will be similar to the course work of full-time students, particular efforts should be made to document at least some of the teaching and learning activities that are unique to continuing education.

Technical assistance programs present documentary problems not only because the record of these activities tends to be dispersed but also because of proprietary concerns. Documentation of the general policies that guide these programs should be available in the centralized office that coordinates these efforts. Where partnership arrangements exist, especially those based on an academic campus, documentation is also available. Problems are more likely to arise when faculty and staff work off site, consulting for governments, businesses, or cultural organizations. If records are retained, they are held by the individual who acted as the consultant; however, potential problems exist for the archivist concerning the ownership of and access to these records. When a consultant works for a business or industry, the records are generally regarded as the property of the company that contracted for the work. Particular concerns arise over the proprietary nature of these records, as they may contain evaluations of future products or directions for the company as well as financial and personnel information. If such records are received, archivists must discuss ownership and access questions with the consultant and the company to determine if the material can be retained, and if so, if restrictions must be imposed for a period of time.

Consulting activities may be reflected more fully in the records of the government or business that received the service. If records of these activities are known to exist in government and corporate archives, they can be described in the finding aids for appropriate collections in the college or university archives. If little evidence exists of these activities in the personal and professional records of the faculty and staff, it is useful to describe consulting work as part of the biographical sketch in the finding aid.

Records of the activities initiated by the faculty, staff, and students are dispersed among all of the participants (e.g., the faculty and students who designed and erected the community playground). For many activities, such as tutoring or serving in soup kitchens, there may be no tangible evidence. Oral history or photographic projects are needed to document those activities that do not naturally generate a record. For instance, the fraternity or sorority that tutors high school students can interview the participants and create a visual record of their accomplishments.

Bibliography

Crosson, Patricia H. *Public Service in Higher Education: Practices and Priorities.* ASHE-ERIC Higher Education Research Report, no. 7. Washington, D.C.: Association for the Study of Higher Education, 1983.

Promote Culture

Academic institutions preserve and promote the culture of a society — its knowledge, values, concepts, and skills — in many ways. Most obviously, colleges and universities promote culture by providing a setting for learned men and women to conduct research and pass on their knowledge. The process of teaching transmits the culture to another generation, while the process of inquiry and research fosters its testing, refinement, and alteration. As creative artists — writers, composers, painters, and choreographers — are included among the faculty, where they teach and practice their crafts, academic institutions can also be seen to promote culture by providing one of the few supportive environments for artists in the United States.

In another sense, however, academic institutions preserve and promote culture by providing a home not only for scholars and creative artists but also for the tools they need to carry out their activities. Henry P. Tappan, in "On the Idea of a True University," expressed the belief that "the very idea of a University is that of concentrating books and apparatus, and learned men in one place" (Hofstadter and Smith, vol. 2, p. 528). The emphasis in this section is on things rather than on people: the role that colleges and universities play as the curators of cultural artifacts. The discussion that follows, therefore, focuses specifically on academic libraries, museums, and archives as promoters of culture.

Books and journals, paintings and sculptures, fossils and stuffed animals, manuscripts and medals — almost every academic campus has some or all of these, and more. Though sometimes modest in scale, these collections are often significant in scope and numbers. Harvard University is probably the extreme case with approximately a hundred libraries, a dozen museums, and more than fifty archival collections. Every institution, however, has collections of one sort or another.

Collecting repositories serve multiple roles at academic institutions. In the terminology of this book, they directly support the functions *convey knowledge, conduct research,* and *provide public service.* This function, *promote culture,* focuses on the responsibilities incurred as a by-product of those functions. Collections of books and objects were originally assembled to enable the faculty and students to study, teach, and conduct research. As these collections grew, however, they took on an additional value and a life of their own. Academic institutions are now the stewards of a significant portion of this nation's cultural heritage, and therefore, perhaps not consciously or willingly, they have accepted the responsibility to preserve these materials. It is important to understand both the primary rationale for assembling these collections and the problems academic institutions incur as stewards of these resources.

While the collections were assembled to support specific teaching and research needs, their value and usefulness have changed over time. When elective courses and research became central parts of the curriculum, books and artifacts were recognized as required to support these activities. As disciplines evolved and research and teaching methods changed, the use of supporting tools changed as well. The establishment of art history programs encouraged the formation of campus art museums. Connoisseurship and museum studies required a close examination of original works of art, but with less emphasis placed on connoisseurship and a growing interest in the social context of art, slides of works of art and reproductions in books often suffice. Nineteenth-century courses in geology, zoology, and botany focusing on taxonomic studies required the availability of collections of rocks, stuffed animals, and live and preserved plants, but advances in these sciences made the examination of specimen collections obsolete by the end of the century. Changing trends in the study of literature and history alter the questions researchers ask and the sources they use. Social and quantitative history create a demand for very different forms of archival records and published materials.

In some cases, the topics studied and the methods used by a discipline appear cyclical. Anthropologists and archeologists may come back to the same set of objects periodically and ask a new set of questions. In some areas, like the physical sciences, however, significant changes in the fields and the methods of inquiry suggest that the collections that once supported the work are now only of antiquarian interest.

During the nineteenth century, academic institutions assembled collections in an effort to build significant libraries and museums to support their academic programs. Self-sufficiency and completeness were the guiding principles. Great collections brought prestige to the institutions and were used to attract faculty, students, and more collections. Early acquisition of materials often came through the gift or purchase of personal libraries and collections of artifacts, each with its particular strengths and idiosyncrasies. Acquiring these large collections fostered the effort to build libraries quickly. Natural history museums were formed around the specialized collections brought to the institutions by their faculty. Holdings grew as faculty purchased books and artifacts in their areas of interest, or donated material gathered during field work. It was not until after World War II that professional library and museum personnel inherited the responsibility of selecting and managing the collections.

The products of these acquisition activities are the substantial holdings of college and university libraries and museums. Judged by modern standards, these collections sometimes appear uneven and divorced from current interests. At the same time, it must be acknowledged that through this process collections of great research value were gathered, and that there are now significant specialized collections scattered throughout American academic museums and libraries. The *Ash Subject Collections* and the *Official Museum Directory* provide evidence of the strengths and diversity of academic collections. Random examples of these extraordinary collections follow:

Libraries and Archives

Children's Literature	Special Collections, UCLA
The Great Lakes	Jerome Library, Institute for Great Lakes Research, Bowling Green State University
Americana	William L. Clements Library, University of Michigan
Architecture	Avery Architecture and Fine Arts Library, Columbia University
James Joyce	Poetry/Rare Book Collection, SUNY-Buffalo

Museums

British Art	Yale Center for British Art, Yale University
Photography	Center for Creative Photography, University of Arizona
Pre-Columbian Art	Krannert Art Museum, University of Illinois, Urbana-Champaign
African Sculpture	University of Iowa Museum of Art, University of Iowa
Anthropology	Museum of Comparative Zoology, Harvard University
Archeology	University Museum, University of Pennsylvania

The manner in which the holdings developed has resulted in collections, sometimes with considerable strengths, in areas that may have little relevance to current curricula or research programs. Twentieth-century professionals must balance their obligation to respond to present curricula and research needs against the continuing responsibility to build on the strengths of their existing collections. Changes in the composition of the faculty, in research interests and methods of the disciplines, and in the curricula may call into question the continuing support of collections that are little used.

While the strengths of existing holdings impose responsibilities on the institution, so too can the role that academic libraries and museums have played in the local community. The development of college and university collections has often forestalled the development of city or town repositories. Especially in communities where the academic institution is the major cultural agency in the area, collections and services are often designed to meet the needs of the local communities as well as the academic institution.

Collections and services thus impose a legacy of obligations. Colleges and universities have assumed a stewardship role toward their collections which forces them to weigh the needs and constraints imposed by their own institutions against the obligations they have to society to preserve and make their collections available. The tensions that arise from this stewardship role are revealed in the debates surrounding deaccessioning and preservation. Institutions attempting to sell portions of their library or museum holdings are subject to the criticism of students, donors, faculty, and community members. The argument that the material is not needed for current academic programs is met with the argument that the institution has an obligation to ensure the continued availability of the material to the scholarly community and the general public. The growing awareness of the need to preserve books, archives, and museum objects places pressure on curators to expend resources to ensure the survival of their collections. Tensions arise when funds needed for long-term care are drawn away from more current concerns such as acquisitions and personnel. How curators respond to these often conflicting demands is influenced by changes in both academic and administrative priorities.

The proliferation of information and diminished resources to care for collections have challenged librarians, museum curators, and archivists to reevaluate their collecting activities and services. Librarians and archivists are responding to the proliferation of information in all forms and the rising costs of acquiring, controlling, housing, and servicing their collections by developing cooperative arrangements and new selection techniques. For many museum curators, the problem is not the proliferation of objects, but rather the scarcity and expense of the objects they seek. Repositories are narrowing the scope of their collections and determining how alternative approaches can be used to fulfill their missions.

Librarians now view the subject strengths of the nation's academic libraries as a foundation for cooperative activities. Collections that were developed to fulfill local institutional needs are now recognized as national resources. Institutions have come to accept the responsibility to share these resources by reporting information about their holdings to national bibliographic databases and, when possible, lending their materials to others. Shared bibliographic databases have transformed impressionistic judgments of collection strengths into detailed analyses by subject area. Signed agreements between members of library consortia designate the collecting and preservation responsibilities of each library and promote access to materials through interlibrary loan and photocopying services. The stewardship of the "collection" has become a shared responsibility.

Cooperative plans oblige individual academic libraries to build and pre-serve collections that are used by researchers from many institutions. At the same time, the primary obligation of these repositories remains to respond to current teaching and research activities at their own cam-puses. Recognizing that collections at each institution cannot be compre-hensive in all subject areas, librarians have developed services to provide ready access to material that they do not acquire. Access to shared sources rather than ownership is now recognized by the library community as the most practical means to fulfill the needs of faculty and students within the limited resources of each institution. Administrators, faculty, and accrediting agencies, however, are accustomed to measuring the value of libraries by the volume of their holdings; they have yet to adapt to the concept of access in contrast to ownership of materials.

Archivists have responded to the proliferation of information by refining collecting policies, developing more systematic documentation efforts, and utilizing records management techniques to cope with current records. As archivists recognize that funding, regulations, and coopera-tive activities link modern institutions to one another, they also perceive that each institutional archival collection is part of an interconnected documentary record. Automated databases on archival sources may support coordinated collecting activities in the future.

Museum curators face a different set of problems. Changes in teaching and research programs may create cyclical changes in use, or total aban-donment of the collections by faculty and students. Administrators are increasingly reluctant to support facilities that are peripheral to the aca-demic program. However, institutional responsibility for the museum collections has meant that on the whole they have remained on the cam-puses. Sources of funding, services, and clientele have changed, but the museums remain. Funds from private and public agencies now support exhibits, programs, and publications sometimes aimed more at the local and national communities than at the members of the parent institution. The ongoing obligation, however, is not just to exhibit and educate but also to preserve the collections and ensure that they continue to be available.

Documentation

This function focuses on the issues of documenting the collections, as they are the resources that are being maintained and promoted by the institution. The documentation should include a record of the policies and procedures that determine the growth and use of the collections; the size, makeup, and use of the holdings; the local and national mechanisms used to report the holdings; the inter-institutional cooperative collecting agreements; the commercial contracts and database services used to enhance access and services; and the unique collections.

Administrative records of library, museum, and archival officers should provide evidence of the changing policies toward the development and management of the collections: acquisition and deaccessioning of materials; cooperative acquisition and loan agreements; reporting practices to the bibliographic networks; policies on access and use of the holdings; and allocation of resources for acquisitions, preservation, and staff.

Libraries, museums, and archives compile extensive statistics on holdings and use that are reported annually both for internal administrative purposes and to external professional associations. The Association of Research Libraries (ARL) publishes information on the holdings, subscriptions, number of staff, salaries, etc., for its 106 member institutions. College and university libraries submit statistical information to the *American Library Directory*. Archives do not have standard external reporting requirements, but statistics on their holdings and activities are submitted to the appropriate academic or administrative officer. Statistical information about museums is reported to the *Official Museum Directory*.

Libraries, museums, and archives require detailed information about their holdings for long-term legal and administrative purposes. Libraries still rely on the shelf list (a card file of information about monographs, serials, and other materials maintained in call number order) as a legal record of their holdings. Automated versions of the shelf list may soon replace the manual file when the machine-readable version is more secure and can be searched in a comparable fashion to the card version.

While for legal and administrative purposes a library must maintain a record of its current holdings, it seems neither necessary nor desirable to retain a detailed record of the collection at specific points in time or of materials that are no longer part of the library. Published catalogs and automated bibliographic databases attest to the publication history and general availability of library materials. National bibliographic databases and the policies of sharing resources shift the emphasis from knowing what an individual library holds to a knowledge instead of what information exists.

Different criteria are required, however, for information about unique holdings. Curators and historical researchers need information about the history or provenance of rare books, archival and manuscript collections, and museum objects. Information about previous ownership and use guides the process of describing and interpreting materials. Knowledge of how the collections were organized, exhibited, and treated guides future preservation, exhibit, and processing decisions. Knowledge of the legal agreements with donors directs the administration of the collections including access to and loan of materials and decisions to remove or de-accession holdings. Special collections librarians, archivists, and museum registrars maintain information about the history of their collections as part of their administrative records. Even when holdings are deaccessioned, curators tend to retain this information.

For rare books, manuscript collections, and art objects, provenance records can include letters of transfer, deeds of gift, descriptions of a collection on receipt, and a record of processing and preservation decisions. For museum objects, such as anthropological and archeological relics, provenance records can include field notebooks of the researchers that include information about excavation sites and the location and condition in which each object was found. All of this information should be retained as part of the archival records of the repository.

Records provide information about the acquisition, care, and use of library and museum collections, but it is harder to capture the experience of the individuals who use the materials: the students who use the library collection to write papers and escape from academic pressures by reading newspapers, magazines, or works not on their reading lists; the scholars who visit special collections for extensive periods to use manuscripts and artifactual collections; the museum visitor who spends twenty minutes or hours viewing the exhibits.

Statistical reports provide information on the number of books loaned from a library, of visitors to a museum, and of researchers that use an archives. These figures, however, provide little evidence about the experience of the users and how (or if) they made use of the information they located. Libraries and archives may publish bibliographies of works that have resulted from research utilizing the resources in their collections. Student papers and faculty publications can both be viewed as works that have relied, in part, on the institution's collections and services. Libraries and museums periodically conduct user surveys to assess their services and programs. These and other studies provide some insight into the use of the collections. The social and public uses of these facilities are even harder to document. Curators who are trying to measure the effectiveness of their collections and services and archivists who want to document the experience of users must seek additional means to capture this knowledge.

Bibliography

American Library Directory. New York: R.R. Bowker, 1990.

Ash, Lee, and William G. Miller, comps. *Ash Subject Collections*. 6th ed. New York: R.R. Bowker, 1985.

Edelman, Hendrik, and G. Martin Tatum, Jr. "The Development of Collections in American University Libraries." In *Libraries for Teaching, Libraries for Research, Essays for a Century*, edited by Richard D. Johnson. Chicago: American Library Association, 1977.

Hamlin, Arthur. *The University Library in the United States, Its Origins and Development*. Philadelphia: University of Pennsylvania Press, 1981.

Kohlstedt, Sally Gregory. "Museums on Campus: A Tradition of Inquiry and Teaching." In *The American Development of Biology*, edited by Ronald Rainger, Keith R. Benson, and Jane Maienschein. Philadelphia: University of Pennsylvania Press, 1988.

Official Museum Directory. Washington, D.C.: American Association of Museums, 1987.

Osburn, Charles B. *Academic Research and Library Resources, Changing Patterns in America*. Westport, Conn.: Greenwood Press, 1979.

Tappen, Henry P. "On the Idea of a True University, 1858." In *American Higher Education: A Documentary History*, edited by Richard Hofstadter and Wilson Smith. Chicago: University of Chicago Press, 1961.

Institutional Documentation Plan

An institutional documentation plan (IDP) is a statement of documentary goals and a delineation of how those goals will be realized by an individual institution.

The preceding chapters describing the seven functions can be used in different ways. Readers can consult the index and refer selectively to the text to help them solve immediate problems about specific records, or they can dwell on sections or functions that are of particular concern to them. The larger purpose of these chapters, however, is to provide the broad understanding of functions and evidence that is needed to formulate a detailed institutional documentation plan.

The chapters on the seven functions are not prescriptive, as there can be no uniform or absolute recommendations about selection. Decisions must be made by archivists in light of their own institutions' history, goals, and resources. The IDP presents a process of translating the general descriptions in *Varsity Letters* into a detailed plan applicable to a specific institution. The IDP uses the functional approach described in this book as well as traditional archival tools such as administrative histories, collection analysis, and surveys. The application of the functional approach to these tools, however, alters the way they are used.

The process of formulating an institutional documentation plan consists of the following steps:

Translate the functions so that they describe a specific institution

Draft documentary goals

Apply a functional understanding to the preparation of administrative histories of individual units of the institution

Evaluate the documentation already under curatorial care and the records still housed in offices, as well as the need to create a documentary record

*Assess the resources (physical, finan-
cial, etc.) available to preserve the
documentation*

*Confirm documentary goals and the
process proposed to achieve them.*

Why Develop an Institutional Documentation Plan?

Archivists have traditionally used collecting policies to articulate their documentary goals. In truth, collecting policies are usually vague general statements about areas of interest and formats that will be collected. A documentation plan, by contrast, encourages the formulation of a detailed program to realize documentary goals. The premise of a documentation plan is that the determination of what is to be documented and a knowledge of the documentary issues must be established before collections are sought. This process is entitled an institutional documentation plan rather than a collecting plan because collecting is only one facet of a documentary program; the term documentation is used rather than appraisal because appraisal is only one part of the documentation program. A documentation plan articulates objectives for the management and appraisal of existing material, the intervention to assure the creation and preservation of desired records in the future, and the creation of supplementary documentation to fill gaps.

Depending on the size of the institution, the mandate of the archives, and the size of its holdings, the development of a documentation plan can represent a considerable investment of time, energy, and resources. So why do it? Planned documentation objectives provide evidence that an archives collects thoughtfully and selectively and that it manages its resources wisely. Archivists foster a negative image when they are perceived as random collectors keeping whatever they obtain. Passively accepting what is offered negates the archivist's role as a selector and active documenter of the institution.

The purpose of the IDP is to turn the documentary process into a planned activity. Of course, the process will never be fully predictable. Archivists will always have to respond to unexpected offers of records prompted by moves or departures of individuals and the closing of offices and departments. Even in these situations, however, the analysis and planning captured in the IDP will guide the decisions that must be made.

The manner in which the IDP is developed must be dictated by the resources of each institution. The plan need not be formulated all at once in a concentrated way. The limited time of the "lone arranger" may dictate a phased, less formal approach. The functional analysis, the first step of the IDP, can be accomplished by a committee composed of curators, faculty, administrators, and alumni or by the archivist working alone. The administrative histories and collection analysis tasks that follow can also be carried out as a concentrated team effort or by one archivist over time. However the study is carried out, the knowledge gained will be well worth the effort.

Background Issues

An institutional documentation plan is formed by understanding the institution, the documentation, and the facilities available to house the documentation. Understanding the character of the institution clarifies the nature of each function and defines what should be documented: the function *sustain the institution* is larger and more complex at the University of Wisconsin-Madison with its 43,000 students, 2,400 faculty, and staff of 14,000 than at Wellesley College with its 2,200 students, 254 faculty, and staff of 550; the characteristics of *foster socialization* differ dramatically at a commuting college from those at a residential campus. The first step in the IDP is to study each function to determine its nature and importance to a specific institution. This knowledge forms the background to all documentary activities.

Understanding the documentation clarifies the availability or absence of specific forms of evidence to document each function. The documentation of an institution exists in many forms — archival, manuscript, published, visual, aural, and artifactual sources — and is housed and cared for by many agencies — archives, libraries, data centers, museums, and records centers. When considering the problems inherent in documenting any function, all evidence must be evaluated in an integrated fashion regardless of where the material will be housed. The football trophies may be in a museum, while the coach's records are in the archives, and the bound souvenir programs are in the library. The primary concern is not the ultimate location or the form of the material, but the information it offers.

Understanding the mandate and resources of the available repositories to gather and preserve the documentation clarifies the extent to which the evidence of each function can be preserved. While the archives may be the only unit with the specific mandate to preserve official records, other collecting facilities have roles to play. For the IDP, the relevant question is not which is the appropriate facility to house specific material. That question will be resolved as specific materials are placed by curators guided by the programs and policies of their repositories. Rather, at this stage, the question is what is the sum total of the resources available — space, staff and funds — to care for the documentary collections.

The Process

Translate the Functions

The first step in the IDP is to apply the functional descriptions to a specific institution. By studying how each function manifests itself — its history, relevance, and importance — the generic descriptions in this book can be transformed into a fundamental knowledge about the college or university in question. This functional understanding is vital, as it defines the general documentary goals and forms the background to all the tasks that follow.

The functional analysis can be done by an archivist alone or by the archival staff working by themselves. If possible, however, a team composed of archivists, curators, librarians, students, staff, administrators, faculty, alumni, and historical researchers should be formed to carry out this process. Their different viewpoints would be of great help in determining the particular characteristics of each function at their institution.

What does each of these seven functions mean to your institution? How has it manifested itself? An institution in an urban area with a long history of town-gown conflicts defines public service quite differently from a liberal arts college that serves as the main cultural and social center for a small town. A community college with no intercollegiate athletic program defines parts of its function *foster socialization* quite differently from a "Big Ten" school. The function *conduct research* permeates almost every facet of a university, while at a college this function may exist mostly in the endeavors of individual faculty members.

This first step, then, is a translation process that makes each function meaningful to a given institution. This task demands different kinds of knowledge and skills. A historical understanding of the institution is fundamental to the process, but analytic methods of many disciplines — historical, sociological, political, and economic — can be applied. Team members should therefore be chosen not only for their knowledge of the institution but also for their varied analytic skills. The analysis requires the use of many sources. In addition to the archival records and published sources, which are essential, the experiences of the documentation team and interviews with selected members of the community will be valuable.

Background research and discussion should provide answers to the following questions about each function:

How important is this function to your institution?

What is the history of this function?

How has the function evolved, and what were the causes of change?

What aspects of the function are most relevant to your institution?

What were the key events, policies, and individuals that affected this function?

What structures have been used to carry out this function?

The time and personnel allocated to answering these questions will determine the level of detail and understanding achieved about each function. A general understanding can be gained by a knowledgeable archivist working alone through a brief thought exercise. Or, if properly prepared, a team can address this task fruitfully in a few days or more fully over many months.

Draft Documentary Goals

The profile derived from this translation exercise describes a particular college or university and delineates the aspects of each function to be documented. This knowledge can then be captured in a statement of general documentary goals. Several factors influence the establishment of these goals. The primary factor is the archivist's traditional legal, administrative, and historical obligations. The documentary goals and the entire IDP must assure that the "vital records" and other sources of enduring value to the institution are identified and preserved. After that, the particular strengths of the institution, the teaching and research programs of the faculty, and the interests of the curatorial units will influence what areas are emphasized in the documentary goals.

The study of each function should include all aspects that are relevant to the institution, and the statement of documentary goals should articulate goals for each one. Here are some examples for a hypothetical institution, Dieterle College in Rego Park, New York.

Provide Public Service:
The relationship of the institution
to the local community

Goal: To document the economic, social, and cultural impact of Dieterle College on the surrounding community. Particular attention will be given to the economic and social impact of changing land-use policies and the role of the Friday Lectures and Spring Concert Series in promoting ties with the community. The role of the Office of Community Relations (established in 1962) also deserves particular attention.

Confer Credentials:
The curriculum

Goal: To document the evolution of the curriculum from its vocational origins to the program in general education. Particular emphasis will be placed on documenting the roles that the 1890 Smith Committee, the 1948 O'Toole Committee, and the 1970 Seiden Committee had on effecting these changes. Documentation of the intellectual and social impact of these changes will be sought from the faculty, administrators, and students (alumni). Due to the regional and national significance of the college's geography and Jewish studies programs, emphasis will be placed on documenting these curricula.

Conduct Research:
Teaching and the facilities

Goal: To document the intellectual and physical changes caused by the increasing emphasis on research. Particular attention will be devoted to documenting the impact of the Thomas G. Anderson Center for Physical Sciences: its effect on the undergraduate and graduate teaching programs in the physical sciences and the impact of this building on the library and other surrounding facilities.

Formulate Documentary Plan

A second translation process takes place as these broad documentary goals based on a functional understanding are developed into a concrete documentary plan. Functional analysis provides the understanding of what is to be documented and why specific documentation is sought. Traditional archival principles and practices determine how that documentation is located. Central to these activities is the archivist's principle of provenance, which relies on a knowledge of the office or unit that created records to locate, arrange, and describe documentation. The principle of provenance underlies archivists' use of administrative histories, surveys, and collections assessments to examine a specific office or unit, chart its history, and evaluate the documentation about that unit that is already under curatorial care and the records still in offices. These tools are used frequently in traditional archival practice but often in isolation from one another. While administrative histories, surveys, and collection analyses will be used to construct the documentation plan, the difference in this application is the sequence in which they are done, the relationship between them, and the questions brought to them.

The first step in formulating a documentary plan is the preparation of administrative histories, but their scope is broadened to encompass an examination of all functions. The development of an administrative history provides the opportunity to describe in detail what is to be documented (the policies, programs, events, and individuals) and the associated documentary problems. The knowledge of what is to be documented and the documentation sought guides the next steps in the process: the examination of the evidence, the surveys, and the collection analysis projects.

Administrative Histories

The administrative history is a valuable tool used by archivists to understand the structure, purpose, and history of specific units of their institutions. The knowledge gained guides both appraisal and descriptive activities. The traditional primary focus of these histories, however, is on administrative matters, or, in the terminology of this book, on issues covered in the function *sustain the institution* (governance, personnel, and finances). For the documentation plan, the administrative history is broadened to encompass an examination of all the functions.

The administrative history of an academic department, for example, must

Examine the enrollment patterns and admission standards for its undergraduate and graduate programs and chronicle the degrees awarded (confer credentials)

Trace the evolution of the curriculum and the methods used to teach the curriculum (convey knowledge)

Examine the clubs and social activities (outings, parties, etc.) offered by the department or run by the students and the relationships between the students and faculty (foster socialization)

Trace the research efforts of the faculty and graduate students (conduct research)

Chronicle how the department was administered: the reporting relationship to senior officers, composition and role of the committees used to govern the department, staffing patterns, and changing sources of revenue (sustain the institution)

Investigate the relationship of the unit with the communities (local, national, and international) it serves (provide public service)

Determine if collections were assembled as a part of the mission of the unit and have been preserved in a library or museum collection (promote culture).

The way in which a specific institution carries out the administrative history project will depend on the time and staff available. Administrative histories can be written by an archivist relying just on the sources at hand, but, like the functional analysis, this process will benefit from the assistance of others outside of the archives. Some or all of the following steps will be useful:

Select the department or unit to be examined and choose the prime person to prepare the administrative history. The prime person can be a member of the archives staff, a student in an archival training or history program, or a current or former member of the chosen department or unit.

Inform the department or unit head of the project and gain his or her cooperation. Ask the head to identify other current or former senior officers, faculty, students, and staff who might be valuable participants in the project. If possible, also involve historians of appropriate areas (disciplines, etc.). The participants can meet as an advisory group, if needed, or serve as individual consultants.

Conduct research in the archives, library, and administrative offices as needed to draft a four- to six-page administrative history. Attention must be given to the manifestation of all seven functions throughout this analysis. The history should cover the following key points:

> Date the unit was established
> Dates of alterations in scope, name, and programs
> Reporting lines
> Individuals in charge
> Scope and programs
> Areas of responsibility (for academic units: areas of teaching and research, laboratories, and links to other academic programs)
> Key events: successes and failures

Prepare an appendix of collections documenting the unit that are already under curatorial care in the archives, libraries, and museums.

Have the draft administrative history reviewed by the members of the archives staff.

Have the draft administrative history reviewed by the unit head and others participating in the project. Members of the library and museum staffs may also serve as useful reviewers at this point. Ask the reviewers to comment on the accuracy of the history and suggest corrections, additions, and deletions. Explain that the history is intended to guide decisions about what is to be documented and ask the reviewers to suggest specific programs, efforts, and events that should be documented as well as individuals to contact for more information and for documentation. From these comments and suggestions or discussions at a meeting about the administrative history, a detailed documentary plan can be formulated.

Before the administrative history can be refined and the documentary plan put into action, several additional activities must be carried out: evaluate the available evidence; address the absence of evidence; evaluate the material under curatorial care; and assess the documentation not yet under curatorial care.

Evaluate the Available Evidence

Following the research required to prepare the administrative history, the author is in a good position to assess the availability and relative value of the sources required: published, manuscript, archival, visual, and artifactual. Each form of evidence contributes some information.

The published record is usually the most widely available as generally there are duplicate copies. Most institutions issue many publications, and it is important to understand the information they contain and the questions that can be answered from these sources. Understanding the value of the published sources of information suggests when and why other evidence is required. For example, the college bulletin states that all freshmen must live in campus housing. The names of the available houses, the cost of room and board, and the process by which the students are assigned housing are discussed. The published record does not, however, reveal the policy and planning efforts behind this decision, nor what this really means to the freshmen themselves. The records of the committee on housing or the president's papers show when and why the decision was made to require the freshmen to live in campus housing; the records of the development office document the tactics used to raise money for new dorms; the planning and physical plant offices hold drawings of the dorms; the photographic record shows the relationship between the dorms and the rest of the campus, the layout of each room, and the students in their living quarters.

A better understanding of the value of each form of evidence suggests when a published record alone is sufficient, as in the following examples. Full documentation of each research project may be impractical, especially in science and technology, and for many research projects the published final product may be sufficient evidence. The automated records and card files in the dean's office keep track of the multiple addresses for students who move during each academic year, but this level of documentation may not need to be preserved. The published annual student directory, which lists the local and permanent address, may suffice.

Address the Lack of a Documentary Record

At the same time, the absence of documentation must be considered, whether it is a result of the intangible nature of the function, the nature of the documentation, or a catastrophic loss of evidence.

Many activities do not leave any documentary evidence. Sometimes the lack of evidence is a side effect of informal decision making or a deliberate choice not to leave a record. More often, no evidence exists because none is created naturally as a by-product of the activity. The interaction between students in their dormitory, the student's learning process, and the conceptualization of a research problem are all difficult to document, as they leave no direct evidence. Photographs can be taken of students in their rooms, interviews can be conducted with students about their learning, and working notes can be collected to document the research activity. Such records are helpful but remain indirect evidence of essentially intangible processes.

The increasing presence of automated records creates documentary problems for the archivist and the real possibility of a loss of evidence. Without effective intervention as the records are created, valuable information may not be created or retained. Without full technical documentation, automated databases cannot be read or reused in the future. Without proper storage and care and the availability of appropriate hardware, tapes and disks will be useless. Archivists must work with the creators of these records (as well as others who create records in fragile, transient forms, such as videos and other magnetic media) to assure that the desired evidence survives.

Specific conditions at each campus may impose additional documentary problems. All too many campuses have lost part of their documentary record to fire, flood, or other misfortune. Often, too, critical sets of records are missing because they were taken away by departing staff members, deliberately destroyed, or given to another institution. In each case, the institution must try to fill in the gaps. The documentary analysis conducted as part of the administrative history project should suggest when plans must be made to assure the preservation of a fragile or transient record or when the creation of a record is needed because sufficient documentation is lacking.

These studies of the evidence — the value of existing evidence, the lack of evidence, and the need to create supplementary evidence — serve as a guide but remain hypothetical until confirmed through a study of the sources already under curatorial care and those that are not.

Evaluate the Material under Curatorial Care

Part of the process of preparing a documentation plan includes the evaluation of those materials already under curatorial care. How well does this documentation contribute to the documentary goals?

In recent years, both the archival and library professions have devoted increasing attention to evaluating their holdings. Archivists are using collections analysis techniques as part of the reevaluation of their collecting activities. (See discussion on page 10.) Collection analyses utilize a subject analysis and quantitative assessment of collections to evaluate holdings and refine collecting objectives.

The collection analysis model provides a useful tool if a few modifications are made. In the projects to date, holdings were evaluated against a list of general subject terms. A quantitative assessment was made to determine how much documentation (how many collections) provided information about specific subjects. The analysis determined how much material existed on a given topic but generally failed to evaluate the quality of the documentation.

When collection analysis is used as part of an institutional documentation plan, the documentary goals for each function and the documentation plan derived from the administrative histories replace the examination of subjects. The collection analysis is therefore guided by a knowledge of what the institution is trying to document and what forms of evidence are needed. Such background information permits the collection analysis process to accomplish a quantitative and a qualitative assessment at the same time. Archivists can determine how many collections they have assembled to document specific units or departments of the institution and, by examining the material in the collections, how adequately the evidence documents them.

To date, most collection analyses have focused primarily on manuscript collections and have not evaluated all of an institution's holdings as integrated sources of information. (The State Historical Society of Wisconsin project went the furthest toward incorporating the published record into its evaluation.) For collection analysis to be useful as part of the IDP, all forms of information — archival, manuscript, published, visual, etc.— must be evaluated together.

The collection assessment should include a consideration of not only the documentation housed in the various collecting agencies at the institution but also the availability of materials housed at other institutions. The IDP makes provision not only for what will be collected but also for sources that are appropriately held at other institutions. Records of state boards of higher education contain information about policy, funding, and planning efforts relevant to all institutions in the state. These records are most likely held at some central repository but should be considered by archivists at all of the institutions involved. While each college or university will have the material that its institution presented to an accrediting agency for reaccreditation, only the agency holds the full record of the process.

Assess the Documentation
Not Yet under Control and
Plan for Future Preservation

Archivists and records managers use surveys and schedules to locate and control the records of institutions. Many archives use surveys as the initial step of their program in order to locate existing records and identify records of long-term value. Records schedules are used to control and dispose of the bulk of routine records created by an institution. These are useful techniques, but they can be improved.

Records surveys provide information about what exists — not necessarily what archivists and researchers want to exist. As was the case for collection analysis, the functional analysis and administrative histories clarify what part of the existing record is needed to respond to an institution's documentary goals. Although many advocate comprehensive surveys, a selective survey may be sufficient for the IDP. It may not be necessary to learn about everything that exists, but rather to use targeted surveys to test assumptions made about the evidence and locate the documentation identified as desirable during the functional studies and preparation of administrative histories. Again, however, whatever the survey process, all forms of evidence must be included.

The examination of the documentation will reveal specific problems: committee files that are passed from chairman to chairman and get lost; record copies of publications that are not preserved; office filing systems that preclude the easy weeding of records and their transfer to the archives; student records that are being routinely destroyed; automated files that are not backed up and are updated or destroyed before they can be preserved. In each case a particular course of action can be designed to address the documentary problem. Some problems might require the strengthening of archival policies (records may not be destroyed without proper authority). Some problems may require educational efforts (regular meetings with committee chairmen and office staff to establish sound records-keeping practices and assure transfer of records to the archives). Some problems may involve formulation and dissemination of advice (publication of general schedules and filing guidelines). The general analysis of the documentary problems will suggest the particular approaches best suited to an institution's needs and resources.

Determine the Need To Create Documentary Evidence

During the process of formulating the institutional documentation plan and writing the administrative histories, the less tangible and poorly documented aspects of each function are examined as well as the available evidence.

The idea of deliberately creating records to fill out the documentary record is certainly not new. Oral history was conceived for this purpose. Archivists have confronted the problem repeatedly as they face the challenge of documenting modern society. And yet, concerns remain about the legitimacy of intervening to shape or create documentation. The traditional view of the archivist as the passive assembler of an existing record lingers. If the archivist's role is perceived as the documenter of an institution rather than the manager of an existing record, then creating a supplementary record is a logical part of the task.

The greatest problem is often resources — the people, money, and time needed to carry out documentary projects. Oral history, photographic, and video taping projects are expensive. The IDP can promote these projects by clarifying their purpose. Such a planning document can be used to work with alumni and development offices to raise money and with students, faculty, and alumni to find volunteers and participants.

Archivists should not feel that they alone must carry out these tasks. Their efforts might be spent more fruitfully defining projects and providing education. Discussions with faculty, students, and alumni will suggest documentary projects that they can accomplish effectively.

Assess the Resources Available
To Document Each Function

The resources available to manage, collect, create, and preserve the documentary record must be evaluated. The assessment should include the following areas:

Inventory of Repositories. What repositories are currently available to house portions of the documentation? In addition to archives, libraries, and museums, nontraditional facilities such as the computing center should be considered. Are these units able to assume responsibility for the retention, description, and use of part of the documentation? The inventory of facilities should include those offices that assume permanent responsibility for specific records; e.g., the registrar's office frequently houses the permanent student transcript.

Authority. Are any of these units operating under legal authority conveyed by the institution or a government agency? Often this will be the case for the archives and for certain offices like the registrar. What are the requirements and limits of these authorities? Are they adequate?

Mandate and Scope. What is the mandate of each repository and the scope of its activities? What responsibility does each have for the documentation of the institution? Does the library collect official, student, and faculty publications? Are these publications retained permanently or weeded periodically? Does the museum collect artifacts associated with the institution's history? If not, can its policy be changed or another institution identified to carry out this task? Can the administrative computer center accept the responsibility to house, protect, and provide access to machine-readable records of long-term value?

Space and Equipment. What space and equipment does each repository have? Are these adequate to support their programs? Are there appropriate security measures, environmental controls, and storage areas?

Staff. What staff is available? Are the personnel properly qualified to do their jobs and are an adequate number of professional and support staff members available?

Funds. What funds are available to support documentary activities? Are there funds to purchase documentary materials (monographs, serials, slides, etc.) and equipment (boxes and folders as well as computer hardware and software)? Are funds available for documentary projects such as oral histories? What are the possibilities of raising special funds for aspects of the documentary program?

Needs. What is needed to strengthen the documentary program? Must stronger legal authority be granted to specific agencies? Do the mandates of some units need to be reconsidered to clarify the scope of their collecting activities? Are better physical facilities required or specific equipment?

Publications such as William Maher's *The Management of College and University Archives*[1] and SAA's *Archives Assessment and Planning Workbook*[2] can support this evaluation, as they provide considerable information about the component activities of archival programs and how they can be judged.

Confirm the Documentary Goals and Establish the Process Proposed To Achieve Them

The findings from the preceding analyses should be used to test and refine the documentary goals. Knowledge about the availability or absence of evidence clarifies the problems involved in gathering an adequate documentation and delineates what evidence is required. The evaluation of the resources indicates how much material can be assembled based on the availability of facilities, staff, and funds. Taken together, this information permits a reexamination of the documentary goals. Can they all be realized? Do documentary problems or resources make some impossible? They do not all need to be realized at once. The lack of resources and staff may suggest that an incremental approach is required.

The final product of the process outlined in this chapter should be a detailed plan that confirms the documentary goals to be pursued and specifies how those goals are to be achieved. These findings can be consolidated into a report that delineates both the detailed documentation plan and the policy issues that must be addressed. The need for adequate legal mandates and sufficient staff, storage, and funding for the repositories should be addressed as broad issues that affect the ability of the institution to preserve its heritage. By assigning priorities, the documentary plan can highlight areas (functions, specific units, or types of records) that need immediate consideration.

The final product, however, must be detailed in its analysis and description of tasks to be done. It is not sufficient to say that increased emphasis will be placed on documenting the teaching-learning process. The plan must evaluate the holdings and specify what material (types of documentation) will be sought from whom (faculty, students, alumni, or administrative offices) for what purpose.

The documentary plan must be used, refined, and altered regularly to keep it current. Again, these reviews and updates can be done by an archivist alone or with outside advisors. In this way, the IDP will continue to be an effective guide for the documentary activities of a college or university.

Notes

1 William Maher, *The Management of College and University Archives* (Metuchen, N.J.: Scarecrow Press; Chicago: Society of American Archivists, 1992).

2 Paul H. McCarthy, ed., *Archives Assessment and Planning Workbook* (Chicago: Society of American Archivists, 1989).

Photography Credits

Index